The Great Maria

THE
GREAT
MARIA

A Portrait of Maria Edgeworth

by

ELISABETH INGLIS-JONES

'. . . Miss Edgeworth; not the great Maria
but one of her sisters'
            —SIR WALTER SCOTT in a letter

FABER AND FABER
24 Russell Square
London

First published in mcmlix
by Faber and Faber Limited
24 Russell Square London W.C.1
Printed in Great Britain by
Latimer Trend & Co Ltd Plymouth

For my dear niece Sara

Contents

	Foreword	page 11
One	1782–1792	17
Two	1792–1798	35
Three	1798–1801	51
Four	1802–1803	61
Five	1803–1812	83
Six	1813	101
Seven	1813–1817	116
Eight	1817–1818	132
Nine	1818–1819	149
Ten	1820–1821	162
Eleven	1821–1822	179
Twelve	1823	192
Thirteen	1824–1829	208
Fourteen	1830–1831	221
Fifteen	1831–1833	236
	Epilogue	254
	Index	256

Illustrations

———————— ✦ ————————

1. Richard Lovell Edgeworth's four wives   *facing page* 20

2. The Edgeworth Family, 1787   32

3. Edgeworthstown House   48

4. Madame Récamier and Laharpe   64

5. The Duchess of Wellington   112

6. Sheep-shearing at Edgeworthstown   128

7. Louisa, Marchioness of Lansdowne   224

8. The Honourable Mrs. Hope   240

The author wishes to thank the following for kindly giving permission to reproduce the illustrations: Mrs. H. E. Butler for plates 1, 2, 4 and 6, the editor of the *Irish Independent* for plate 3 and the engraving on page 215, the Bodley Head for plate 5, the Marquis of Lansdowne for plate 7 and the Trustees of the British Museum for plate 8.

Foreword

———————————— ⟨⦿⟩ ————————————

In spite of the fame Maria Edgeworth enjoyed in her lifetime and for long afterwards and though her children's stories were still read at the beginning of this century, today her name is almost unknown. *Practical Education* is remembered by educationists as the first attempt at introducing more enlightened and imaginative methods of teaching the young, but the novels and stories that once had world-wide popularity are forgotten. In this account of her life I have not attempted to discuss Maria Edgeworth as a writer. My only aim has been to give a truthful picture of one whose character and abilities in any age would make her outstanding and who in her own was regarded as almost phenomenal. As all her life long she steadfastly refused to be drawn or painted even by her sisters, no other likeness exists of Maria than that in the family group by Adam Buck.

The devoted and obedient disciple of her remarkable father, his influence on her has often been unjustly criticized by earlier biographers who had not the opportunity of reading the many hundreds of letters written by Maria to members of her family, and other unpublished papers, which have provided the material for this book. To Mrs. H. E. Butler who generously placed these letters at my disposal and has been unfailingly kind and helpful in every way, I owe a deep debt of gratitude. Extracts from many of these letters, sometimes much edited, form a large part of Mrs.

Foreword

Edgeworth's *Memoir of Maria Edgeworth*, which was privately printed in 1863. Hitherto this has been the chief source of information for biographers and I have found it very helpful. So also have been *The Black Book of Edgeworthstown* by Harriet Butler and H. E. Butler and *Maria Edgeworth's Tour in Connemara* edited by H. E. Butler, while for the account of Marc-Auguste Pictet's visit to Edgeworthstown I turned to his little book, *Voyage de Trois Mois en Angleterre etc.*

I have also to thank Lord and Lady Longford for taking me to see Edgeworthstown and helping me in various ways; Miss Ruth Butler for family information and the loan of papers; and Lady Studholme for information about Lady Elizabeth Whitbread. For permission to quote from *Byron, a Self-portrait*, by Peter Quennell (John Murray, Publishers, Ltd.) and *The Genevese Background*, by H. W. Hausermann (Messrs. Routledge and Kegan Paul), I wish to acknowledge my indebtedness to the authors and publishers.

Family and Descendants

‘The Edgeworths, originally it is said, established at Edgeworth, now called Edgeware, Middlesex, settled in Ireland in the reign of Elizabeth, about the year 1583. Two brothers Edward and Francis Edgeworth went to Ireland, probably under the patronage of Essex and Cecil.’ (Burke's *Landed Gentry*, 1879.) The elder brother, Edward, beneficed by Queen Elizabeth, became Bishop of Down and Connor in 1593. He died without issue. From the younger brother Francis, Clerk of the Hanaper in 1619, who married Jane, daughter of Sir Edward Tuite of Sonna, Westmeath, Richard Lovell Edgeworth was directly descended.

Richard Lovell Edgeworth of Edgeworthstown, Co. Longford, was born at Bath, 31st May 1744. He married first in 1763, Anna Maria, daughter of Paul Elers, Esq., of Black Bourton, Oxfordshire, and by her (who died in March 1773) had one son and three daughters:

Richard, b. May 1764; settled when young in America where he married Elizabeth Knight; d. 1796. His descendants are still living in the U.S.A.

Maria, b. 1st January 1767; d. 21st May 1849.

Emmeline, b. 1770; m. 1802, John King, a surgeon of Clifton, and d. 1847, leaving issue Zoë and Psyche Emmeline.

Anna Maria, b. March 1773; m. 1794, Dr. Thomas Beddoes, and d. 1824, leaving issue, Thomas Lovell; Charles Henry; Anna Frances Emily and Mary Eliza.

13

He married secondly in June 1773, Honora Sneyd, daughter of Major Edward Sneyd of the Royal Horse Guards, and by her (who died 1780) had one son and one daughter:

Lovell, b. 1776; d. December 1842.

Honora, b. 1774; d. 1790.

He married thirdly, 25th December 1780, Elizabeth, daughter of Major Edward Sneyd, and by her (who died in November 1797) had five sons and four daughters:

Henry, b. 1782; d. 1813.

Charles Sneyd, b. 1786; m. 1813, Henrica Broadhurst, and d.s.p. 1864.

William, b. 1788; d. 1790.

Thomas Day, b. 1789; d. 1792.

William, b. 1794; d. 1829.

Elizabeth, b. 1781; d. 1800.

Sophia, d. an infant 1784.

Charlotte, b. 1783; d. 1807.

Honora, b. 1791; m. 1837, Admiral Sir Francis Beaufort, K.C.B.; d. 1858.

He married fourthly, 31st May 1798, Frances Anne, daughter of the Rev. D. A. Beaufort, Rector of Collon, Co. Louth, and by her (who died 10th February 1865) had two sons and four daughters:

Francis Beaufort, b. 1809; m. 1831, Rosa Florentina Eroles; and d. 1846, leaving five sons and one daughter; William, b. 1835, d. 1863; Antonio Eroles of Edgeworthstown, b. 1841; m. Françoise Delcher and d.s.p. 1908; David Reid, b. 1842, d. 1871; Richard Lestock, b. 1843, d. 1869; Ysidro Francis of Edgeworthstown, b. 1846, Drummond Professor of Political Economy at Oxford, d. unm. 1926; Mary, b. 1839, m. 1871, Rev. John Sanderson, d. 1891 leaving four daughters.

Michael Pakenham, b. 1812; m. 1846, Christina Macpherson and d. 1881, leaving one daughter, Harriet Jessie, m. 1877, Rev. A. B. Butler, and d. 1946, leaving one son, Harold Edgeworth, and three daughters.

Frances Maria, b. 1799; m. 1829, Lestock Peach Wilson; d. 1848.

Harriet, b. 1801; m. 1826, the Very Rev. Richard Butler, Dean of Clonmacnoise; d. 1889.

Sophia, b. 1803; m. 1824, Major Barry Fox of Annaghmore, King's Co., and d. 1837 leaving two sons and two daughters.

Lucy Jane, b. 1805; m. 1843, Rev. Thomas Romney Robinson, D.D.; d. 1897.

At the death of Professor Y. F. Edgeworth in 1926 the estate passed to trustees for his nieces Maria Sanderson and Rosa Montague. The house and most of the property were sold in the early 1930s.

Chapter One

1782-1792

His friends tried to dissuade him when in 1782 Richard Lovell Edgeworth announced his intention of taking his third wife Elizabeth and the children of his two previous marriages to live in Ireland, at Edgeworthstown in the wilds of County Longford. What, they asked, would a man with his scientific and intellectual tastes find to satisfy him in that half-civilized country, cut off from every enlightened and stimulating idea and the society of his equals? As an unusually skilful amateur several of his mechanical devices had been awarded medals by the Society of Arts and he was equally well-versed in chemistry, engineering and moral philosophy. Only quite recently his friend Sir Joseph Banks had welcomed him as a newly-elected Fellow of the Royal Society.

Since Edgeworth's twenty-third year, having proved by experience that pleasure-seeking did not appease his urge to improve himself or solve the problem of how to achieve a satisfied, contented frame of mind, his chosen friends were men with similar aspirations. At Lichfield in the serious-minded coterie of philosophers and scientists revolving round Dr. Erasmus Darwin he found what he sought. All agreed that only through hard, unselfish work, losing one-self in a steady stream of useful employment, could enduring happiness and peace of mind be obtained. Unless a man exerted himself to conquer his faults and cultivate the virtues of industry and altruism no saving grace would avail him. They taught him, too, to accept pain and pleasure, life and death, with the same equanimity; a principle requiring almost superhuman fortitude that earned them an undeserved reputation of heartlessness.

Having for the past fifteen years resolutely practised these exacting doctrines, Edgeworth now felt compelled to turn his back on the life he enjoyed in order to go and look after his neglected Irish estate and the tenants who provided his income. He also intended to educate his children along lines of his own. Any terrors their banishment might have held for his family were smoothed away by their devotion and trust in his infallible wisdom. And when on a June day as shivering and cheerless as the desolate bogs and hills which they saw through the windows as the coach carried them towards Edgeworthstown, one glance at his keen, blue-eyed, authoritative countenance brimming with confidence, resourcefulness and vigour, was enough to dispel any melancholy impressions their introduction to Ireland may have evoked. The swarming beggars who closed in on them the instant they landed at Dunleary, fighting and scrambling to get hold of their bags and boxes before the porters drove them off; the unsavoury, poverty-stricken hordes thronging the narrow Dublin streets; the wretchedness and squalor pervading the countryside—'towns' consisting of a row of miserable huts with dung-hills at the doors and weeds and grass flourishing on the thatch, and whole families squatting in the ditch alongside the road by a little hovel huddled together with branches and turf. Broken-down fences, gates half off their hinges—the trail of disorder followed them to their own front door. After standing empty for six years Edgeworthstown House, blotched by damp, the paintwork peeling, and here and there a broken window-pane, presented a dismal appearance.

To Maria it looked very odd and unfinished, a slice of a house, all front with nothing behind. Set at an angle from the village, approached by a drive across the field, the big yard at the back opened on to the main street. Hardly a tree broke up the undeviating flatness stretching sombrely towards a far horizon; a dreary vista of flat fields, black bogs and dirty roads as Maria often remarked in years to come. But quite undaunted the happy, united little party entered their new home and as Maria wandered through the rooms and peered through the windows she saw roses blooming on the over-grown bushes in the garden. Running out to pick them, her sense of strangeness, of being in a foreign land, grew even more acute as she saw snowflakes glistening on the petals.

Maria, aged fifteen and a half, was the second child of her father's first and only unhappy marriage. Her mother, Anna Maria Elers, had been one of the penniless, almost illiterate daughters of a gone-to-seed lawyer of German extraction married to the Hungerford heiress of Black Bourton in Oxfordshire. As a sociable, impressionable Oxford student, young Edgeworth used to spend his vacations at Black Bourton, reading with Paul Elers and philandering with the pretty girls. He was quite out of love with her when, determined to do what was right, he eloped with Anna Maria to Gretna Green. Their son Richard, born before his father was twenty and brought up in imitation of Rousseau's *Emile*, grew up wild and uncontrollable. He was at sea, serving under Edgeworth's friend Lord Longford, when the family moved to Ireland but very soon afterwards he ran away from his ship at Goa and nothing more was heard of him for years. Maria, three years younger than Richard, was succeeded by two more girls—Emmeline who was still at school at Derby, and Anna born in March 1773, the day their mother died.

Next in age were Honora and Lovell, eight and seven respectively, the children of Edgeworth's second wife and his life's great love—Honora Sneyd of legendary beauty and merit, who dying of hereditary consumption seven years after their marriage, enjoined him for his own sake and his children's to marry her sister Elizabeth as soon as he could. Though at first neither of them wished it, so compelling was the power of Honora's last injunctions that Elizabeth ran away from her father's house in Lichfield to take charge of her broken-hearted brother-in-law. Supported by the fondness and sympathy of this handsome, dark-eyed young woman, his grief yielded at length to the unruffled serenity of their domestic life. They had been married for eighteen months in June, 1782, their little Bessy was nine months old and Henry was born the following September.

From her 'mother Honora' whose beauty took her breath away though her strictness chilled her heart, Maria learned obedience and the scrupulous neatness and orderliness in whatever she did that characterized her through life. Later at Mrs. Latuffière's school at Derby where she spent five years, she acquired perfect French and became a skilled needlewoman, and from her father's friend, the austere philosopher Thomas Day, whose moral disquisitions formed part of the pattern at home, she learned to reason impartially and the correct understanding and use of words. When she came home for the holidays to the little house near Berkhamstead where they lived, her father encouraged her to listen while he and his friends talked, arguing and debating some knotty ethical or scientific problem, and at school he watched over her from afar, admonishing her in long letters to control her temper and regulate her conduct in order that

Anna-Maria Elers
m. 1763 d. 1773

Honora Sneyd
m. 1773 d. 1780

Elizabeth Sneyd
m. 1780 d. 1797

Frances Anne Beaufort
m. 1798 d. 1865

1. RICHARD LOVELL EDGEWORTH'S FOUR WIVES

she might become 'a very excellent and an highly improved woman'. He encouraged her gift for inventing stories and when she was thirteen was writing: 'It would be very agreeable to me my dear Maria to have letters from you familiarly —I wish to know what you like and what you dislike—I wish to communicate to you what little knowledge I have acquired, that you may have a tincture of every species of Literature and that you may form your taste by choice and not by chance.' With his sharp insight into a child's nature he realized that his little ugly duckling, inside the stifling coils of her nervous diffidence, had qualities and capacities of a high order. As for Maria, who adored him ever since she could remember, the desire to please him, to be as he wished, was her guiding star. Without him she felt sure she could not go on existing, an unkind fate having burdened her not only with every physical disadvantage but a hypersensitive disposition as well. Her pale, narrow face looked altogether too small for her big, beaky nose and wide mouth, and her fair hair was thin and straight. Her little hands were square and stumpy-fingered, her feet tiny as a child's because she grew no taller. She was almost a dwarf, measuring only four feet, seven and a half inches tall when she was twenty-one.

To make matters worse, for the last eighteen months she had been badly disfigured by an inflammation of the eyes that distorted her whole face. As it was thought likely she would lose her sight she was taken away from the fashionable school in Wimpole Street where she spent nine unhappy months, looked upon as very odd and pedantic by her companions. Though this danger was over and she could read and write with impunity the effects of the disease were still painfully visible. Her only bulwark was the ever-strengthening intimacy with her father whose power over her was magical. Caught in its vital beam, her crushing sense of inferiority dissolved like vapour in the sun, turning her into quite a different person, alert, confident, capable of anything. His favourite sister Margaret Ruxton, so like him in character and looks, and almost as fond of Maria, braced and exhilarated her in the same way. Aunt Ruxton, who lived at Black Castle in Navan, half a day's journey from Edgeworthstown, was the wife of a badly-off retired army officer and of their numerous offspring only three lived on to be Maria's lifelong friends—Sophy, Margaret and Richard. Always passionately grateful for any sign of approval or affection, her aunt's kindness when she first came to Ireland won Maria's devoted and unfaltering allegiance. 'How can I forget my Aunt Ruxton,' the famous novelist wrote long afterwards, 'who has been constantly partially kind to me from the time I was a child with enflamed eyes and swelled features for whom nobody else cared.' Nor did she ever forget the delight of driving to Black Castle (only a 'bowery cottage' in spite of its name) with her father; of how, as the carriage entered the avenue, she would shut the book she was reading to him and start fidgeting with impatience to be there, and his warning: 'Take care my child and don't eat your cake beforehand—don't wear out your pleasure by anticipation. Read on, Maria, read on and don't think of Aunt Ruxton till you see her.' Maria's visits to Black Castle, a joy all her life, were the subject of a perennial joke. If her aunt had not a bed to spare, wrote Maria, 'I am so small I can sleep in a drawer', to which Mrs. Ruxton duly answered that though Maria was always welcome, she must at least have a day's warning 'to get the drawer ready'.

Also from gratitude sprang her affection for Fanny Robinson whose kindness was her only solace at Wimpole Street, as Maria later reminded her when Fanny had cause to reproach her for not writing. 'I hate you? and pray now my dear what in the name of Fortune put that into your head? Pray why should I hate Miss Fanny Robinson?

Because she has uniformly showed me more affection and kindness than any friend of my own age ever showed me before? Because three years ago she preferred me to twenty girls from whom she had to chuse? Because after a three years' absence she still continues to think of me with partiality—or because where no one liked me she defended me? When I was half blind and could not read, she read to me and because since I have been idle and negligent and have not written to her this four months she has written me three kind letters.'

Letters passed regularly between Edgeworthstown and Fanny's home at Cranford, Kettering (her father, Sir George, was Member for Northampton). To Fanny Maria sent the tales and poems she wrote and confided that she was making an English translation of Madame de Genlis' *Adèle et Théodore* which she hoped to get published, and talked of the books she read. In French she was reading the works of Voltaire, Marivaux and Molière and in English everything from Blackstone's *Commentaries* and Lesolme *On the Constitution of England* to Dryden's *Fables*, Smith's *Moral Sentiments* and Gray's *Letters*. *Evelina* which in her excitement she read straight through twice from cover to cover, introduced a livelier note but as a rule she was adamant in refusing to read the novels that were Fanny's favourite literature: 'Though I am as fond of novels as you can be I am afraid they act on the constitution of the mind as Drams do on that of the body' she pointed out discouragingly. Their paths were already diverging. Absorbed in the busy, useful life at Edgeworthstown Maria could not visualize the bright stream of frivolity upon which Fanny was launched or plumb its depths of satisfaction. Her determination to discover what it really amounted to caused her to reveal her innermost feelings with a frankness that is seldom heard again in her usually reticent, self-effacing letters.

'I have an odd question to ask you—are you happier at a Ball than anywhere else? You will laugh and say to be sure I am, and perhaps you will ask me why I make such an uncommon inquiry?—I will tell you why—because I am inclined to believe it is the preparations, the Musick, the dress, the praise and the bustle which constitute the charms of a Ball—therefore you will my dear Miss Robinson favour me with an exact and clear answer to this question . . . Our tastes do not in these respects, *I believe*, agree—but I see the obvious cause for their disagreeing—You have a very agreeable person, agreeable manners and many external accomplishments which I want. You are active, nimble and dance well, I am awkward and dance very ill—It is not therefore in the least surprising that you should be happy in a ballroom where you are praised and at least equal to others in those qualifications which shine most in public assemblies, or that I on the contrary with every *personal* disadvantage and others which arise from awkwardness and *mauvaise honte* should feel myself much less at my ease in company than amongst friends who set little *comparative* value on such Qualifications. Comparative value I said for because I want them myself I would not deprecate them in others—I know their value, for I know the want of them—and the pain arising from that want is certainly the most exact measure of their worth.'

Cut off thus from a girl's usual destiny, Maria lived vividly in her imagination. Inventing wonderful romances or simple tales around everyday happenings came quite naturally; at school in bed when the candle was blown out she used to regale her shuddering companions with flesh-creeping narratives and at home her small brothers and sisters listened with glee to her 'wee-wee' stories. Though her father was proud of her gift he was determined to make a capable, useful woman of her as well as a blue-stocking.

Soon after they came to Ireland he started teaching her how to keep accounts and manage his business affairs, work she became so efficient at and took such pride in that in a comparatively short while she was looking after all the household and estate finances. Continuing this all-round training, when she was eighteen little Henry was handed over to her by, as she said, 'so kind a Father and Mother who trusted him to my care to teach me the art of Education and instructed me every day and all day long in the theory and practice'. She loved her 'ward' dearly though she often feared later that his gentle, timid nature might be partly due to 'having been brought up by one who had very little experience and a great deal of cowardice herself'.

Edgeworthstown was the happiest of homes for the children, surrounded as they were by loving, sympathetic elders who regarded each child in its own right as an important person. At regular intervals a new baby arrived and almost as soon as it could toddle it became the object of that kindly vigilance which was the basis of Edgeworth's system. However busy he was with public or private affairs, his children always had first claim, he and Elizabeth and later on Maria keeping records of their sayings and doings as a key to their tastes and character. They were brought up entirely in the family, kept away from servants whose ignorant talk and uncontrolled emotions were considered harmful. There was a playroom at Edgeworthstown but never a schoolroom. They read their books and played with their toys in the library, the general sitting-room, where their father did most of his business, discussing it openly with his wife, and Maria at her desk cast up accounts or wrote a story. They were treated from the first as rational beings, their high spirits encouraged, sensible questions patiently replied to, by precept and practice growing to realize the natural consequences of good or bad behaviour. Edgeworth who did not approve of too much learning by heart or written work, egged his little pupils on to find things out for themselves. Prints and maps lying about on the library table were a great source of interest, prompting questions that often led to a history or geography lesson without their realizing it. Handicrafts like modelling and basket-making satisfied their constructive instincts while their father's indoor workshop, fitted up with every sort of tool and contrivance for mechanics and carpentry, where he was always busy constructing anything from a clock to a carriage-wheel, was the scene of instruction for old and young alike. 'No tears! No tasks! No masters!' was his boast and tears and squabbles were almost unheard of. There was always time too for games and amusements, digging their gardens, flying kites and playing battledore, with an older sister watching over the tiny ones, and seldom was their father to be seen setting off across the lawn on his rounds without several children beside him, all agog to help the men mix mortar or set up a fence.

Maria who instinctively understood little children and their needs and loved to have them about her however busy she might be, shared her father's fervent interest in education. Any book that had a bearing on it, though few they were, was always bought and contributed something at least to the collection of notes and extracts that mounted up year by year to form the staple of the great work which later made Maria and her father famous. It was already in their minds at Christmas 1785 as she mentioned it to Fanny Robinson. *Adèle et Théodore* had long been put aside, a rival translation having appeared 'in all its glory', and now she said 'my Father prefers the thoughts of an original work upon Education—including remarks upon Mad^me de Genlis, Rousseau, etc. Have you seen a book of my friend Mr. Day upon education—Sandford and Merton—Pray read it for my sake and tell me how you like it.'

Living as they did on the edge of a market town the air
resounded with primitive country noises, a distant vocifer-
ation and clatter that appealed strongly to Maria who relished
all the facets and signs of life. On fair days the house rang
with the noise of 'pigs squealing, men bawling, women
brawling, and children squealing' and by afternoon with the
uproar of drunkards fighting in the road and homeward
bound peasants shouting as they belaboured the beasts they
drove before them. Her curiosity about people of all degrees
was insatiable and from the moment she came to Ireland
she was fascinated by the different types of 'lower Irish'—
loungers, agents, tenants and petitioners—who invaded the
yard and pushed their way into the garden, to seek a favour
or to air their grievances. Her father could scarcely cross his
yard without being waylaid by some lurking figure, with his
head as likely as not bound up in a blood-stained garter, and
a tortuous, rambling tale to tell that Maria drank in with
every look and inflection that went to its telling. She followed him everywhere during those first months, as he
walked round the demesne setting in train a long-term pro-
gramme of fencing, levelling, draining and planting. A great
deal required doing, indoors and out, and at the head of a
large band of workmen he directed operations, attended by
his steward John Langan.

Maria was immediately attracted by this fine-looking,
picturesque countryman in his battered broad-brimmed hat
and old frieze greatcoat slung over his shoulders and but-
toned at his neck like a cloak, whose passionate loyalty to
'the family', scraps of country lore and wonderful super-
stitions permeated his talk. Though Maria in these early
days was usually so silent, she could when she chose make
everyone rock with laughter by her gift for mimicry; her
retentive memory and sharp eye for the ludicrous losing

none of the idiosyncrasies of a comical character and enabling her to tell some complicated, highly-coloured history word for word as it fell from his lips. She listened for hours to John Langan's descriptions of the strange things that had happened at weddings, death-beds and wakes within his own memory, flavoured by his grudging respect for the *good people* (fairies) and their friendly and unfriendly feats. When the wind raised an eddy of dust on the road the country people knew that the fairies were travelling from one fairy-mound to another. 'God speed ye, gentlemen, God speed ye' they would say as they passed for otherwise the *good people* might be offended and do them some harm. Though to the practical Edgeworths fairy-mounds were nothing but common or garden ant-hills, when the lawn was being levelled the labourers flatly refused to demolish one of these humps and Edgeworth had to take the pick and do the job himself.

Many curious figures besides the invisible fairies were to be met on the roads; itinerant harpists and fiddlers or a dancing master accompanied by a piper, travelling from cabin to cabin to teach old and young the jigs which were danced with such furious zest at village weddings. Or they might meet one of the long funeral processions winding slowly across the hills to some remote family burying-place, the countryside reverberating with gusts of wild sobbing and wailing, certain old women with very strong lungs being hired to give vent to their vociferous lamentations. As a man once remarked to Maria: 'Everyone would wish and be proud to have such at his funeral or at that of his friends.' Their natural grace in expressing themselves was enchanting; a gossoon given a message to take to a distant house promising to 'be off at the flight of night' or a would-be tenant assuring her father 'I should be proud to live upon your honour's land as long as the grass grows or water runs.'

As she grew stronger, every day Maria went riding with him, forgetting her fear of horses as she trotted beside him along the lanes and across the fields, listening to what he was telling her. His brain worked faster than ever on horseback, thinking, inventing, composing at an astonishing rate, while his shrewd eyes assessed the state of the land they rode over and the crops of potatoes and flax. He had taken the management of his estate into his own hands, determined that no middleman should come between him and his tenants, examining every acre himself and judging the farmer by what he found. He saw much that displeased him; farms let for ninety-nine years or three lives which looked exactly like tribal settlements, swarming with a ragged population and dotted with cabins, having been divided and subdivided among the sons of subsequent generations. Directly these leases fell in he put an end to the system. He made many benevolent changes, abolishing the old feudal fines and penalties that were still enforced, the unjust 'duty work' which many landlords insisted upon and the 'duty fowls'—turkeys and geese—that had to be supplied free and in great quantities to the 'Big House'. Owing to the severity of the Popery Laws, Roman Catholic tenants were entirely at the mercy of Protestant landlords, but Edgeworth, ever the champion of justice, treated Catholics and Protestants exactly alike. Slowly and prudently he set about improving his farms and the buildings and twice a year he held his own rent day in his house, Maria sitting beside him filling in the ledger as the tenant paid him the money.

Within a few years Maria, imbued with his high principles, was managing most of his estate business, work that brought her closer still to the people. She could sum up the different types and see through the complicated webs they wove around their words and deeds, though her father maintained that she was always too ready to throw prudence to the winds when her heart was wrung by a tale of woe. Her credulity worried him: 'Maria will swallow anything like a gudgeon' he would say, though it did not prevent him from writing: 'Anybody my dearest Daughter who knows you are entirely in my confidence, that you transact all my business and that I love you as much as a father can love a daughter. . . .'

His many interests and the active part he played in the county brought people of all kinds to hospitable Edgeworthstown where sometimes as many as thirty sat down to dinner. Government officials and members of the learned professions from Dublin and local lights of every degree found their way to his always well-spread table. Quiet in her corner, looking the very emblem of meekness, Maria listened intently to what was said, especially if the talk turned to the old days and the doings of some wild Irish gentleman in his lonely castle. One of the first of such stories she heard was that of the fortune-hunting Colonel McGuire who, having married a rich Lady Cathcart, kept her locked up in a room in his house for more than twenty years. An old Mr. Nugent who came to Edgeworthstown described how when the Colonel died he rescued her from her filthy lair, a scared, half-stupefied creature in a red wig and rags, and took her back to her friends in England. Maria could not get it out of her mind; when her curiosity was awakened, with tireless pertinacity she would follow a trail year after year, leaving no stone unturned or likely person unquestioned, in her determination to get to the bottom of it. This passionate curiosity about people and their motives agitated her as violently in old age as when she was young. It served too to pass the time at the large, dull dinners which were the only form of entertainment in the neighbouring houses, when course after course was wolfed down without speaking and the gentlemen spent hours over their wine while the ladies sat on hard stiff-backed chairs in a silent circle in the drawing-room.

At nearby Fox Hall Edgeworth's elder sister resided with her husband, Mr. Fox, and they counted themselves lucky at being within visiting distance of Castle Forbes in one direction and Pakenham Hall in another. At Castle Forbes Lord and Lady Granard were a very young couple in 1782, he extremely good-natured but not very wise and she always too much the fine lady to please critical Maria. All the same she often went there to see Lady Granard's mother, Lady Moira, an accomplished woman of the world, renowned in Dublin for her wit and learning. Lady Moira who enjoyed talking to such an unusually well-read and intelligent girl always sent for Maria when she came to Castle Forbes. At Pakenham Hall the Edgeworths were very much in their element, the long-standing family friendship dating back to the beginning of the century when a step-daughter of Edgeworth's grandfather had married the father of the first Lord Longford. The second Lord Longford, a naval captain, now lived there with his amiable wife and a long string of sons and daughters, keeping open house to innumerable relations and friends. To get there needed considerable fortitude: 'there was a vast Serbonian bog between us; with a bad road, an awkward ferry, and a country so frightful and so overrun with yellow weeds, that it was aptly called by Mrs. Greville "the yellow dwarf's country".' Mrs. Greville, Fanny Burney's 'penetrating, puissant and sarcastic fairy queen', authoress of a much-admired *Ode to Indifference*, brought a whiff of literary London to Pakenham Hall which Maria must have enjoyed.

Her father knew and so did she that some day she would be an authoress; out riding they often discussed the plots and characters she made up, his zest for romancing as strong as her own. He would make suggestions and widen her knowledge by telling her stories of his own experiences as a young man when he lived for two years in London with the fashionable, raffish friends of that gay rake Sir Francis Delaval. As she grew older she applied herself more seriously to her writing, taking much greater pains with the stories she told the children to illustrate a particular lesson or precept, and in collaboration with her father beginning a novel.

Five years went by. Elizabeth Edgeworth was recovering from her sixth confinement and to amuse her, her husband made up a long history called *The Freeman Family* which he told every evening to the whole party clustered round her bed. Out riding next day he repeated it to Maria who was able when she got in to write it down exactly as he told it. On this story she practised her craft for years, eventually using it as a plot for her novel *Patronage*, published in 1815.

As for her 'wee-wee' stories, having scribbled a tale on a slate she would read it out to the children, watching their reactions as they afterwards talked about it. According to what they said she wrote it out again, often making several versions before her young critics were satisfied. From the first her books were very much a family affair, written for the general amusement and freely talked about and pulled to pieces as they sat round the library fire in the evening. Although Maria as a rule was easily discouraged, terrified of unfriendly critics and being laughed at, she never minded how frankly her family expressed their views, reading her stories aloud with so much gusto that her father complained that even badly written passages sounded quite excellent. As her critic-in-chief and collaborator he corrected and cut as she wrote, attending to the grammar and composition and seldom interfering with the course of the tale unless she appealed to him—again and again his fertile invention

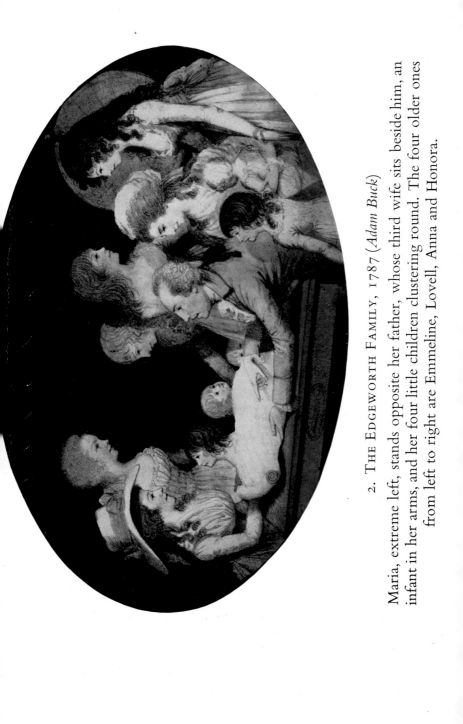

2. THE EDGEWORTH FAMILY, 1787 (*Adam Buck*)

Maria, extreme left, stands opposite her father, whose third wife sits beside him, an infant in her arms, and her four little children clustering round. The four older ones from left to right are Emmeline, Lovell, Anna and Honora.

helped her out when her own ran dry. She often sent what she wrote to Black Castle to hear what her aunt and cousin Sophy thought of it—Sophy several years younger than Maria was fast becoming her closest friend.

Though two little children died in the course of these years such minor misfortunes were only to be expected, but when in the winter of 1789 lovely, angelic-tempered Honora lay on the library sofa fading away with consumption at the age of fifteen, the whole family was heart-broken. Endowed by her fatal heritage with vivid beauty and a precocious brilliance, she was beloved by all; on her father particularly her premature death inflicted the cruellest of wounds. In despair Maria entreated Aunt Ruxton 'to come in one of the coaches to chear my poor Father's heart and my Mother and all our Hearts—It is the most melancholy thing imagineable to see my Father preparing to bear the loss of his second Honora.'

Though he strove hard when she died to accept it calmly the strain was too much for him: 'we cannot help seeing his feelings at intervals'. Maria's heart ached for him for many months. Although she had achieved such a position in the family, placing her in a category apart from the others, her dependence on him grew greater rather than less. This was by no means his wish. He did everything he could to make her independent, giving her money of her own so that she might be, he said, 'independent for subsistence'. He very much hoped she would marry, a hope he never concealed. 'What sincere satisfaction I shall feel in seeing you united to a man worthy of your merit. My whole mind has been turned to forming your character for the enjoyment and the power of conferring permanent happiness.'

This marriage theme runs through his letters to her from the time she is seventeen, a wish that was ever uppermost. Frank and outspoken as he was and loving her as he did, he probably often talked about it too. What Maria felt, always morbidly aware of her ugliness (even late in life she never cared to look in a glass) can only be conjectured. She was much too well-trained in the habits of cheerful compliance that were essential to an improved woman, to show her distress. With exemplary self-control, her rigid sense of what a daughter owed her parent never allowed her to contradict or criticize. She bore it meekly, blaming herself perhaps for whatever pain his affectionate wishes caused her.

Early in 1791 when he and his wife went to England, Maria was left in charge at home, given *carte blanche* where business was concerned. Luckily for her peace of mind the good effects of his educational system were never in better evidence as she told her aunt, whose comparative proximity was a great solace: 'I feel much more cheerful than I had any idea I should . . . because my sisters and Lovell are so kind to me.' But Lovell whose auburn locks and sweet smile were so like his mother's looked wretchedly ill, torn by a hacking cough. That summer he joined his parents at Clifton, the great place for consumptives, where they had taken a house for Elizabeth's approaching confinement. Besides the Hot-wells where the invalids congregated, Clifton was a popular resort among the fashionable and well-to-do; just the place in Edgeworth's opinion, to give his three grown-up daughters the opportunities they should have for making new friends.

For Maria, rising twenty-five, this was important; at Clifton she could hardly fail to meet the right man. Fired by this splendid conviction he sat down and wrote to her: 'I never see a Gentleman of tolerable promise, that I do not immediately think of you; and instantly consider whether we should like him.' And soon afterwards, in what seemed to her the 'kindest possible letter', he ordered her to bring the whole family to Clifton as soon as she could.

Chapter Two

1792-1798

Six years went by. Though two were passed at Clifton no suitor came courting Maria; it was vivacious, elegant Anna who was wooed and won by the celebrated Dr. Beddoes who was just setting up in practice there. The other outstanding event was the return of the errant Richard from the rice-fields of South Carolina where he was scraping a living for his wife and family; he crossed the Atlantic on two future occasions to visit his father before his death in 1796. Maria was full of affectionate concern for him and all he might still become but he was too much of a rolling stone and Edgeworth when he announced Richard's death to his old friend Miss Mary Powys, did not mince his words: 'All that he received from me in two years about £2,000 was spent and his way of life had become such as promised no happiness to himself or his family—it is therefore better for both that he has retired from the scene.'

From Clifton Maria went to Roehampton to spend a month with her friend Fanny, now Mrs. Charles Hoare, wife of the young Fleet Street banker. Though she politely insisted in her letters home that 'Mrs. Hoare is exceedingly kind to me' the reunion after ten years was a dismal fiasco. Learned, serious-minded Maria, awkward and tongue-tied as ever in company, and the fashionable young married

35

lady, had so little to say to each other as they sat in Fanny's large drawing-room that it was quite a relief when the tea-urn was brought in and its 'bubbling and whizzing created some sensation'. Worst of all Maria could not play cards and the Hoares and their friends did little else and if they talked it was of nothing but 'chariots and horses, curricles and tandems. Oh to what contempt I exposed myself in a luckless hour by asking what a tandem was!' Her father's well-meant injunction, starting off hopefully: 'If you can find any situation in the world more agreeable to you than our family . . . 'must have rubbed salt into her sores for had she been endowed with the attractions that elicit soft glances and flattering attentions from hovering swains Fanny might have been kinder. Those unhappy weeks gave the *coup de grâce* to the friendship. Twenty years later on when Fanny's nephew, Sir Thomas Acland, called at Edgeworthstown to pay his respects to the novelist, Maria refused to revive it. 'He pressed me much to send my love to his aunt Mrs. C. Hoare, and to promise that I would go to see her again whenever I went to England—My love I sent her—that is as much of it as she wants or he could carry—but no promise to trust myself again in the fine lady's den, could be extorted from me. *'Deceived for once I trust not friends again.'* Not but what I forgive her with all my heart . . . but there is no occasion for my quitting my happy home a second time to go and see one who could not find out that I was a good friend till the public told her I was an authoress.'

While they were at Clifton builders were busy at Edge-worthstown finishing off the house which Edgeworth had been adding to by slow degrees. They returned to find it looking much as it does still, a spacious, white-walled square with big light rooms and a plentiful supply of bedrooms—very different from what it was in 1782. Young trees were growing up fast to shade the park-like lands beyond the

garden that were always called 'the lawn'; an arched doorway led into a walled kitchen-garden close by the house;
granaries and barns gave a look of solidity to the yard and
a nearby wood where in spring the herons nested was
tattered and stained by approaching winter.

Maria was glad to be home and again within reach of
Aunt Ruxton and Sophy's sympathetic and invigorating
society. She could never read a new book without immediately wondering what her aunt would think of it and now
as her father read Gay's *Trivia* aloud, 'I wished very much
dear aunt that you and Sophy had been sitting round the
fire with us . . . I had much rather make a bargain with
anyone I loved to read the same book at the same hour than
to look at the moon like Rousseau's famous lovers.' And
'I like to read as well as to talk with you my dear aunt
because you mix the grave and gay together and put your
long finger on the very passages which my short stumpy
one was just starting forward to point out if it could point.'

In the summer Sophy must come to Edgeworthstown.
'I will tell you what is going on that you may see whether
you like our daily bill of fare. . . . There are an' please you
ma'am a great many good things here. There is a balloon
hanging up and another going to be put on the stocks—
there is soap made and making from a receipt in Nicholson's
chemistry—there is excellent ink made and to be made by
the same book—there is a cake of roses just squeezed in a
vice by my father according to the advice of Madame De
Lagaraye. . . . There are a set of accurate weights just completed by the ingenious Messrs. Lovell and Henry Edgeworth partners—for Henry is now a junior partner and
grown an inch and a half on the strength of it.'

The bad state Ireland was in at this time, due to the anti-
popery prejudices which the French Revolution aroused in
the English politicians, was the reason for Edgeworth's

return. A spirit of tolerance that had led to various concessions and the repeal of many of the penal laws, had suddenly
turned into dislike and terror. Ireland accordingly became
a fruitful field for French agents who arrived with tempting
offers of liberty. The United Irishmen under Wolfe Tone
plotted with France while the Protestants, shocked at the
thought of a priest-ridden state, formed the Orange Society.
Wider issues were soon forgotten in the fury and turmoil
of a bitter religious feud.

Although for some time things were quiet in County
Longford, the treacherous tide crept on across the bogs
until quite unexpectedly it broke almost against their walls.
'Last night,' wrote Maria in consternation, 'a party of forty
attacked the house of one Hoxey about half a mile from us.'
In the ensuing panic Edgeworth took command. Men came
hurrying to him with their fire-arms for safe-keeping, meetings were called, soldiers billeted. 'The poor people here are
robbed every night—Last night a poor old woman was
considerably roasted—My father has been at it all day.'

Besides organizing the county against the Defenders and
commanding a squadron of horse, the danger of a French
invasion made Edgeworth take up again one of his early
inventions—a telegraph by means of a series of signals.
'Telegraphic affairs' kept the family occupied for months
and while he vainly tried to persuade the Government to
adopt it he was also preparing to contest a local constituency.
Night after night Maria sat up into the small hours, 'working her fingers to the stumps' writing his electioneering
letters. She gloried at the welcome he met with as he rode
about the country on his grey horse, 'hailed as "the poor
man's friend" with joy and eagerness'. With the landowning
gentry, however, his liberal ideas and championship of the
peasants made him unpopular and as Lord Granard and
other magnates refused their support, he withdrew before

the election. Later he was elected for one of the Longford boroughs.

In 1795 Elizabeth Edgeworth's two unmarried sisters, Charlotte and Mary Sneyd, left Lichfield and came to take up their abode at Edgeworthstown. These gentle, fluttering ladies settled most happily into the busy communal life, their many good works in the village causing them to be known as 'the two good ladies'. Almost as soon as she got there, Aunt Mary found her special vocation as Maria's 'copier in chief'.

Though death and destruction stalked without, and indoors from her desk in the library, Maria was 'eternally being called to something else', she went steadily on with her writing. *The Freeman Family* had been abandoned in favour of a serious treatise, a plea that the wretchedly rudimentary education accorded even to the daughters of the greatest in the land might be improved. She and her father had talked of it for a long while and now as she wrote he corrected her pages, disfiguring them she told Sophy 'by all manner of crooked marks besides various abusive marginal notes, that I would not have you see for half a crown sterling'.

Letters to Literary Ladies was published by Joseph Johnson, the bookseller of St. Paul's Churchyard, in 1796 and later that year he brought out a collection of Maria's children's stories under the title of *The Parent's Assistant*. With two successful books to her credit she was now well launched on her career; by the autumn of 1797 Johnson was planning to print second editions of both. That of *The Parent's Assistant* was to be illustrated and Aunt Ruxton solved the problem of the artist by recommending her talented young friend Frances Beaufort, one of the daughters of their former rector at Navan who now held the living at Collon.

Maria in the meantime was hard at work getting her

39

third and most important book ready for the press—the great work on education so long discussed and now written in close collaboration with her father. He, with his advanced views, had always realized how important it is to begin inculcating good habits and the right ideas from an early age. Taking into consideration the character and tendencies of each child, as a general rule all children, he insisted, should be taught to pay attention, to take an intelligent interest in what goes on around them and encouraged to find things out for themselves. Then, with such habits as industry, perseverance, unselfishness and self-control firmly implanted, and the ability to use their hands as well as their heads, children have every chance of growing into useful, independent and contented men and women. As we have seen he, and more recently Maria, had devoted a great deal of thought and care to perfecting his theories, studying and often adapting to suit his purpose the rules and suggestions put forward by such writers as Rousseau and Madame de Genlis. Now in *Practical Education* all the fruits of their reading and experience were garnered, in an eloquent attempt to bring home to all classes how urgently reforms were needed in the nursery and schoolroom. The book spans the whole range of childhood and adolescence, every aspect of a child's life being taken into account, from its toys and pastimes to its moral and mental welfare. Higher standards of education for girls were again warmly advocated and the advantages of a modern instead of a classical education for boys who were not destined for one of the learned professions. The inclusion of elementary science in the curriculum was another revolutionary suggestion, together with the simple experiments that were an important and exciting feature of Edgeworth's lessons. The Edgeworthstown children at work and at play are to be encountered throughout the book, reports of their questions and conversations serving to prove or exemplify particular points. Thus the whole family had a part in it, Lovell writing the chapter on *Chemistry* while that on *Obedience* was woven round Elizabeth's notes.

All that summer of 1797 Elizabeth Edgeworth lay on the sofa, looking like the wraith of her once beautiful self, going carefully over the proofs of *Practical Education* until she was too feeble to turn the pages. For wars and rebellions were not the only calamities overshadowing the house; ever since the birth of her youngest child William in 1794 her health had been failing, a slow, inexorable decline that her husband could not endure to watch. Again that fell disease was destroying his domestic happiness, depriving him of a wife who as he said 'more than fulfilled the promises made by her generous sister'. To be happily married was essential to him, the key to all else. During the years of his wife's illness home was no longer the same happy place. To appease his troubled heart and as an outlet for his abounding energy he threw himself into politics which involved a great deal of travelling about and frequent trips to Dublin. But now the stricken years were nearly at an end; as winter drew in Elizabeth became much worse. As she lay dying, in another room Bessy was dangerously ill with smallpox from which she was to recover sadly disfigured, only to die at Clifton of galloping consumption in three years' time. Elizabeth Edgeworth died on November 27th and, having laid her to rest in the vault in the churchyard, life at Edgeworthstown went on as usual unhindered by vain regrets.

Edgeworth was never a man to let the grass grow under him. Though close on fifty-four now he was in splendid fettle, interested in everything, ready for anything. On his way to Dublin he often stayed at Collon with John Foster the Speaker whose house was not far from the rectory, and latterly he and the Reverend Daniel Beaufort had become increasingly intimate. The rector was an interesting man of French-Huguenot parentage, a noted cartographer, with nice taste in literature. Quite lately he had vetted 'Maria's great work' and his report pleased her: 'the prophecies of so good a judge as Dr. Beaufort are most comfortable words'. Mrs. Beaufort was a Waller of Allenstown, Co. Meath and their family had been brought up to be as well-informed and industrious as the Edgeworths.

Fanny Beaufort, aged twenty-nine this winter and her father's favourite companion, whose 'beautiful drawings' for Maria's stories were much admired, was as Edgeworth saw at a glance a very exceptional young woman. When in his blunt, outspoken way he criticized and corrected her work, instead of taking offence she listened with the utmost good nature and intelligence. Besides being sensible she was pleasing to look at with her sea-green eyes, russet locks, serene expression and small, trim figure.

Conjectures as to who would be the fourth Mrs. Edgeworth were already rife among those who knew him best— Margaret Ruxton and Charlotte and Mary Sneyd; all felt sure he would marry again as soon as ever he could. No such thought seems to have entered Maria's head until the name of Frances Beaufort suddenly riveted her attention and she found herself threatened by a situation that might easily ruin her life. She had seen her once and had not liked her. All through this dark December with this dread at her heart, her loyal devotion must have been sorely tried by her father's high spirits when he returned from his trips to Dublin. In January when her aunt and Sophy came to stay they cross-questioned Maria about his intentions almost before they were inside the house, declaring to her dismay that Frances Beaufort was just the right wife for him. Though Maria, who could be as downright as her father, disagreed with every word they went on praising Fanny to the skies.

When the Ruxtons left her father told her everything but nothing he said reconciled her to it: 'I have told my father in much stronger terms than ever I used in speaking to you, *the exact state of my mind* in the whole progress of this business', she wrote to Sophy. She was just as unyielding when in February the Beauforts came to stay though on closer acquaintance her opinion of Fanny improved somewhat. While they were there he made his formal declaration but Fanny, overwhelmed by the size of his family and daunted by Maria's downcast looks, begged for time to think it over.

During these emotion-racked weeks whilst he was on tenterhooks, desperately in love and his fate in the balance, he spared nothing to propitiate Maria, to make her see his beloved through his eyes. He loved and relied on Maria, he reiterated, just as he always would but he must have a wife. He poured out his feelings without any reserve, determined that she should realize how groundless her fears were. 'I believe no human creature ever saw the heart of another more completely without disguise, than you have seen mine,' he said. His fervid confidences soothed and warmed her heart, proving beyond doubt how dear she was to him. Never had he been so affectionate, so confiding, showing her letters and telling her things 'which have layed Miss B's character and disposition thoroughly open to me'. Her prejudices were softening when he took her to stay at Collon where a satisfactory understanding between all three was reached and the way cleared for that golden alliance delineated by Fanny which united them from that time forth.

'Say that you give me your friendship,' she wrote to Maria when the visit was over, 'as I give you mine; that instead of lessening your dear father's love to you by taking part of it myself I have only awakened in his heart another equal portion of affection, only made the third side of an equilateral triangle—all equal all necessary to each other.'

Endless letters were exchanged in the course of the three months' engagement and with each new instance of Frances Beaufort's kind, unselfish nature Maria saw that her father by no means over-estimated her. All she asked was to be allowed to slip as unobtrusively as possible into the existing pattern; the two aunts must not dream of leaving their home and nothing must be changed. Happiness was already returning to the house as everyone looked forward to her coming and Maria shared in her father's delighted 'preparations for June'.

'I flatter myself,' wrote Maria a week before the wedding, 'that you will find me gratefully exact *en belle fille* . . . I think there is a great difference between that species of ceremony which exists betwixt acquaintances and that which should always exist between the best friends—the one prevents the growth of affection—the other preserves it in youth and age. Many foolish people make fine plantations and forget to fence them, so the young trees are destroyed by the rude cattle and the bark of the old forest trees are sometimes injured by rubbing—You need not Dear Miss B —fence yourself round with very strong palings in this family where all have been early taught to mind their boundaries—as for me—you see my intentions, or at least my theories are good enough, if my practice be but half as good you will be content, will you not?'

A grave threat to their happy expectations lay in the state of the country; after a long lull it was again becoming so dangerous that many families (and the Ruxtons among them) had left Ireland. Dublin was actually under arms when on May 31st, his birthday, Edgeworth and Frances Beaufort were married there. Outside St. Anne's Church his carriage waited to take them straight home, a drive that was not without hazards as part of the country they traversed was in open rebellion. When they reached Edgeworthstown late that evening the whole family was waiting to welcome them: 'the two Miss Sneyds, Maria, Emmeline, Bessy, Charlotte (Lovell was then in Edinburgh), Henry, Sneyd, Honora and William'. Never was a young stepmother greeted with greater affection; never, as Maria in old-age declared, did a marriage bring greater happiness to so many people. Essentially a home-maker, she took them all to her heart, by her affectionate care for each and all filling the void left empty by Elizabeth's long illness. Between her and Maria it was exactly as she predicted, an exquisitely balanced interdependence and intimacy with Edgeworth as its central figure, neither wife nor daughter ever encroaching on the other's claims. From the night of her arrival Maria addressed her as 'mother' and deferred to her in everything.

Though their neighbourhood was quiet for the next few weeks the reports of what was happening elsewhere were alarming. 'Why cannot we be left in peace to enjoy our happiness? that is all we have the conscience to ask; we are indeed happy my dear good Sophy . . . The more I see of my friend and mother the more I love and esteem her . . . I never saw my father at any period of his life appear so happy as he does and has done for this month past . . . We laugh and enjoy the good of every day which is more than sufficient . . . I am going on in the old way writing stories —as I cannot be a captain of Dragoons and as my sitting with my hands before me will not make any one of us one degree more safe . . . I know nothing of Practical Education it is advertized to be published—I have finished a vol of Parents Assistant wee-wee stories.'

While Maria wrote these tales which children all over Great Britain were beginning to clamour for, fearful omens and rumours ran wild in their once peaceful county. As their house was only a mile from the border of rebellious Westmeath, Edgeworth, helped by Lovell and Henry, raised a corps of infantry from among the peasants, true to his usual policy enlisting Catholics as well as Protestants. This made him still more unpopular with the Protestant gentlemen, their agents and hangers-on, many malicious reports being circulated. But when at the end of August the French landed at Killala the Edgeworthstown Infantry were still without weapons. The next news was that the French were marching inland. 'The Carbineers, Longford Militia and a large body of Yeomanry who opposed them' were entirely cut off; Athlone was said to be their objective, then Dublin. 'Most fortunately for us,' wrote Maria, 'they have left us behind in their route—My father's corps of Yeomanry are extremely attached to him and seem fully in earnest but alas! by some strange negligence their arms have not yet arrived from Dublin . . . You would scarcely believe perhaps . . . that he goes on regularly every morning a lesson in Algebra.—My mother has made a charming picture of St. Peter.'

These peaceful pastimes were brought to an abrupt conclusion, and face to face with the horrors of war they were forced to flee from home and take refuge at Mrs. Fallon's Inn at Longford.

'We are all safe and well and have had two most fortunate escapes from Rebels and from the explosion of an Ammunition cart—My father's Yeomen were at this moment gone to Longford for their arms . . . We were ordered to decamp with each a small bundle—the two chaises full and my mother and Aunt Charlotte on horseback were all ready to move when the report was contradicted—only 20 or 30 men were now as it was said in arms and my father hoped we might still hold fast to our dear home.—Two officers and 6 dragoons happened at this moment to be on their way through Edgeworthstown escorting an ammunition cart from Mullingar to Longford—They promised to take us under their protection and the officer rode up to the door to let us know he was ready—My father most fortunately detained us—they set out without us—Half an hour afterwards as we were quietly sitting in the portico we heard as we thought close to us the discharge of a pistol or a clap of thunder which shook the house—The officer soon returned almost speechless with terror—He could hardly explain what had happened. The ammunition cart containing nearly three barrels of gunpowder packed in cases . . . took fire and burst half way on the road to Longford; the man who drove the cart was blown to atoms—nothing of him could be found; two of the horses were killed—others blown to pieces and their limbs scattered at a distance—the head and part of the body of a man was found at 120 yards distance from the spot . . .

'An hour or two afterwards we were obliged however to fly from Edgeworthstown—The pike men 300 actually were within a mile of the town—My Mother Aunt C and I rode —passed the trunk of the dead man—bloody limbs of horses and two dead horses by the help of men who pulled on our steeds—all safely lodged now at Mrs. Fallon's inn— two and but two good large rooms for the whole family— lucky we have those for town full—An hour after we left Edgeworthstown four or 500 pike and blunderbuss men came and pillaged and shattered every protestant's house in the town except Mr. and Mrs. A Bond's and my father's— said they would do my father no harm for that he had never oppressed them—touched nothing in the house—Went off in a few hours to Ballynalee of which they have now possession—My father has written to the Commanding officer at Athlone for 100 troops to defend Edgeworths-town—Whether we return thither—or whether we go to

Dublin is yet all in uncertainty—depends on L<u>d</u> Cornwallis —if he gains a victory over the French these rebels are undone—if not we are undone.'

Five anxious days were spent in their cramped and noisy quarters, officers and men for ever tramping in and out, up and down, and panicking crowds surging past the windows talking, clattering, loitering, in whispering, confidential knots. The tension worsened with every scrap of news about the French who were advancing unopposed and coming nearer every instant. Other rumours were current as well; sinister reports about the Edgeworths whose house the rebels had spared. Oblivious to public opinion Edgeworth was here, there and everywhere, sitting up all through one night to guard the gaol against a possible attack, whiling away the weary hours reading a newspaper by the light of a farthing dip. Next morning he was away reconnoitring outside the town while Henry kept watch with a telescope on the Court-house roof.

As Maria and the rest waited anxiously in an upstairs sitting-room the air suddenly rang with cheers and shouts: an express had brought the great tidings of General Lake's victory at Ballynamuck where 1,500 rebels and French lay dead upon the field. But thankfulness was quickly turned to terror when they saw a man who had started haranguing the crowd, point up at the Court-house and just as they heard him bawl out, '*That* young Edgeworth ought to be dragged down from the top of that house', their housekeeper burst into the room.

'My master, ma'am—it is all against my master, the mob say they will tear him to pieces if they catch hold of him. They say he's a traitor, that he *illuminated* the gaol to deliver it up to the French.'

Yelling for Edgeworth's blood the crowd went off to find him and, while his wife and Maria, in a dreadful state, drove

3. EDGEWORTHSTOWN HOUSE

towards Edgeworthstown in fruitless search, he got safely back to the inn and it was not until the evening that he was attacked. Great preparations were in full swing for illuminating the town, 'all hands were busy scooping turnips, and potatoes for candlesticks, to stand in every pane of every loyal window'. Accompanied by an English officer who had changed into coloured clothes, he was walking back from evening parade when a screeching, yelling mob set upon them, pelting them with stones and turf. A stunning blow on the side of his head almost brought Edgeworth down but somehow he managed to keep going until he was within a few yards of the inn's open windows. His companion had been seized by the collar and as Edgeworth shouted out 'Major Eustace is in danger', the officers sitting at dinner sprang up and rushed out with drawn swords—a sight that made the mob turn tail and vanish like smoke. The great illumination went on as though nothing had happened, every window ablaze to celebrate the victory.

Early next morning they left Longford and when they drove through their shattered village joyful faces greeted them. Only the new houses in Charlotte Row (built with money lent by Charlotte Sneyd) were untouched, 'the mob declared they would not meddle with these because they were built by the two good ladies.—Everything within these gates we found exactly as we left it—not a border trampled upon—not a flower broken—All looked fresh and cheerful in the lawn. . . . In the Hall, in the library, in the dining-room every thing precisely as we left it—a pansy which Sneyd had been drawing stood just as he left it in a glass of water upon the chimney piece—a map we had been consulting lay on the table—and the last pencil figures which Charlotte had made the last morning we took our lesson in Algebra were fresh upon the slip of paper. All that had passed since we left home seemed like a dream.'

A day or two later Maria with her parents rode towards the hills to see Lord Cornwallis's camp, sixty bell-tents pitched in a field by a pretty stream, and to dine with the officers, though she still felt badly shaken by her experiences. It was many weeks before she recovered and the echoes of the mob yelling for her father's blood finally faded from her ears. He in the meantime was pressing for a Court of Inquiry and had this not been granted he planned to leave Ireland for good. By November everything was settled to his satisfaction and he was able to turn his attention to keeping his family happy during the winter.

'My father has taken me into a new partnership with him —We are writing a comedy . . . My father is making a charming theatre in the room over his study. . . . I believe the play will be acted sometime in January and hope the Pakenhams—Mr. Fox and Lady Anne[1]—Mrs. and Dr. Beaufort, Harriet and Louisa will be here.' All her brothers and sisters were taking part and her mother was painting the scenery and planning the dresses. 'Lovell has bought a fine apparatus and materials for a course of Chemical Lectures which he is going to give us—The study is to be the laboratory.' But by far the most important news, though apparently not in Maria's estimation, was that *Practical Education* had just been published.

[1] Maria's cousin Richard Fox of Fox Hall married Lady Anne Maxwell, daughter of the last Earl of Farnham.

Chapter Three

———————— ⟲⊕⟳ ————————

1798-1801

Nothing like *Practical Education* had appeared in England since Locke's *Thoughts on Education* in 1693 and the stir it made was sensational. Its appeal was widespread. Because such scanty attention was given to bringing up children, the entirely different methods advocated by the Edgeworths aroused storms of praise and protest that whirled Maria and her father into eminence as the most talked about authors of the day. Many of the numerous letters it brought them roundly abused the book's pervading rationalism, the omission of any religious thought or teaching, even some of their warmest admirers deploring it. Although his children were all brought up to read their Bibles and to go to church on Sunday, Edgeworth had purposely avoided attaching his Protestant tenets to a subject of universal interest. This he explained in a preface to the second edition, arguing that as children are generally taught the faith professed by their parents 'could any particular system meet with general approval?' Though his detractors remained unconvinced the book went on selling and was almost as well known on the Continent as it was in Great Britain.

Though several chapters were written by him, he always gave Maria full credit, infinitely prouder of seeing his tiny, ill-favoured daughter transformed by her titanic exertions into a prodigy. As he told her: 'There is a sweeter musick to an honest ear than his own fame—that of a beloved daughter—whose unaffected manners (which God long preserve from the effects of flattery) and whose talents are ready to burst from all lips when she is spoken of.'

At the turn of the century Maria Edgeworth writing her remarkable books in her remote Irish home was a source of speculation and wonder—a phenomenal and intriguing figure. When *Castle Rackrent* was published anonymously in 1800 so many false claims and rumours were current that the second edition was published under her name. She wrote it at a time when her father was immersed in other matters, seized by an urge to write a family history just as John Langan might tell it. While through the mouth of an old steward, 'honest Thady', she unfolded the disastrous tale of the Rackrents she felt as though he was beside her dictating every word. All she knew of the country and people around her was poured into the story, the strange goings-on of the spendthrift gentry in their down-at-heel mansions dashed upon the paper by a pen that was possessed. Again she was breaking new ground as she depicted these untamed gentlemen, their retainers and their tenantry. Inevitably it reflected much of what she saw and heard though she insisted it was all imaginary. Lady Cathcart's incarceration was adapted to a rich Lady Rackrent, while a house called Donore in Westmeath whose owner Sir Peter Nugent (of the Rackrent tradition) died shortly before she wrote it, was said to be the original Castle Rackrent.

Although all the world talked of her, Maria showed no signs of elation. Having learned from her father to despise every affectation of pride and vainglory, she was also quite convinced in her own mind that she owed it all to him. Without him to breathe energy and confidence into her wavering spirit, to incite and prod her along the hard uphill road of endeavour, she would dwindle into nonentity. Not for one moment did she flag in her efforts to live up to what he preached, defying the blinding headaches that every week or two kept her in bed. All the same she was not much liked by her grown-up sister and brother. Deep down and unperceived ran little hostile undercurrents. Easy-going Emmeline whose talents were mainly domestic and who was often away at Clifton with Anna, resented her influence and, Maria felt, judged her unfairly. Lovell, a clever, studious young man without great strength of character, expressed his feelings in a letter to his friend Peter Mark Roget (the future physician and author of the *Thesaurus*) in August 1801: 'Miss E the authoress bears the laurel so meekly and her temper seems so much improved that she is quite agreeable and she does not appear to interfere with anybody the consequence is obvious nobody interferes with her, and we all go on as if there was no such serpent in the house.'

Maria sensing their animosity was hurt and perplexed by it, quite unable to imagine what caused it. Acting always with the highest motives she was sure she did her best for everybody, never (at least in her letters) saying a critical or unkind word. She had nothing but praise for Lovell, his excellent example at Edinburgh which her dear Henry was determined to emulate; and when he was in London, haunting Johnson's bookshop and thinking ten times more of her books than her publisher did. Though her stern principles and relentless activity must often have exasperated those of weaker clay, she was still curiously defenceless, hungering for the reassurance and approval of those she loved. Early in 1800 when her books were selling hot from the press she was writing: 'I wish to send my aunt a few *Popular Tales* which I have just finished: as they cannot be wanted for some months by Mr. Johnson I should wish that she would take the trouble of reading them over before they go to the Press—but if I mentioned this to my father . . . he would call me Goose and leave me there.'

Her books that year came out in a steady stream. First 'An octavo Ed. of Prac. Ed.' a French translation of which was appearing monthly in the *Bibliothèque britannique*; then 'two wee-wee vols' containing the first two parts of *Early Lessons*, and *Moral Tales* in four volumes with frontispieces 'beautifully engraved by Neagle doing justice to the designs two of which are by my mother and two by Charlotte'. On no account, she told Sophy, must her uncle subscribe to the French publication as it only contained extracts without remarks, and she added: 'Tell my aunt that her friendship and yours are more valuable to me a million times than all the fame that ever was blasted through the trumpet of fame.'

Written from her heart every word of it was true as an unfortunate incident that happened the following spring goes to prove. She was staying at Black Castle when the advance set arrived of *Belinda*, a three-volume novel she had written without saying a word about it to her aunt. Maria who was always given to playing little tricks and springing surprises on her friends, after tearing out the title-pages gave the books to Mrs. Ruxton who was so much amused by the story that she insisted on reading bits of it aloud. The more she praised it, the more silent was Maria, her nose buried in her work. At last much provoked, her aunt turned on her sharply: 'I am sorry to see my little Maria unable to bear the praises of a rival author.' Bursting into tears Maria confessed what she had done, Mrs. Ruxton listening coldly, not at all amused at having been taken in. Never again did she care about *Belinda* and for many a long month afterwards Maria smarted under her unjust accusation.

The scientific and literary monthly, the *Bibliothèque britan-*

nique, had lately been founded by two learned brothers, Marc Auguste Pictet, professor of philosophy at the Academy of Geneva and Charles Pictet-de Rochemont. Both were confirmed Anglophiles, well versed in English literature, admiring the developments that were taking place in English thought and counting among their friends many distinguished Englishmen. When the *Parent's Assistant* appeared they were sufficiently interested by it to publish translations of two of the stories and *Practical Education* impressed them profoundly. Like others they regretted that no thoughts of a religious nature leavened the rationalist bias, a criticism that led to an exchange of letters between Edgeworth and Pictet-de Rochemont. Their high opinion of Maria's work and their interest in her never diminished; they always had room for her stories and early in the summer of 1801 two long extracts from *Belinda* were given with many flattering comments. Though it somewhat lacked excitement and the heroine was too consistently reasonable to be very interesting, they found it nevertheless admirable as a guide to young people of how to behave in society. 'We must welcome this agreeable and moral work and hope that she will continue to employ her great talents for the instruction and amusement of our readers.'

Shortly after this was printed, at the beginning of August, Marc Auguste Pictet and his young friend Richard Chenevix, arrived in Ireland in the course of a three-months' tour of the British Isles. The grey-haired philosopher whose notions of the Emerald Isle were mainly derived from *Castle Rackrent,* was consumed by his impatience to see the remarkable Miss Maria whose books made such an impression on him. Richard Chenevix, a clever, scientifically-minded young man, an ardent lover of everything French in spite of having spent fifteen months locked up in a Paris prison during the Revolution, was already acquainted with the

Edgeworths. His sister was married to a distant neighbour, Mr. Tuite of Sonna, and it was to Sonna that he and Pictet drove straight from Dublin.

The morning after their arrival they set out for Edgeworthstown in the Tuites' coach, the professor in a veritable frenzy of anticipation as every turn of the wheels brought him closer to Miss Maria. The two hours' drive in a comfortable carriage was an agreeable contrast to yesterday's journey from Dublin when the rickety post-chaise, the wild little horses, the rotting harness and the reckless postilions caused him frequently to commend his soul to God as they careered at breakneck speed down the hills. But the little ruse he had up his sleeve of concealing his identity was frustrated; news of his arrival at Sonna had already reached Edgeworthstown and as the carriage drew up at the door Edgeworth was standing in the portico delightedly welcoming him by name.

On entering the library Pictet was amazed at the size of the family sitting round a tea-table eating a midday repast and as room was made for him he glanced eagerly from face to face trying to make out which could be the authoress. Nothing escaped Edgeworth who immediately exclaimed: 'I see that it is not only I who you have come to see; perhaps Maria even has precedence of her father, though this I do not grudge her. However, to punish you I will tell you that she is thirty miles from here and you cannot see her today.' He pressed them to stay the night and Maria should immediately be sent for from Castle Sanderson where she was staying. It was impossible—a large dinner was taking place at Sonna that evening; but when they undertook to return in the morning a gossoon was despatched forthwith with Maria's marching orders.

What he recognized at once as a most singular household, diverted the professor exceedingly, the whole scene striking him as simply a background for his astonishing host. Such a display of physical and mental vigour in a man approaching sixty was phenomenal but so also were his domestic affairs—seventeen children by four successive wives whose portraits hung in the entrance hall; ten children still living and an eleventh on the way. The impression they gave of a happy, united family was very agreeable and so was the intelligent curiosity with which the young people listened to what was said and scrutinized anything of interest. When he showed their father his little pocket sextant, Edgeworth after examining it carefully handed it to his wife, explaining it in detail. She then passed it on to the eldest daughter and so on round the entire family down to the very youngest, Pictet in the meanwhile trembling for the safety of his fragile treasure. When they spoke of Maria he felt that they truly appreciated her; he was shown the desk where her great works were written in the midst of all the noise and chatter before his host took him out for a walk round and to meet John Langan, 'the original of honest Thady who amused you so much'.

After Langan had been called up from the hayfield where the men were working and asked a number of questions so that Pictet might hear for himself that Maria's description of the country folk was not exaggerated, a labourer was sent for to describe how quite recently when he was working on the roof putting back slates, he actually saw fairies on the grass in the garden below. Up they came, one after another and started to dance in a circle—fairies as tall as his leg and wearing boots as he noticed particularly. But when he was asked what else they had on he could not say for in the dust that blew up around them they vanished. And before they were allowed to depart the visitors had to be shown all over the house which was as unusual as everything else. Whichever way Pictet looked he saw with startled admiration proof after proof of Edgeworth's mechanical ingenuity—doors opening as if by magic; windows, shutters, drawers fitted with contrivances that doubled their usefulness—even bedposts unscrewing and doubling up handily for travelling.

On the following morning as Pictet relates, it was with the utmost relief that 'we flew to our appointment at Edgeworthstown'. Irish society as he saw it at the Tuites' dinner had absolutely disgusted him. Though the company was distinguished—a peer, several important landowners, officers from the garrison, and their ladies—the deplorable entertainment consisted solely of devouring enormous quantities of food and consuming a vast amount of liquor for what seemed like eternity, without a word being uttered. The enlightened conversation at Edgeworthstown and the longed-for meeting with the brilliant authoress shone all the brighter in consequence.

An even larger party awaited them as Lovell also was absent the day before. Again as he approached the library the professor could scarcely control his feelings for surely, he told himself, a writer so talented must have *something* very remarkable either in her looks or expression. But as he entered the room 'with eyes only for her' one glance was enough to disillusion him. There stood Maria, that dwarf-like figure, with downcast eyes, her whole being 'stamped by a look of utmost reserve and modesty, and with very little expression in her features when she was not speaking'. She hardly opened her mouth at all, being at her very worst this morning, annoyed at having been brought back from a delightful visit. Though it never crossed her mind to disobey she was determined not to simulate a pleasure she was far from feeling. Uncompromisingly she stood before her discomfited admirer, silent as an effigy, staring at the carpet. But her father already had charge of the conversation, characteristically setting his guests a chemical conundrum that plunged them into an abstruse technical discussion which much to Pictet's relief was soon interrupted by the announcement of breakfast.

During the meal he noticed that when Maria did speak, which was all too seldom, what she said was extremely well thought out and expressed though proffered always with great diffidence. Breakfast over, he was presented with a little apparatus for drawing perspective which the young Edgeworths invented and manufactured themselves, and the rest of the afternoon was agreeably spent debating moral and intellectual problems with Maria and her father. Pictet who did most of the talking, noticed how often his listeners glanced at each other in surprise that a foreigner should share so many of their views. When eventually the ladies retired to dress for dinner a walk in the park and a few chemical experiments whiled away the time. Whatever his opinion of Maria may have been, he and Edgeworth had any amount of common interests, innumerable things to ask and to tell. When still talking hard they went in to the dining-room, what a contrast it was to last night's dinner! In spite of the animated conversation he still managed to study the younger members of 'this intelligent family'. Lovell, 'freshly moulded by Edinburgh University and a very learned young man', pleased him much and so did 'Miss Charlotte—a young girl of sixteen, pretty, fresh as a rose, her eyes full of intelligence'. All too swiftly the evening came to an end though when at last they regretfully took their leave Edgeworth prolonged it by accompanying them part of the way, his carriage following behind. As they drove along under the stars they must surely have discussed Pictet's suggestion that in the near future he should bring Mrs. Edgeworth and Maria to Geneva.

Several months later when the *Bibliothèque britannique*

arrived with the account of Pictet's visit to Edgeworthstown, Maria when she read it was much displeased. His description of her and *les yeux baissés* rankled for a long while.

Chapter Four

1802-1803

The suggested trip crystallized into a definite plan, though Paris and not Geneva was the goal. Tantalized by Pictet's account of the society to be enjoyed there Edgeworth decided to take his wife, Maria and Lovell for a winter after first making a little tour in the country. In Paris Maria who spoke French like a native and was as well read in its literature as she was in English, would be in her element, and as a celebrated authoress she need not fear even the coruscating sallies of Madame de Staël.

Travel and change were in the air throughout the spring and summer of 1802, raising a breeze that shook the calm of every day. Lovell's friend, Roget, having taken a travelling tutorship, invited him to go with them to Geneva, a suggestion conjuring up tempting visions of freedom and adventure that appealed to Lovell far more than travelling with his family. Though Edgeworth thought it a somewhat purposeless journey, his wife at last persuaded him to agree and in May the young man joyfully departed. Rumours that later reached his father of the carefree, mildly extravagant life he was leading did not reassure him, nor did Lovell's retort that this was the first chance he had had of amusing himself in the last twenty years. Emmeline too was on the wing, spending her last months at home before her marriage in the autumn to John King, a Clifton surgeon. And in September when the travellers set out, pretty Charlotte taking Lovell's place, she went as far as Holyhead with them, leaving them there 'for Clifton and we hope for happiness' as Frances Edgeworth wrote to the aunts at home.

Travelling in two chaises they proceeded on their leisurely way through North Wales and England. 'I have the delightful hope', wrote Maria, 'that Charlotte and I shall every day and hour and minute become better known and consequently more agreeable to each other—This is the best thing I have to expect from our journey—we have one chaise, one green bag—one bed in common it is my fault if I cannot take advantage of this—I have indeed so much confidence in myself that I expect to be loved as soon as I am thoroughly understood—Not to be loved as Sophy and my Aunt Ruxton and my father love me—but soberly—reasonably.'

So much was to be seen, so many friends to be visited along the route, that often the events of a single day sufficed to fill the folio sheets across which Maria's pen flew in straight, close lines whenever there was a moment to spare, keeping the family at home informed of their doings. Factories, visible proofs of the power and ingenuity of the human mind, appealed to them more than anything. The copperworks at Holywell, 'a vast manufactory' which Maria thought very sublime; at Etruria their old friend 'Jos' Wedgewood showed them his flint mill worked by a steam engine, and at Derby they inspected Mr. Strutt's cotton mill and a china factory. At each big town Edgeworth called on the bookseller to inquire about Maria's books which at Leicester led to a strange encounter.

'Whilst dinner was getting ready,' wrote Maria to Mary Sneyd, 'we walked to a circulating Library—With you my dear partner-aunt I need not in speaking of self or works make use of any of the customary circumlocutions commonly called humility. I shall speak of myself and my works without ceremony—My father asked for Belinda, Bulls,[1] etc. found they were in good repute—Castle Rackrent in better—The others were often borrowed but Castle Rackrent was often bought.—The bookseller an open hearted man begged us to look at a book of poems just published by a Leicester lady a Miss Watts ... My father told the bookseller that we would pay our respects to Miss Watts if it would be agreeable to her.' After dinner the bookseller guided them to the house where they were shown up to a 'neatish room', Mrs. Watts prim and dragon-like keeping in the background while her tall, fresh-coloured daughter darted forward with her long, thin arms outstretched, exclaiming as Mrs. Edgeworth entered, OH WHAT AN HONOUR THIS IS! —each word a syllable rising in tone till the last reached a scream ... Instead of embracing my mother as her first action threatened she started back to the farthest end of the room which was not light enough to shew her attitude distinctly—but it seemed to be intended to express the receding of awe-struck admiration—stopped by the wall—Charlotte and I passed by unnoticed and seated ourselves by the old lady's desire ... Miss Watts was all ecstasy of hands and eyes speaking always in that shrill theatrical tone a puppet show man supplies his puppets—I all the time sat like a mouse—My father asked 'Which of these three ladies Madam do you think is your sister authoress?' 'I am NO physiognomist (in a screech) but I do imagine that to be the lady'—bowing as she sat almost to the ground and pointing to Mrs. E. 'No—Guess again'—'Then that must be *she*' bowing to Charlotte—'No'—Then this lady looking forward to see what sort of an animal I was—for she had never seen me till this instant—To make me some amends she now drew her chair close to me and began to pour forth

[1] *Essay on Irish Bulls* by R. L. Edgeworth and Maria Edgeworth.

praises on all my works. Lady Delacour! Oh! Lady Delacour! Lady Delacour Oh! Letters to Literary Ladies Oh!
she had never known who they were written by but had so
admired them—Oh! (hands lifted and splashing about) . . .
I am sure she must have thought me an insensible dolt for
her extravaganzas entirely quieted me—If I had taken a
lethargic potion I could not have been more inert.'

Six days were spent in London at Nerot's Hotel, King
Street, while a comfortable coach was being bought to take
abroad. The first person Maria ran into was Humphry Davy,
the ungainly, petulant young scientist whose sensitive brown
eyes mirrored a poetical imagination. She had made his
acquaintance at Clifton in 1799 when she and her parents
spent several months there for the birth of her little sister
Fanny. At that time, fresh from his native Cornwall, Davy
was employed by Dr. Beddoes to superintend his Pneumatic
Institution, and was already arousing great interest by his
experiments with various gases. He was now professor of
chemistry at the Royal Institution in Albemarle Street, and
took the Edgeworths all over it. He seemed to Maria 'much
improved indeed since I saw him last—talks sound sense and
has left off being the Cosmogony man'. Her publisher,
'good generous Johnson', who was just bringing out a
fourth edition of Rackrent, dined with them and one afternoon she and Charlotte went to Saville House to see the
exhibition of Miss Linwood's needlework reproductions
of great paintings which she sold for enormous sums,
works they decided that were better worth seeing than the
lady.

'One morning Charlotte and I had been waiting some
time for breakfast—a knock at the door—'Mr. Philips
Ma'am'—Enter Mr. Philips, a fat rosy chubby man with a
black wig and whiskers. 'Miss Edgeworth I presume'—'Yes
Sir etc.'—'Ma'am there's a lady waiting below in the Hack-

4. MADAME RÉCAMIER AND LAHARPE

"Ah ma belle Julie, que je vous aime aujourd'hui, vous voilà
bien habillée."

(From a sketch by Charlotte Edgeworth)

ney coach in which I came who wishes to pay her respects here—Miss Linwood——'

Enter Miss Linwood who looks not unlike a strolling player—in a very dirty tumbled white dress—riding hat covered with black feathers all on one side—She did not seem capable of feeling timidity but very well able and willing to push, if not to win her way through the world . . . I *wish* she had a nail brush . . . Philips is a bookseller. In the course of conversation my father talked of writing his own life—'As an anecdote in it', said Philips, 'You may if you please say that Philips offered you a thousand pounds for the copyright.' He actually gives Mrs. Inchbald a thousand for her life.'

On October 4th they landed at Calais and next day 'set out for Gravelines with whips cracking in a manner which you certainly could not forget . . . We left Gravelines in an equipage at which Sobriety herself could not have forborne to laugh—To our London coach were fastened by long rope traces 6 flemish horses of different heights but each large and clumsy enough to draw an English cart or waggon; the nose of the foremost was thirtyfive feet from the body of the coach—their hoofs all shagged, their manes all uncombed and their tails long enough to please Sir Charles Grandison himself . . . High!—high! upon their backs sat perfectly perpendicular two long waisted postillions in jack boots with pipes in their mouths.' As they jolted along the paved roads through a country looking like 'one vast flat common' they amused themselves by reading 'the charming story of Mademoiselle Clermont from Mad^{me} de Genlis Petits Romans. I never read a more pathetic and finely written tale.'

At Dunkirk they spent the evening at a dirty, ill-lit playhouse, a grimy municipal officer sitting behind them mis-

E

taking Maria for Madame 'as I looked so much the oldest of the party. "Ah Madame il faut que je vous fasse voir une de nos jolies femmes de Dunquerque—Comment la trouvez vous?" "Mais—plutôt belle que jolie—Eh voilà une jolie femme—celle qui a la rose à sa coiffure; qui est elle?"—"Ah Madame, c'est une femme du monde." As I looked stupid I suppose my municipal officer was determined to explain himself better and added "C'est une femma publique. Et voilà une autre qui entre—Madame a-t'elle jamais été à Paris?" "Non monsieur jamais." "Ah! est-il possible?" Then I was no longer worth talking to.'

Though the desolate-looking towns still bore traces of the Revolution, as they drove along the broad straight Flemish roads through scenes that reminded Maria of a child's Dutch picture book, they noticed that the 'money-making, money-loving people were fast recovering their activity'. As enthusiastic educationists they made a point of visiting the new Ecole Centrale at every town where they stayed and as the *Bibliothèque britannique* was taken at all the schools and libraries they were welcomed wherever they went with the cordiality due to such distinguished visitors. A French translation of *Belinda* by 'Miss Edgeworthy' was in all the shops. When they glided away from Bruges by canal through a bright morning landscape that might have been painted by Teniers, in a 'barque as elegant as any pleasure-boat that ever adorned the Thames', the Mayor and other notables who were on board were overjoyed at meeting the interesting father and daughter about whom they had read. As gradually it dawned on her to whom she owed this gratifying reception, Maria felt more and more contrite: 'We have received many civilities to be charged to the credit of that poor M. Pictet to whom I was so ungrateful.'

Four days were spent sightseeing at Brussels. What an advantage it was, thought Maria, 'to travel with friends who have a variety of tastes and information: even though I am perfectly ignorant of farming and painting and architecture I cannot help being interested in the observations they make on these subjects. . . . My father thought it would be advantageous to us to see inferior pictures before those of the best masters that we might have some points of comparison, and upon the same principle we went to two provincial theatres at Dunkirk and at Brussels—but *unluckily*—I mean unluckily for our principle—we saw at Brussels two of the best Paris actors, M. and Mad<u>me</u> Talma. The play was Racine's *Andromaque*.' She was much impressed by her first introduction to fine acting; what she liked next best at Brussels were the dogs harnessed to carts and hampers, trotting about the streets.

The sun had never ceased to shine from the moment they left home and one beautiful afternoon on the way to Paris they visited Chantilly, 'the antient residence of the great Prince of Condé' and the scene of Madame de Genlis' wonderful story.

'After going through for an hour and a half a thick dark forest in which Virginia might have lived secure from sight of mortal man, we came into open day and open country and from the top of a hill we beheld a mass of magnificent buildings shaded by woods. I imagined this was the palace, but I was told these buildings were only the stables of Chantilly—The palace alas!—is no more. It was pulled down by the Revolutionists—the stables were saved by a petition from the war minister stating that they would make stabling for troops—to this use they are now applied—As we drove down the hill we saw the melancholy remains of the palace . . . We walked to look at the Riding house built by the Prince de Condé—a princely edifice!—Whilst we were looking at it, we heard a flute played near us and we were told that the young man who played it was one of the poor Prince de Condé's *chasseurs*—The person who shewed us the ruins had lost some hundred pounds which he had earned in the Prince de Condé's service—He is a melancholy-looking man of 60 years of age who during his whole life had been employed to shew the gardens and palace of Chantilly to strangers—He now shews the ruins and tells where the Prince and Princess once slept and where there were fine statues and charming walks . . . We asked for l'Isle de l'amour and this poor man told us that it was once beautifully planted but now it is all destroyed.'

Next day their coach rattled into Paris under the great archway of Porte St. Denis, filling the narrow dirty streets and forcing pedestrians to fly for shelter as it bore westwards towards the Champs Elysées and the Hôtel de Courlande, Place de la Concorde. A city that despite the mellow beauty of its famous buildings and the kaleidoscopic animation in the squares and boulevards, for Maria was stained by the blood-drenched shades of the Revolution. When she looked out from the hotel she reflected with a shudder that only a few yards separated her from the spot where its worst scenes were enacted to the murderous howls of the mob. 'In this square the guillotine was once at work night and day—Here Louis Seize and Marie Antoinette and Madame Roland died! Opposite to us is the Seine—and LA LANTERNE! On one side of this square are les champs elisées where the famous courtisanne de l'ancien régime drove her triumphal car with horses shod with silver!—What a mixture of things in the best of all possible worlds.' When they ran upstairs to the roof to see the view, 'the first object that struck us was the Telegraph *at work*—This is as nearly as possible my father's.'

Within a few hours attentions such as were rarely accorded to English visitors were paid them. At the hotel

Edgeworth met his friend James Watt, the inventor of the steam-engine, who carried him off at once to introduce him to the engineer de Prony, head of Ponts et Chaussées, and le Breton of the Mint, introductions which resulted in his meeting many scientists and inventors—chemists, clock-makers, inventors of air-balloons, with whom he could talk on a level. Though Pictet was still in Geneva he had pre-pared the way by introducing them to the family of Etienne Delessert the banker whose wife presided over a salon as famous though far more exclusive than Madame de Staël's. The day after they arrived the eldest son called with an invitation from his mother and sister for the following evening, an evening that was an unqualified success. Madame Delessert was one of the many friends of Edgeworth's former idol Rousseau, who still venerated his memory; it was for her daughter, the widowed Madame Gautier, that his *Letters on Botany* were written. Maria at once saw a likeness to her Aunt Ruxton while the charming, un-affected younger son François reminded her of Henry. If Madame Gautier was not quite as engaging as her mother, she was very obliging and unmistakably a gentlewoman— 'neatly dressed—not at all naked'—and devoting most of her time to educating her two children.

Next day they drove out to Madame Gautier's country house at Passy where besides a whole clan of Delesserts they met many distinguished people who immediately became their friends. Among others were charming Madame Pas-toret, 'a literary and fashionable lady', and her husband, 'a man of diplomatique knowledge', who had suffered much during the Revolution. The young politician Lord Henry Petty was there with his former tutor, that distinguished Genevese and man of letters Etienne Dumont who, in England, was as much at home at Holland House as he was at Bowood. Though he and Lord Henry were about to leave

Paris there was still time for an acquaintanceship to be formed which was to be of great importance to Maria later on. And this day too she met the old writer and *économiste* the venerable Abbé Morellet who enchanted her with his 'vivacity and feeling and wit of youth'. When the Abbé was presented to her he said: 'A Paris on lit votre livre sur l'éducation—à Genève on l'avale. A Paris on admire vos principes—à Genève on les suit.' They dined at his house next day which he shared with his widowed sister. This lady's daughter, whose first husband Marmontel wrote instructive books for children, was so eager to meet Maria that she made a special journey to Paris from her remote country estate. The only disappointment was the absence of Madame de Staël. Maria was particularly anxious to meet this brilliant woman, only a few months older than herself though in other respects how different! A difference that was provocative, echoes of the turbulent genius and passionate amours of Necker's emancipated daughter having carried to remote Edgeworthstown. Though Maria read her books with admiration her logical mind could not accept the romantic conceptions that inspired them, nor could she approve of a woman who meddled with politics. It was Madame de Staël's political intrigues that accounted for her absence from Paris, Buonaparte having warned her that she would do well to remain where she was on the shores of Lac Léman.

They soon left the expensive hotel for an apartment in Rue de Lille and every moment of their days was taken up with sightseeing, visiting and entertaining the numerous callers who climbed their steep stairs. Though Pictet had told them that their name was as well-known in Paris as at Edgeworthstown and their relationship to the saintly Abbé Edgeworth who supported Louis XVI on the scaffold, earned them the regard of the old aristocracy, the ovation they received far exceeded even Edgeworth's most sanguine expectations. The triumph undoubtedly was Maria's; her tiny form exhaled the magic that threw open doors to admit them to drawing-rooms where visiting foreigners never set foot. Everyone was reading *Belinda*, translated by a young Count de Ségur, elderly ladies recommending it to their nieces and granddaughters as a model of what a young woman of the world ought to be. The ease and fluency with which Maria discussed their books and spoke their language amazed them, and her well-reasoned observations admirably suited the intellectual trend of these evenings when the Edgeworths formed part of the choice company who met together to solve the problems of the universe in endless conversation, refreshed by a light supper or a delicious collation of cakes, fruit and cream. At least one evening each week was spent at Madame Delessert's and another at Madame Suard's, a *bel esprit* of the old days and a friend of Madame Geoffrin, Madame du Deffand's hated rival. At the Suards' literature predominated, at Madame Lavoisier's science as befitted the widow of the most enlightened chemist of the century whose head was one of the first to fall under the guillotine. It was at Madame Lavoisier's one night that Maria, sitting next to M. de Prony who was generally very agreeable and informative, became the victim of one of his embarrassingly indecent outbursts. As he regaled her with a graphic account of what he had recently suffered after taking a purgative, Madame Lavoisier sharply interrupted him, upbraiding him for his 'grossièreté'— 'Vous ne savez pas l'état dans lequel vous mettez Mademoiselle Marie en lui disant ces choses.' There were evenings at the theatre with the Pastorets and other friends when the ladies carried nosegays to ward off the smells, and Madame Récamier came on purpose to meet them when they visited Madame Campan's fashionable boarding-school for

young ladies. Invitations followed for dinners and balls at
the splendid Récamier house in Rue du Mont Blanc, a
house that was one of the marvels of Paris with its spacious,
flower-scented rooms decorated with all the sumptuous
opulence of the Directoire, making a perfect foil for the
classic simplicity of the lovely hostess.

Nearly always guests breakfasted with the Edgeworths
and on December 2nd two poets came, Samuel Rogers who
was spending a few weeks in Paris and the Chevalier
Edelcrantz—famed also as an inventor—who was private
secretary to King Gustavus IV of Sweden. Born forty-six
years earlier as Abraham Nikolas Clewberg, son of the
professor of theology at d'Abo University, he later taught
physics, philosophy and history there before a poem he
published exalting the royal house of Sweden drew Gustavus III's attention to him. A place at court and his present
style and title were the outcome of those successful verses,
the forerunners of many poems and plays. Maria had met
him on several occasions among many others who offered
her their incense and came to their apartment to sit in
earnest discussion for hours at a time. A very ugly man, her
family thought him, apart from his fine eyes.

Monsieur Pictet had also arrived: 'he gives up his whole
time to us and seems to think of nothing but our interests
and pleasures—Tell my Aunt Mary that I am grown as fond
of her favourite as her heart could wish and have forgiven
him for les yeux baissés and for bringing me home from
Castle Sanderson, etc.—Indeed I did not know the extent of
my obligations to him till I came to Paris—His account of
us and his extracts in the *Bibliothèque britannique* have been
our best introductions to all the most agreeable society we
have enjoyed—I had no idea the way men of letters and
science are received here, till I actually saw it—They mix
with people of wealth and fashion—with the *nouveaux*

riches and *anciens nobles*—the latter are the most agreeable as you may well imagine.'

She was writing to Aunt Ruxton, her little head so full, she said, of interesting things she had treasured up to tell her that unless she emptied it it would certainly burst. All their new friends must be described and the people they met at their houses—one night at the Suards for instance there were the Count and Countess Crillon, eloquent Lally Tolendal of Irish extraction looking 'just like Father Tom', and the Marquis de Montmorency 'a polite man of honor worthy of his great name'. Politicians and political writers like Boissy d'Anglas and Camille Jordan; a dinner at Madame Récamier's where Charlotte (who was having a great success) sat beside the richest man in Paris; Polish and Russian aristocrats of prodigal splendour who were living there, and so on. At Monsieur and Madame de Vindé's, whose gallery of paintings and musical evenings were famous, what charmed her most was their 'little granddaughter of three years old, very like my sweet Fanny, with stockings exactly the same as Aunt Mary knitted for her, and listing shoes precisely like what Fanny used to wear— she sat on my knee and caressed me with her soft warm little hands—and looked at me with her smiling intelligent eyes.

'Dec. 3. Here comes the brink of the last page and I have said nothing of the Apollo—of the paintings at the museum —of the Louvre—Versailles—La Petite Trianon—La Monnaie . . . I cannot speak of everything and when I speak to you so many things——'

She broke off as the door burst open and a gentleman was bustled into the room by her father who withdrew again, closing it behind him. Only much later and in great agitation did Maria resume:

'Here my dear aunt I was interrupted in a manner that

will surprise you almost as much as it surprised me—Monsieur Edelcranz a Swedish gentleman private secretary to the King, of superior understanding and mild manners came in—he came to offer me his hand and heart—My heart you may suppose cannot return his attachment as I have seen but very little of him and have not had time to have formed any judgement, except that I think nothing could tempt me to leave my own dear friends and my own country to live in Sweden.' The Chevalier's objections to leaving *his* are torn away, nothing remaining but 'he would be materially injured by' [torn] and 'a mother who is old and dependent on him'.

'My dearest aunt,' Maria went on, 'I write to you the first moment as next to my father and mother no person in the world will feel so much interest in all that concerns me—I need not tell you that my father "Such in this moment as in all the past"—is KINDNESS itself—kindness far far superior to what I deserve—but I am grateful for it and for yours my dearest aunt and friend.'

Only lately in *Belinda* she had written that every girl naturally hopes to be married, to have a husband and home of her own, and no one ever loved children more than Maria did. When earlier this year at breakfast one day, Sneyd, seeing how fondly she gazed at little Fanny, asked, 'Would you exchange all your fame as an authoress, Maria, to have a little thing like Fanny of your own?' without an instant's hesitation she exclaimed, 'That I would!' From girlhood onwards she must have suffered acutely from her conviction that nothing of this sort could ever be for her. And now with a few stumbling phrases, an earnest declaration, this mild-mannered Swedish gentleman broke through the thorny entanglement, opening up a vista from which she shrank with alarm. For the road winding through it and out of sight led not only to a shadowy northern country scarcely known to the English, but still worse to its Court. Though he could sweep aside barriers, Chevalier Edelcrantz could not awaken in Maria the love that casts out fear and faces the unknown with shining confidence. Her overwhelming dread of exile at that distant Court exceeded for the time being every other consideration.

Next day Edgeworth conveyed the tidings to Charlotte Sneyd.

'Before I left England I stated as one of my reasons for wishing at this period to take Maria abroad that it was the only probable means of giving her excellent qualities an opportunity of engaging a partner for the remainder of her life and yesterday a Swedish chevalier . . . offered his hand and I most sincerely believe his heart to Maria . . . She objects with reason and kindness to his distant settlement—as her heart is still her own she may without injury to her future happiness take time to consider. . . . She sees that she is *truly* respected and much liked in this country and the first offer should not be instantly accepted.

'I like the gentleman and no selfish considerations shall on my part obstruct his wishes.'

This was the day of the Grand Review which they watched from a window overlooking the Louvre and Place de Carousel, seeing for the first and only time the Maître de l'Univers as Maria called Napoleon. 'He rode down the lines on a fine spirited white Spanish horse, took off his hat to salute various generals and gave us a full view of his pale thin woe-begone countenance—he is very little but much at ease on horseback.' From a little notebook she kept intermittently the rest of the day was as follows: 'Dinner Pictet—before carriage came Edelcrantz—evening at Morellet's.'

To Sophy Ruxton 'to whom every thought of my mind is open', she wrote on December 8th: 'Now for love and wisdom. I have nothing new to tell you about our Swedish knight. I persist in refusing to think of leaving my country and my friends to live at the court of Stockholm and he tells me (of course) that there is nothing he would not sacrifice except his *duty*—he has been all his life in the service of the King of Sweden, has places under him and is actually employed in collecting information for a large political Establishment—he thinks himself bound in honor to finish what he has begun—says he should not fear the ridicule and blame that would be thrown upon him by his countrymen for quitting his country at his age, but that he should despise himself if he abandoned his duty to gratify any passion—All this is very fine and I must add reasonable but it is reasonable for *him only*; not for me. I have not felt any thing for him but esteem and gratitude—and he says he could never be contented to be loved next to a father—I wish you were here!'

There is only one other reference to him, on January 10th, when she agreed with Aunt Charlotte 'that with such a father and such friends as I have much merit and strong affection must combine in a husband to make me happy in marriage'. Evidently she found Edelcrantz wanting in both respects and with his ardour quite likely damped down by her singular and wounding qualification, he does not appear to have put up much resistance. An entry in the notebook for January 26th, 'breakfast Ed.' may signify that he came to bid them farewell before he returned to Sweden. Thereafter the dark north swallowed him up; she never saw or heard from him again.

But the tumult of warring emotions he stirred up took many years to subside. Once back in Ireland her feelings for him grew softer, much tenderer sentiments than gratitude and esteem colouring her thoughts. Memories and dreams of what might have been haunted her the more persistently as time slipped by and never another chance of marriage came her way. Something that happened seven years later proves how long and how painfully it troubled her, and suggests too that in Paris her father thought more highly of her lover than she did, and even regretted her decision. When she heard that her Aunt Ruxton had encountered a Mr. Knox who was acquainted with Edelcrantz, she was thrown into great agitation. She wrote at once imploring Sophy: 'Do for mercy's sake write directly and tell me all you know—even if you know nothing at all. Tell me at what period Mr. Knox knew him—What he thought of his understanding, his manners, his character? Whether he ever spoke of us—what he said—whether Mr. K. knew then or knows now that he had any connection with us. Tell me all this I charge you for I am distracted about it.'

To her aunt who had a bad habit of handing Maria's letters about among her friends, she wrote more guardedly. Having read what Mr. Knox wrote to Mrs. Ruxton about the Chevalier, she merely observed: 'How gratifying it is to hear those we love spoken of as we feel they deserve', though it shows a surprising change in her sentiments. Mr. Knox who evidently admired and thought highly of him, not long afterwards expatiated on the subject to Sophy who faithfully reported all he said. This time Maria's reply was fraught with unhappy implication.

'I wish excessively that my father could have the just pleasure of knowing Mr. K's opinion exactly in the words he expressed it to you on the only subject on which we ever materially differed—I owe this to him and yet for the life of me I could not tell it to him—Do you—if you can and if you think it prudent.'

At Paris the days flew by as busy and varied as ever, Maria's letters losing nothing in vivacity and amused observation. Breakfasting with the Abbé Morellet one morning they met Madame d'Houdetot, 'the lady who inspired Rousseau with the idea of Julie in the Nouvelle Héloise—Rousseau's Julie is now 72 years of age—a thin woman in a little black velvet bonnet. At first she appeared to me shockingly ugly—she squints so much that it is impossible to guess who she means to look at—Yet no sooner did she begin to speak than I began to like her . . . She is possessed of that art, the art of seizing the best side of every object . . . She told me a great many anecdotes of Rousseau . . . I asked if he was grateful for all the kindness she shewed him—"No —he was ungrateful—he had a thousand bad qualities, but I turned my attention from them all and thought only of his genius and of the good he had done mankind".'

To her 'Very dear Henry, her dear great boy' his 'little old nurse' wrote: 'The title of a philosopher or rather of a man of letters or science is the best possible title here—We see the French scavans mixing with most polite and elegant societies of both sexes, not only without being considered as heterogeneous beings but as essential to the formation of good company—At La Harpe's we met a few days ago the celebrated French beauty Madame Récamier—the celebrated English wit Lady Elizabeth Foster—and a Russian Princess Dolgorouki . . . Nothing but fashion could have brought her there and therefore I mention her as the strongest proof that literature and literary men are in high esteem here—La Harpe lives in a miserable house, in a miserable street, in a miserable room waited upon by a miserable-looking old woman yet he had a levee or rather a coucher of fine ladies who all vied with each other in flattery and invitations—Madame Récamier dressed in a robe of white satin trimmed with fur seated herself on the arm of La Harpe's elbow chair and hung over the philosopher who was in a dirty night cap and old robe de chambre in the grand costume of a literary valetudinarian—He took hold of her arm, stroaked the white satin and fur and said "Ah ma belle Julie que je vous aime aujourd'hui, vous voilà bien habillée" —He is very fond of seeing ladies well dressed ... La Harpe told us some entertaining anecdotes of Voltaire and repeated some of his poetry which I did not think extraordinary.'

Their stay was proving such a success that Edgeworth decided to rent a house and bring his whole family over for a couple of years. A house near the Luxembourg Gardens was actually being negotiated for when one morning towards the end of January an officer arrived at their apartment with a *lettre de cachet* from the Government ordering him to leave Paris instantly. On the advice of the British ambassador Lord Whitworth, he and Maria drove out to Passy that same evening while their friends rallied to his aid, doing all they could to get the order cancelled. A petition signed by many imposing names was presented to the *Grand Juge* at a public audience next day and when it was explained that Edgeworth was only a second cousin and not the Abbé's brother as had been rumoured, the Judge declared it was all a mistake and revoked the order. But this alarming experience made Paris seem much less attractive and though they lingered on through February they were unsettled by the rumours of war breaking out and anxious as well about Henry who was lying ill at Edinburgh with the first symptoms of consumption.

Maria was always exceedingly interested in Madame de Genlis, a woman 'of the first talents in Europe—who has lived—who has shone—in the gay court of the gayest nation in the world'. Governess to the children of the magnificent Duc d'Orléans Philippe Egalité, she was said to be the mother of his daughter the lovely Pamela (widow of the ill-fated Irish patriot Lord Edward Fitzgerald). Because of her equivocal position and past history Edgeworth put off visiting her until they were on the brink of departure. She was living in rooms at the Arsenal and thither one evening at the end of February he and Maria drove through a maze of ill-lighted streets; when at last their coach drew up before a huge, straggling range of buildings they had great difficulty in discovering her whereabouts. At last groping their way up a dirty, ruinous staircase they rang the bell. The door was opened by a pretty little girl with dark, sparkling eyes and fashionable corkscrew ringlets, who on hearing their name smiled graciously: 'Maman is at home.'

She led the way across two miserable-looking antechambers 'into a small room in which the 2 candles were so well skreened by a green tin skreen that we could scarcely distinguish the tall form of a lady in black, who rose from her arm chair by the fire-side as the door opened: a great puff of smoke came from the huge fire-place at the same moment —She came forward and we made our way towards her as well as we could through a confusion of tables and chairs and work baskets and china and writing desks and ink stands and bird cage and harp—She did not speak and as her back was now turned to both fire and candle I could not see her face or anything but the outline of her form and her attitude—Her form was the remains of a fine form—her attitude that of a woman used to a better drawing-room— I being foremost and she still silent was compelled to speak and spoke first to the figure in darkness—"Madame de Genlis nous a fait l'honneur de nous mander qu'elle vouloit bien nous permettre de lui rendre visite et de lui *offrir nos respects*" said I or words to that effect—To which she replied by taking my hand graciously and saying something in which "*charmée*" was the only intelligible word. Whilst she spoke she looked over my shoulder at my father whose bow I presume told her he was a gentleman, for she spoke to him immediately as if she wished to please—seated us in fauteuils near the fire. I then had a full view of her face and figure

... She looked ... very thin and melancholy—dark eyes—
boney—sallow—compressed thin lips—two or three ugly
black ringlets on a high forehead ... altogether an appearance of fallen fortunes, worn out health and excessive but
guarded irritability. To me there was nothing of that engaging captivating manner that I had been taught to expect
by many even of her enemies—she seemed to me to be
alive only to literary quarrels and jealousies; the muscles of
her face as she spoke or as my father spoke to her, quickly
and too easily expressed hatred and anger when ever any
not of her party were mentioned ... My father spoke of
Pamela—Lady Edward Fitzgerald—and explained how he
had defended her in the Irish House of Commons—instead
of being pleased or touched her mind instantly diverged
into an elaborate and artificial exculpation of Lady Edward
herself ... Madame de G. seems to have been so much used
to be attacked that she has defences and apologies ready
prepared as some have books of prayer suited to all possible
occasions and capacities—She spoke of literature—of
Madame de Staël's *Delphine* with detestation—of another
new and fashionable Parisian novel *Amelia* with abhorrence
—Kissed my forehead twice because I had not read it—"Ah
vous autres angloises vous êtes modestes!" Where was
Madame de G's delicacy of conscience when she penned and
published *Les Chevaliers du Cigne* and the heroine who ran
between the two camps *en chemise et chemise bien courte*, etc.
... There was something of malignity in her countenance
and conversation that repelled love and of hypocrisy that
annihilated esteem ... But my father judges her far more
favorably than I do ... and he says he is sure she is a person
over whose mind he could gain a great ascendancy—he
thinks her a woman of violent passions ... one who has
been so torn to pieces that she now turns upon her enemies
and longs to tear in her turn.'

Having been secretly warned by M. le Breton that Napoleon was ready at any instant to declare war, they left Paris and only just in time—luckier than Lovell who never received his father's warning letter. When war broke out he was on his way across France but like many other English civilians he was arrested and interned at Verdun, a fortified town among the ague-infested marshes of the Meuse. A dismal end and a heavy price for his one brief year of pleasure and independence; eleven more were destined to drag by before he was free again.

As the party driving to Calais was convinced that he also was making for the coast, and as the last news of Henry was more reassuring, they could laugh and talk to their hearts' content and look forward to seeing their friends in London. And at Edinburgh Henry was waiting impatiently to introduce his famous sister, not only to his chosen companions, but to the object of their veneration, Dugald Stewart, the Professor of Moral Philosophy whose lectures pointed the way and steeled the high endeavours of countless young men of his time. Maria's heart overflowed: 'When I reflect upon the kindness that has been shewn us abroad, and upon the affection that awaits us at home, I feel I shall never be able to deserve all this happiness.'

Though the plan was that only Maria and her father should go on to Scotland, when they reached London she refused to hear of their happy party breaking up, rearranging things so effectively that Frances Edgeworth told Charlotte Sneyd: 'Now I believe that Charlotte and I will have the pleasure of seeing Henry and continuing the journey without separating from our dear fellow travellers—And this double advantage and double joy has been procured for us by Maria's great kindness ... I am heartily glad she did not quit her friends for Sweden—and as sincerely hope she may find a man who may be her match in mind and situation.'

Chapter Five

—————————✦—————————

1803-1812

They got home in April after seven months of an unbroken succession of triumphs for Maria. At Edinburgh her arrival caused such excitement that county grandees as well as all the doctors and professors, tumbled over one another to make her acquaintance; the literary Earl of Buchan even rising from a bed of sickness to see, as Maria said, 'what was so little worth seeing'. No amount of applause shook her level-headed detachment. It was noticed how modestly she stood beside her father at the various gatherings given in her honour, though Joanna Baillie the poetess was told that he monopolized most of the conversation when everyone would sooner have listened to his daughter. But when they reached Edgeworthstown their adventures receded into a treasure-house of reminiscences, as they took up once again the more satisfying reality of home life.

In the following years Maria was busier than ever, appeasing her troubled heart and justifying her rejection of Edelcrantz by making herself even more indispensable. Added to account-keeping, estate work and her writing, endless matters arose from her father's public activities. When in 1804 a French invasion was feared the Government commissioned him to set up a telegraph between Dublin and Galway. After two years' hard work he established a highly efficient service which flashed messages across the 125 miles in eight minutes. As soon as this was finished and out of his hands, he was appointed one of the commissioners for inquiring 'into the education of the people in Ireland'. However busy Maria might be in other directions, he would not allow her to neglect her profession. Time must be made and she made it, never leaving an instant unoccupied throughout the long days when she often rose at six and went to bed after midnight. If compelled to sit quiet she was always busy with her needle, embroidering sleeves and other pretty trifles for her friends: 'after breakfast, you know when my father reads Homer, or when there are long sittings'.

In 1804 *Popular Tales* written for 'the respectable middling classes such as farmers and tradespeople' were published in three volumes and a short novel, *Griselda*, written as a surprise for her father; while several stories with a French background were begun for a future collection of *Fashionable Tales*. By the autumn she was working on *Leonora*, told in a series of letters, illustrating the harm wrought by the rash, irresponsible behaviour of a romantic, ambitious heroine modelled after Madame de Staël. Drawn from her memories of Paris, it was a silent offering to Chevalier Edelcrantz, whose image can never have been far from her mind as she wrote it in a style that he liked. If she hoped for some word or sign from the palace overlooking the island-strewn Baltic, she hoped in vain. Though her writing suffered from her emotional stress her father did not guess the cause when he read and corrected it during a visit to Dublin.

'Your critic partner father friend has finished your Leonora—He has cut out a few pages one or two letters are nearly untouched; the rest are cut and scrawled and interlined without mercy. I make no doubt of the success of the book amongst *a certain class of readers* PROVIDED it be reduced to one small volume and provided it be polished *ad unguem* —so that neither flaw nor seam can be perceived by the utmost critical acumen . . . You will perhaps be surprized to hear that I have corrected more faults of style than in anything I have ever corrected for you. Mr. Ruxton's criticisms have except one been adopted by me—and I hope when you have corrected it again, that he will have the goodness to revise it a second time.'

Long before *Leonora* was published she was preparing to write a pendant to *Practical Education*. 'I am now laying myself out for wisdom, for my father has excited my ambition to write a *useful* essay upon professional education; he has pointed out to me that to be a mere writer of pretty stories and novelettes would be unworthy of his partner, pupil and daughter and I have been so touched by his reasons or his eloquence or his kindness or all together, that I have thrown aside all thoughts of pretty stories, and put myself into a course of solid reading . . . Now Sophy, dear Sophy! Mixed with this filial piety and obedience, and goodness etc., which I see you ready primed to praise, there is one little tiny grain of folly, which is visible to no eye but that of conscience, and which I might keep snug concealed from you if I pleased, but I do not please to cheat —I have the same lurking hope, which first prompted me to write *Leonora*; that it will be read and liked by——'

Though they lived in the depths of the country the house always buzzed with visitors, large parties of Ruxtons, Foxes, Beauforts and other connections and friends as well as men of learning and affairs. Into their little home festivities Maria threw herself heart and soul; she never tired of the games and romps in which everyone joined with gusto. 1805 opened gaily with a houseful of Beauforts and January

29th, Mrs. Beaufort's wedding day, was celebrated 'with a sort of masquerade without masks—a Twelfth Night such as we used to have . . . We were very merry and wonderful noisy.' Everyone dressed up and took part, even Mrs. Edgeworth joining in the revels though a few weeks later she gave birth to her fourth little girl.

'This morning', wrote Maria, 'as she lay beside her mother all the children, Fanny, Harriet and Sophy, came to be introduced to her—Their words seemed exactly in proportion to their ages—Sophy took to kissing her very cordially without asking by words or looks, who or what she was or whence she came—Harriet, after observing with some indifference the smallness of its hands, suddenly exclaimed, "I'll go and tell Charlotte, I'll go and call Charlotte" and she pushed her way off the bed and out of the room to Charlotte who was making breakfast.—Fanny waited with the conscious dignity of 5 almost 6 years old till she was summoned from the foot to the side of the bed, then after examining "the poor little thing" joint by joint and feature by feature, she ended with kissing it most maternally—and when her mother observed that she would be able to nurse Lucy a little—Fanny added with pride and joy in her eyes, Yes and I can teach her her letters too.'

There were theatricals at Castle Forbes at the end of March. 'We were much entertained at the play at Castle Forbes—a very pretty little theatre, beautiful dresses. *Of Age Tomorrow* and *The Jew and the Doctor* were the pieces that were represented—*The Jew and the Doctor* splendid Spanish dresses with spangles and feathers and vandykes in abundance. The lady Forbes act as well as gentlewomen ought to act and upon the whole we were extremely amused—particularly with Lady Moyra's conversation. She has at 75 a wonderful portion of the spirit of animation and as warm sympathy in the pleasures of her grandchildren as if she were in the bloom of fifteen—How well she understands the arts of living!—Between the acts, when cakes and jellies were handed about she said to me, "It was I begged Selina would let us have these things for people may say what they please but I who have lived long in the world know that you must gratify the palate as well as the eyes and ears— Some are to be taken by the eyes and some by the ears, but all more or less by the throat!"'

Soon after this Edgeworth fell ill and though it lasted only a day or two the attack was alarming enough to terrify Maria. 'What would become of me without my father?' she cried to Aunt Ruxton, 'I should sink into that *nothing* from which he raised me.' Swift on the heels of her alarm, her beloved Henry came back from Edinburgh 'coughing, deaf and hollow-eyed'. Though he eventually recovered sufficiently to practise as a doctor at Rostrevor for a short time his health was unequal to it and in order to escape the damp Irish climate he afterwards migrated to Madeira. When later on they heard he was dangerously ill there, Maria begged her father in vain to be allowed to go out to him. But years of suffering and frustrated hopes proved too much for sensitive, aspiring Henry who was brought back at last to a mental hospital at Clifton.

That April 1805, Maria was taken ill, poisoned by opium that had been applied to an aching tooth. When she was convalescent she lay on the library sofa listening enraptured as Charlotte read aloud a new poem, *The Lay of the Last Minstrel*, which Lady Granard sent to amuse her. Maria who thought it touched the highest peaks of sublimity was carried away by an admiration that never abated for Walter Scott. Later that summer another present arrived, this time from Pakenham Hall. 'Lady Elizabeth has sent me a little pony, as quiet and almost as small as a dog on which I go trit trot, trit trot, but I hope it will never take it into its head to add

> *When we come to the stile*
> *Skip we go over.'*

Though her father was away in London on business, his birthday on May 31st was celebrated as usual. 'Sneyd who is ever the promoter of gaiety contrived a pretty little *fête-champêtre* which surprised us most agreeably—After dinner he persuaded me that it was indispensably necessary for my health that I should take an airing; accordingly the chaise came to the door and Anne Nangle and my mother and little Lucy in her arms and Sophy and Maria were rolled off and after them on horseback came rosy Charlotte all smiles and Henry with eyes brilliant with pleasure—riding again with Charlotte after eight months' absence!' Upon their return, 'our ears were suddenly struck with the sound of music and as if by enchantment a fairy festival appeared upon the green—in the midst of an amphitheatre of verdant festoons suspended from white staffs, on which the scarlet streamers of the yeomen were flying, appeared a company of youths and maidens in white with their heads adorned with flowers, dancing merrily—whilst the matrons, their mothers, with their little children—the united families of the Bristows and Langans . . . were seated on benches round the amphitheatre. John Langan the delighted father and grandfather sat upon the pier of the dining-room steps with little Harriet on one knee and Sophy on the other and Fanny beside him—In the course of the evening William danced a reel with Fanny and Harriet to the great delight of all the little and large spectators—The cakes and syllabubs served by good Kitty formed no inconsiderable part of the pleasures of the evening. William who is at present in the height of electrical enthusiasm proposed to the dancers a few electrical sparks to complete the joys of the day—All, men and women, flocked into the study after him to be shocked and their various gestures and expressions of surprise and terror were really diverting.' When darkness fell the little amphitheatre was illuminated, 'the lights mixed with the green boughs and flowers were beautiful and various men and boys with flambeaus waving about had an excellent effect', the young ones joining in the dance on the green while Maria and the elders watched from the window.

Visits to Pakenham Hall were always greatly looked forward to. Lady Longford, now a widow, kept house for her eldest son who had succeeded to his grandmother's earldom and as a gay bachelor with his own pursuits and pleasures was seldom there. His old friend's widow was ever the object of Edgeworth's chivalrous devotion while his praise of her daughter Kitty's well-bred politeness, indefinable beauty and sweet disposition rang sky-high. As three of the four younger sons were away at the wars only the two unmarried daughters, Kitty and Caroline, and their aunt Lady Elizabeth, were usually at home. This autumn Maria wrote: 'I have lately been at Pakenham Hall and Castle Forbes—I was the better for the first and the worse for the last. Not but what all the inhabitants of Castle Forbes were extremely and exuberantly polite and kind but I could not help being tired out at a large dinner and room full of company—At Pakenham Hall I was delighted with "that sweetest music" the praises of a friend—from a person of judgement and taste . . . hearing sweet Kitty Pakenham speak of Sophy— I never saw her look more animated or more pretty than when she was speaking of her.'

When six months later 'in a warm kind letter to my father' Lady Longford announced Kitty's engagement to her early love, Sir Arthur Wellesley, back, covered in glory, after ten years in India; they were all so excited that as

Frances Edgeworth said 'waking or sleeping the image of Miss Pakenham swims before our eyes'. Maria, thirsting for details, had to wait until a fortnight after the marriage for a description of the bridegroom. 'Doctor Beaufort, tell Charlotte, saw Sir Arthur Wellesley at the Castle—handsome, very brown, quite bald and a hooked nose.'

The doom that marked down one after the other, the children of Elizabeth Edgeworth was closing in on lovely, talented Charlotte whose health in 1806 was swiftly declining. 'She looks terribly like her poor mother,' wrote Maria in December, 'and my father's manner of speaking of her alarms me more than I can tell.' When she died in April 1807 he broke down completely under a grief that shattered them all for many months though Maria's sorrow was soon absorbed by her concern for him. 'Sad, silent and utterly passive' he went about like one half-dead. All her thoughts and energies were bent on rousing him, bringing him back from the twilight into which he was slipping away from her. So intent was she on this single purpose that she was quite oblivious to what others were feeling, writing at the end of May to Sneyd who was away in London: 'I wish you would make haste back to enliven us and to revive my father's interest in life.'

Sneyd who adored Charlotte and to whom none of the tough moral fibre and resilience which Maria inherited had descended, was incapable of casting his sorrows aside by sheer force of will. Feeling quite heart-broken, he hardly knew how to face going back to Edgeworthstown with Charlotte no longer there. To his young brother William he turned for sympathy, pouring out his unhappiness in a letter.

'I am a sanguine little animal and thank God not of the cold-blooded type,' Maria sometimes said. When she read this letter of Sneyd's she was appalled; it was something that had never entered her head. It was 'so pathetic that I have not yet recovered my wits after reading—I sat stock still in the arm chair in the cabinet where I read it for I believe a quarter of an hour afterwards ruminating sweet and bitter and bitterly sweet thoughts—My dear Sneyd I sympathize in all your feelings—Your return to this house will not, however, be quite as painful to you I hope as you imagine—for you will be *forced* to break old associations as you will probably come in company with Admiral P(akenham) and Mrs. P. and children whom my father has promised to bring from Coolure . . . My father's spirits are much recovered latterly . . . All July he will have U and troops of friends about him.'

On the strength of a 'most kind and pressing invitation' from that dark and debonnair bachelor Lord Longford, Christmas was spent at Pakenham Hall, Maria with her parents and seventeen-year-old Honora driving over the day before.

'Found here Lady Longford Miss P.—Lady Eliz P.—Mrs. Fortescue and Miss—A few minutes after we came arrived Captⁿ Hercules P.—the first time he had met his family since his return from Copenhagen—I never saw such mild calm joy as Lady Longford shewed—She is a charming woman and it is delightful to see her in the midst of her family—What a contrast this family is to Castle Forbes—at least in their manner of shewing the same feelings, for granting the feelings to be equal, which I no more believe than that the moon is made of green cheese, yet there is such a quantity of sentimentality and *chère* maman-ing—and dearest Lady Granard-ing as makes one almost sick even of maternity . . . Now to return to Hercules P. My father has scarce ever quitted his elbow since he came and has been all ears and no tongue. He has given a full account of all their proceedings in that *piratical* expedition to Copenhagen. . . .'

Maria was writing to Henry and Sneyd who were spending a melancholy Christmas in London, both in bad health and low spirits. To amuse them she covered pages with Captain Pakenham's adventures though she complained he talked so fast and indistinctly that she and Honora were left in a 'Miz-Maze'. 'He did not change my opinion one whit as to the injustice of the whole proceeding and tho' I am sure he is a very gallant officer I did not like his soldier *slang* nor his way of speaking of the poor people whom he called dogs and scoundrels and *rollikin* fellows, etc. . . . I got my father and Mrs. E. to repeat to me and make sense of—which they did—not without interlarding their discourse with execrations against my stupidity and suggesting perpetually that I was so prejudiced by Captain P.'s ugliness that I would not give him credit for any sense. . . .

'Lord L. has finished and furnished his castle which is now really a mansion fit for a nobleman of his fortune. The furniture is neither Gothic nor Chinese, nor gaudy nor frail, nor so fashionable that it will be out of fashion in six months . . . The immense hall so well-warmed by hot air that the children play in it from morning till night. Lord L. seemed to take great pleasure in repeating 20 times that he was to thank Mr. Edgeworth for this . . . Now Lord L. has made such a comfortable nest he must certainly get some bird with pretty plumage and a sweet voice to fill it.'

Much disgusted, Maria opined, 'by a near view of the domestic lives of some fine ladies' this eligible peer remained unwed, the intercourse between the two houses going on without interruption for many years longer. One snowy night a whole procession of carriages set out from Pakenham Hall for a 'grand ball at Mrs. Pollard's' where three beauties from Tipperary with 'white feathers as long as my two arms joined together, stuck in front of what was meant for Spanish hats . . . towered above their sex, divinely vulgar, with brogues of true Milesian race! Supper so crowded that Caroline Pakenham and I agreed to use one arm by turns and thus with difficulty reached our mouths.' Driving back in the small hours, the drunken postilion galloping the horses through the snow, 'laid the coach fairly down on its side in the ditch', Maria clinging like a bat to the hand-string until Admiral Pakenham rescued her, lifting her up and carrying her in his arms 'as if I had been a little doll' and setting her down on the step of Mrs. Tuite's carriage. On another winter's night there she read aloud a story from *Fashionable Tales*, the Pakenhams 'sincerely kind and well bred' listening with the utmost politeness, 'taking it as a mark of kindness from me and not as an exhibition'. One summer the great, many-towered house was filled with excited children who danced their little paste-board puppets at the end of 'gossamer strings' while a footman played the fiddle and 'my father as usual was the soul of the dance and the joy of the children'. And snug in the well-warmed, candle-lit rooms some other winter's evening Maria watched in bewilderment while her father and Lady Elizabeth played cribbage. 'They count so quick, 15 two 15 four that I was never able to keep up with them and made a sorry figure— Worse again at understanding some genealogies and inter-marriages which Lady Elizabeth undertook to explain to me, till at last she threw her arms flat down on each side in indignant despair and exclaimed, "Well! you are the stupidest creature alive!" '

Another house where she always enjoyed going was Sonna. Although she never really liked cynical Mr. Chene-vix 'who loves to collect scandalous anecdotes of our sex and who prides himself on the knowledge of the bad', if he happened to be staying there she was certain of hearing entertaining reports of her friends in France. He was there when she dined there in the autumn of 1809, and told 'a number of Parisian anecdotes. You know Bonaparte has forbidden Madame de Staël to come to Paris but she had a great desire to see Talma and she obtained permission to go to Lyons when he was there to see him—In the midst of the play one night she started up and stretching her arms and breast far out of the box towards the stage, exclaimed in a voice that all the house could hear, "Toute la puissance de mon âme est dans la sienne."—Fine stage effect! A la Corinne! . . . Mr. C. says the Parisians now are as eager to go to the new Court as ever they were to go to that of Lewis the 14$\underline{th}$—That it is magnificent to Eastern profusion —but ill-bred as you may guess when officers make no scruple of elbowing and pushing ladies to get into the magic circle—7 Queens sit all in a row with more diamonds than are to be found anywhere but in the Persian or Arabian Tales—The Queen of Spain—the Queen of Holland—the Queen of Naples—the Queen of Etruria—the Queen of etc.—Poor creatures!'

Shortly after this Maria had fresh proof of the inconsistencies which delighted Richard Chenevix. 'I see by today's paper that my friend Madame Pastoret is made Countess de Pastoret and that she and the pretty Countess de Ségur are making fine figures presenting reports of la Charité de la Maternité to the Empress—It struck me much to see among the list of the ladies presented by Madame de Pastoret Madame Gautier, Madame Grivel, Madame Portalés all of whom we lived with 8 years ago and used to hear abusing Bonaparte and his court à gorge deployée!'

The war never prevented her from corresponding with her friends abroad and a copy of everything she wrote was always despatched to M. Pictet for the *Bibliothèque britannique*. Their other Genevese friend M. Dumont was in England all this time and Maria was delighted with the flattering letter he wrote to her from Lord Henry Petty's country house where her *Tales from Fashionable Life* were read aloud to an appreciative audience. Such was their success that her publisher asked her to write a second series and when these appeared in three volumes two years later, among them was *The Absentee*. This short, exceedingly amusing novel was written first as a play to please the children in the summer of 1808 when Anna Beddoes, recently widowed, brought her little family to Edgeworthstown. It was always Maria's unfulfilled ambition to be a successful playwright and her father was so pleased with this piece that he sent it to Sheridan. But as she told Aunt Ruxton, Sheridan replied 'as I foresaw he *must* that in the present state of this country the Lord Chamberlain would not license the "Absentee"—besides there would be difficulty in finding actors for so many Irish characters'.

Though her fame increased with every book she counted it no more than a tinsel thread running through the good plain stuff of everyday when such down-to-earth matters as leases, repairs and the depredations of an absconded tenant often took up her time, or she fretted herself 'to an atomy' over letting an inn. Nevertheless this gleaming thread drew many distinguished strangers across the bogs, among them two lion-hunting ladies. On a summer evening in 1808 as a large party were sitting down to dinner, the butler came in and announced 'Mrs. Apreece, sir, she is getting out of her carriage'. This rich, vivacious young widow was known to be travelling in Ireland and many stories were going the rounds of the way she was pushing to make friends with the highly-placed and celebrated people she longed to be acquainted with. They thought it was a hoax, 'some nonsense of Sneyd's', when Edgeworth returned with the elegantly dressed little woman whose pretty dark eyes flashed forth from a face as brown as a berry. She stayed three days, monopolizing Maria who at last was quite worn out by her continuous chatter and resisting repeated invitations to stay with her in Berkeley Square. A year later when the elderly blue-stocking Lydia White, who entertained at her house in Park Street the best literary society in London, appeared upon the scene Maria was not impressed either by her affected manner, golden locks and excess of rouge and pearl powder. She much preferred a clever, modest young man like Josiah Wedgwood's great-nephew Henry Holland (son of a Knutsford surgeon) who stopped there 'in the course of a pedestrian tour' and whom she thought uncommonly well-informed. He became her devoted servant and 'literary intelligencer'; from that time forth keeping up 'an unbroken and affectionate correspondence for more than forty years', as Sir Henry Holland wrote in his *Recollections*.

Thanks to him Maria was *au fait* with the doings of Mrs. Apreece. 'She is at Edinburgh and charmed with all the wits there and as I hear from Mr. Holland she is much admired by them.' And later: 'She has already philosophers enough at her feet, viz.—Mr. Davy and Mr. Chenevix—one at each foot—it is doubted which will succeed.' As they knew both the suitors, the race for the widow was particularly interesting. Davy often stopped at Edgeworthstown ('the moral and intellectual paradise of the author of *Castle Rackrent*', was his dry description) on his way south to fish, and in 1810 a large party went from there to hear him lecture in Dublin. In the end he won the day, was awarded a knighthood and carried off the widow. When not long afterwards Mr. Chenevix married Madame de Riou, an ageing French beauty of dubious reputation, pensioned, it was said, by one of the Royal Dukes, Maria declared he only got what he asked for.

During these years that carried her ever farther across the smooth, apparently endless plain of middle life, Maria's character expanded and strengthened though subservient ever to her father's wishes. Accustomed as he was to an assenting, admiring family circle, now as he approached seventy his readiness to hold forth in company and his out-spoken contempt for any signs of affectation or insincerity, sometimes put a great strain on the watchful indulgence of his wife and Maria. He was liable to rate a young lady at dinner because she mispronounced a word, his outbursts often startling their more timid guests. When a very shy young couple, the Aclands, called there, Sir Thomas 'seemed to be quite astonished by my father's eloquence in a charac-ter he gave—indeed most eloquently—of Lady Wellington —and looked and looked! *avec des grands yeux ébaubis!* When my father struck the table I am sure he thought heaven and earth were coming together! . . . Lady A.—is rather pretty when she does not poke out her chin and close her eyes—which she does regularly when spoken to or preparing to speak. My father mimicked it once (by mis-take) in answering her and she colored all over and kept her chin in better order thenceforward.'

This was nothing however to that awkward occasion in Dublin when they met Mr. Parnell Hayes. She and her father went with Fanny and Harriet to see the celebrated young aeronaut, Windham Sadler, go up in his balloon. As owing to bad weather the ascent was postponed they spent the time sightseeing, and as they drove through the city one day they met Henry Hamilton who had married Caroline Pakenham, riding with a friend.

' "There," said my father, "is Mr. Parnell Hayes who wishes so much to be acquainted with you, Maria." Im-prudent I replied (now mother do not be angry with me) "Then I have no particular ambition to be acquainted with him, for I don't want to stoop to conquer one who I know abuses us and all our works."—Scarcely were the words out

of my mouth than Mr. H. H. called to coachman to stop.—
"How do you do, Mr. E. Is Miss E. in this carriage? Here's
a gentleman who is particularly ambitious of the honour to
be introduced to her."—Bows on each side scarcely made
when my father stretched from the farthest part of the coach
out of the window quite into the street to Mr. Parnell and
in a loud distinct voice exclaimed, "Ha! Mr. P., how do
you do.—We know you abuse us and all our works but we
don't mind that."—Drove on and all my hope was Mr.
Parnell was so much surprised that he did not clearly comprehend or hear.'

Mr. Parnell Hayes, however, heard every word, and as he,
like the Edgeworths, was on his way to Dr. Philip Crampton's to see the interesting discovery of a muscle in an
ostrich's eye, it might have been very embarrassing if
Maria's tact and his good nature had not covered up every
vestige of unpleasantness.

'Thursday morning to our inexpressible joy was fine and
the flag, the signal that Sadler would ascend, was to the joy
of thousands flying from the top of Nelson's Pillar.' The
balloon was tethered in Belvidere Gardens and as the vast
crowd hurried towards the two narrow doorways, forcing
their way in, Maria, clinging to Fanny for ten agonizing
minutes 'thought we must have been flattened and the
breath squeezed out of our bodies . . . My father quite pale
calling in a stentor voice to the sentinels . . . he fairly kicked
off the terrace a man who was intent upon nothing but an
odious bag of cakes which he held close to his breast,
swearing and pushing. . . .

'Music and the most festive scene in the gardens—the
balloon—the beautiful many-colored balloon, chiefly mar-
oon colour with painted arms of Ireland, hung under the
trees and filling fast from pipes and an apparatus which I
leave for William's scientific description: terrace before

Belvidere House—well-dressed groups parading on it—groups all over the gardens, mantles, scarves and feather floating—all the commonalty outside in fields at half-price. We soon espied Mr. and Mrs. Hamilton and joined company and were extremely happy . . . Presently we met the Solicitor-General—he started back and made me such a bow as made me feel my own littleness, then shook hands most cordially and in a few moments told me more than most men could tell in an hour . . . curtsy bow and pass on. Soon hear Sol Genl voice again behind me.—"Miss E." (running) "Here's a greater man than I am and who cannot run so well, trying to overtake you." Turned, saw Sir E. L. and Lady L. and Lady Isabella, very civil all—talked about nothings and passed on. Next came in full flowers, rouge, veil and scarf Mrs. Austin with speeches as long as my arm. . . .' And so it went on, everyone of note making a bee-line for Maria.

'The drum beats! the flag flies! balloon full! It is moved from under the trees over the heads of the crowd . . . Mr. Sadler quite composed, this being his twenty-sixth aerial ascent, got into his car—a lady—the Duchess of Richmond I believe—presented to him a pretty flag—the balloon gave two majestic nods from side to side as the cords were cut. Whether the music continued to play at this moment nobody can tell. No one spoke while the balloon successfully rose—rapidly cleared the trees and floated above our heads —loud shouts and huzzas, one man close to us exclaiming as he clasped his hands, "Ah, musha, musha, God bless you! God be wid you." Mr. Sadler, waving his flag and his hat and bowing to the world below soon pierced a white cloud and disappeared—then emerging the balloon looked like a moon, black on one side, silver on the other—then like a dark bubble, then less and less and now only a dark speck is seen, and now the fleeting rack obscures it.'

The day was made quite perfect for Maria by meeting some of the Ruxtons and her father insisting that she should do as her uncle suggested and go back with them to Black Castle for at least a week.

Chapter Six

1813

In 1813 her father decided that Maria as a celebrated and widely-read authoress should have a season in London. As neither she nor his wife had left Ireland since 1803, significant years in an age of progress, they arranged to make a little tour of the principal commercial and manufacturing towns in Lancashire on the way. The inseparable trio accordingly set out at the end of March and as soon as they got to Liverpool Edgeworth 'found out' the great William Roscoe—the market-gardener's son whose business acumen and extraordinary erudition brought him to wealth and fame as a savant and philanthropist.

'Mr. Roscoe is a benevolent-looking chearful gentleman-like old man, tall—neither thin nor fat—with a peaked forehead—thick grey hair . . . looks as if it was blown by the wind in a picturesque style—his manner frank and prepossessing free from pretension of any kind . . . He has a quick recollective memory, speaks excellent language but with a strong provincial accent . . . but in a short time his chearful kindness effaces the recollection of this—Mrs. Roscoe is an honest-faced, fat, *hearty*, good-natured hospitable body without the least pretension to polish, but with a downright, plain good understanding and uncommonly warm heart which throws out all her thoughts and feelings in a broad Lancashire dialect . . . Neither sons or daughters have any polish of manner or appearance. In short though it is in the power of a father's genius to drag a whole family up in the world, yet unless the mother be a woman of education and good manners it seems impossible to give an air of gentility to the family—Now I have written this I wish to blot it out because it seems ungrateful to make such observations on a family by whom we were so hospitably received and among whom there appeared such genuine goodness and warm family affection . . . Mr. Roscoe gave himself up to us the whole day.'

He walked them round the Botanic Gardens for which he did so much, complaining that the town and neighbourhood paid scant attention to it and its wonderful collection of rare flowers and trees, and afterwards they drove out to Allerton Hall. Maria who far preferred seeing people to pictures did her best to be interested in her host's great collection which covered the walls of his fine, spacious rooms, but was far more diverted when 'towards dinner-time the room filled with sons, tall black-eyed bashful young men who spoke not at all. It was a considerable time before I knew them asunder—The eldest a little man a banker with the most frightened look I ever saw was however the first to enter into conversation, and we soon happily found one common subject of interest—Wully had been at Harrowgate and he had met Mrs. Foster and the two Miss Fosters . . . It was very droll to hear Mrs. Roscoe complaining in the broadest of the broad Lancashire dialect of the "*aldest* young lady's having so *mooch* of the *haccent* that she could scarce understond her at the furst going hoff".'

'Mr. Roscoe could converse at dinner and so could a Mr. Shepherd . . . His conversation is not too literary . . . it has a happy mixture of anecdote and facts—He has been much taken notice of by the great since he rose to celebrity and I particularly admire the simplicity with which he talks of them. He never introduces Dukes and Princes to do himself honor but to tell some characteristic anecdotes of them.'

Factories were cropping up all over the place, an industrial prosperity that already was bringing disconcerting changes to the social scene. From 'Mr. Holland's house at Knutsford' Maria wrote: 'I feel rejoiced to be at this quiet clean place after Liverpool and Manchester—I sh^d dislike extremely to live in a manufacturing town . . . It is curious to see rich manufacturers growing into fine people with pictures and gildings and mirrors and democratic principles and aristocratic tastes.'

At some point on the road to London the news reached them of Henry's death, an event that could only be regarded as a merciful release. True to his precepts Edgeworth decided to proceed with their plans, though in deference to the Sneyd aunts, mourning must be donned on the journey home. In London the story leaked out and went the rounds as an astonishing instance of expedience overruling the natural emotions. Lord Byron, years later, recalling the Edgeworths, jotted it down in his notebook though the actual circumstances seem to have eluded the gossips.[1]

In London where they rented two floors at 10 Holles Street, the arrival of the diminutive lioness created an absolute furore. Lady Davy was in high feather this May giving

[1] In his Notes for October 1821 Lord Byron who was about to read Edgeworth's *Memoirs* wrote: Old Edgeworth, the fourth or fifth Mrs. Edgeworth and *the* Miss Edgeworth were in London, 1813. Miss Edgeworth liked, Mrs. Edgeworth not disliked, old Edgeworth a bore —the worst of bores—a boisterous Bore. I met them in society once at a breakfast of Sir H. D.'s. . . .

When on the road they heard of *her* brother's, and *his* son's, death. What was to be done? Their London Apparel was all ordered and made! So they sunk his death for the six weeks of their Sojourn, and went into mourning on their way back to Ireland. *Fact!*

parties and introducing her to everyone. People stood on chairs at assemblies to catch sight of her, the greatest in the land elbowing one another in their eagerness to be introduced and angling for invitations to meet her. Mrs. Edgeworth wrote of 'Maria's *prominent* position—visited and noticed as she is by everybody . . . We laugh at Maria for having been visited by Lady Besborough and [Lady] Melbourne—and the Duchess of Sussex and Princess of Wales[1] and all the demireps who are setting up new reputations on the strength of wit and blue stockings—when beauty and white hose could charm no more.' When Madame de Staël who was also expected in London this May failed to arrive, someone at a large dinner inquired when she was likely to come. 'Not till Miss Edgeworth is gone,' replied Samuel Rogers, 'Madame de Staël would not like two stars shining at the same time.' Almost before he finished speaking a gentleman rose up at the other end of the table—her son Auguste whom Rogers had never seen till now. 'Madame la Baronne de Staël est incapable d'une telle bassesse,' he solemnly declared and sat down again.

Though another royal encounter awakened old memories it looks as though Maria's friends had other plans in view. 'Mrs. E. has been much diverted by my meeting with Sweden, its king and its courtiers, wherever I go and to whomever I talk. In the most unexpected manner this flashes up on me continually in company.—But I don't care about it now in the least—only when Madame de Staël comes I shall ask her a few questions—but I only ask for information, totally damn me, etc. . . .

'What do I think of M. Dumont? I will tell you not only what I think—but what I have thought—what I may think hereafter it is out of my power to predict. The evening of

[1] Though the Princess of Wales informed Maria that she wished to see her, Maria wrote to the Princess declining her invitation.

the day after our arrival I had a dreadful *customary* headache
and had gone to lie down. Mrs. E. came to summon me
downstairs—"Do come if you possibly can for Mr. D. has
come a long way on purpose to pay his respects to you."
I was so sick and in such pain I could hardly bear to move
—however I crawled down . . . and I would have given
five guineas well counted that he had not called this un-
lucky evening.—But so it was and there he was!—a fattish,
Swiss-looking man in black with monstrous eyebrows and
a red large face like what the little robbins described the
gardener's face when it looked down upon them in their
nest—I felt at once que l'amour n'avoit jamais passé et ne
passeroit jamais par là—au reste he is and will be always to
us, an excellent friend, a man of first rate abilities, superior
in conversation to any one I have met with except Sir James
McIntosh. Dumont lives the life of a French savant in
society—wants nothing more and seems to have sold himself to Bentham as Dr Faustus sold himself to the devil. This
point settled *completely*, I will now my dear Sophy go on
with our public history . . .

'The first persons who came to see us were Sir H. and Lady
Davy—they have been uniformly and zealously kind and
attentive to us and Davy is just the same in his manners as
he always was—We have been frequently at their dinners
and parties—They see all the world of wit and much of the
world of fashion and rank . . . I will just name a few of the
most conspicuous of both classes. Lord Byron, Malthus,
2 Smiths (rejected addresses) Miss Baillie—Mrs. Opie—Mrs.
Marcet—Sir James and Lady McIntosh—the Miss Berrys—
Miss Fanshaws—Lady Crewe—Mrs. Weddell—Lady Carysfoot—Lord and Lady Carrington—Lord Lansdowne[1]— Mr.
and Lady Elizth Whitbread—Miss Fox—Lord and Lady

[1] Lord Henry Petty succeeded his half-brother as third marquis in
1809. In 1808 he married Lady Louisa Fox Strangways.

Darnley, Lord and Lady Hardwicke, Lady Charlemont, Lady Charlotte Lindsay, Lord Gore, Dutchess of Somerset —I am tired and so are you of this list of names—Of Lord Byron I can tell you nothing but that his appearance is nothing that you would remark in any other man—he stood behind the door all night with the Dutchess of Somerset who penned him up effectually and I hear he complained that he could not get out—but all the time I am sure he was flattered by it—Nobody but her Grace heard him say one word—This is in imitation of Lady Hertford and P. Regent —we are to breakfast quite in private with Lord B. in a few days—Malthus is plain and sensible in conversation and agreeable notwithstanding a defect in his pronunciation— the two Smiths, nothing but the Rejected addresses— . . . Mrs. Marcet *plain* and sensible and good-natured . . . Mrs. Opie! my curiosity is satisfied—The Miss Berrys all that you have heard of them from people of various tastes—consequently you know that they are well-bred and have nice tact in conversation—Catherine Fanshaw—her manners and conversation are what I most like . . . well-bred—not labouring at the oar of Bel Esprit or any oar—but quite easy, natural and sprightly—Lady Crewe has still the remains of much beauty—*Buff and blue and Mrs. Crewe*—I looked at her with Charles Fox in my head . . . The difference between her really fashionable air and that of the strugglers and imitators struck me much. Her style is quick, rather reserved —wishing to have people exert themselves for her amusement with the air of an idol long used to be worshipped and expecting it—but still a well-bred idol. Lady Eliz. Whitbread in one word delightful . . . Miss Fox very agreeable —Lady Charlotte Lindsay ditto.—

'Lady Hardwicke was much more pleasing than I expected to find her and both her Ladyship and her Lord peculiarly gracious to us. Lord Somerville is so much charmed with Lady Delacour and Lady Geraldine whom he pronounces to be perfect women of fashion, and who he says are in high repute in the Equerry's room at court, that you know I cannot help being charmed with his Lordship's good breeding in return. He was quite indignant against certain pretenders to fashion. Lady Derby[1] he says is always acting. There is continually a stage *aside* which betrays her —I told him the remark of a friend of ours that a gentleman or gentlewoman cannot be made in less than two generations. "In less than *five* Ma'am."

'Lady Lansdowne taking in beauty, character, conversation, talents and manners I think superior to any woman I have seen—perfectly natural—daring to be herself . . . I long to see more of her and feel afraid I shall like her so much that I shall be sorry to part with her.

'Lady Spencer—dined at her house—clever and in the Lady-Granard-style—taking snuff—pulling her lace shawl and giving her opinions of Windham, Fox, Pitt, etc. in a *loudish* quality voice—laughing at what she says herself and très capable—In elegance she is not all I expected . . . Lord Spencer puts me I cannot tell why in mind of my uncle Ruxton—not in figure but in his quiet reserved way of enjoying conversation in his snugs. I was quite at ease with him and placed quite to my satisfaction between him and Lady Lansdowne—The dinner *au reste* was stupid tho' very grand—24 candles on the table in superb branches—sideboard of gold plate at one end and silver at the other and a prodigiously fine desert of which no creature eat—I mean that literally that nobody touched anything except a biscuit—This I perceive is *an air*—very ridiculous! Lady Georgina Spencer very pretty, Lady Sarah Littleton the other daughter I am told is uncommonly well informed and had a prodigious desire to be acquainted with me for

[1] Eliza Farren, the celebrated actress, m. 1797 twelfth Earl of Derby.

whom she had the highest admiration, etc. *but* she seated herself on a sofa at a distance from me and never *could* cross the room or speak one word to me—But they were one and all potent starers and so near sighted as to be compelled to have frequent recourse to their glasses ... Lady Besborough was there—her manner soft and sentimental—beseeching you to like her with voice and with eye ...

'Charming! amiable Lady Wellington! As she truly said of herself "She is always Kitty Pakenham to her friends"— She received us just as she would have done at Pakenham Hall. After comparison with crowds of others, *beaux esprits*, fine ladies, and fashionable *scramblers* for notoriety her dignified graceful simplicity rises in one's opinion and we feel it with more conviction of its superiority. She let us in in the morning. Talked about her children, shewed them to us ... Delightful children!

'We have been to one of Mrs. Siddons' readings *Measure for Measure*—it did not come up to my expectations ... the tones of tenderness and sorrow were wanting and the looking through spectacle glasses at the book from time to time breaks all illusion. We hope to see her act on 25th.—it was thought impossible to get a box but the moment my father pronounced the name Edgeworth Mr. Brandon the box-keeper said he should have one ...

'We have been to a grand night at Mrs. Hope's—furniture Hope—rooms really deserve the French epithet superbe. All of beauty rank and fashion that London can assemble I may say in the newspaper style were there and we observed that the beauties past fifty bore the belle. Prince Regent stood holding converse with Lady Eliz. Monk one third of the night, she leaning gracefully on a bronze table in the centre of the room in the midst of the very small space or circle etiquette could keep round them—The other two thirds of the night he sat on a window sofa with Lady Hertford.

About 900 people were at this assembly—the crowd of carriages was so great that after sitting waiting in ours for an hour the coachman told us there was no chance of our getting in unless we got out and walked.' And so they did, though they would never have got up the crowded staircase 'but for the gloriously large body and good-natured politeness of the Archbishop of Tuam[1] who fortunately met us at the door and recognized us . . in the wake of his greatness we sailed on prosperously and never stopped till he presented us to his beautiful daughter who received us with a winning smile. It is fortunate that the mistress of such a house should be so beautiful—I don't think Mr. Hope is at all a *bête* though she is a belle. But perhaps I only think well of his taste and understanding because he was very civil to us. Asked him who somebody who was passing was and he answered, "I really don't know—I don't know half the people here nor do they know me or Mrs. Hope even by sight—Just now I was behind a lady who thought she was making *her speech* to Mrs. Hope but she was addressing her compliments to some stranger." Among the old beauties the Dutchess of Rutland held her pre-eminence and looked the youngest.

'And now my dear Sophy I have done with the chapter of Lords and Ladies with which my letter is filled—Pray do not think because I name these fine people and their civilities that my poor little head is turned or turning with them—Be assured that the whole panorama passes before me as a panorama—It amuses me but I would no more pass my life in this way than spend it looking at a panorama.'

Far more satisfying was the meeting they went to at the

[1] Most Rev. and Honble. William Beresford, third son of Earl of Tyrone, Archbishop of Tuam, created Baron Decies 1812. His daughter Louisa m. Thomas Hope 1806. They were sometimes called 'Beauty and the Beast'.

Freemason's Tavern, when the future of Joseph Lancaster's schools (the forerunners of a national system of day schools) was discussed. Though they went as spectators they were immediately recognized; Edgeworth was given a seat on the platform with two Royal Dukes and a crowd of grandees, while Dumont sat between Maria and her step-mother in the audience. Suddenly without warning Maria heard Lord Lansdowne appeal to her father for his support and in his 'sonorous voice' the Duke of Kent called out 'Mr. Edgeworth'. Her panic was groundless: he spoke better, she thought, than any of the others except Lord Lansdowne and when he sat down the applause was loud and long. Many flattering remarks made to him on this and other occasions, proved that his hard work on behalf of education in Ireland had not been overlooked.

'My dear Sophy, you and my aunt would be delighted if you saw how GOOD my father is in all companies—You would not believe (as he desired to tell my aunt) how pretty behaved he is—What a comfortable thing it is to see our dearest relations *look* and act like gentlemen and gentle-women—Mrs. E. is so much liked by everybody who has head, heart or eyes.

'Now for the history of yesterday by which you may judge of our life—9 o'clock dressed and thought it pretty early because up late night before . . . breakfast scarce ended than visitors came in—Wakefield with a letter from the Duke of Bedford who is anxious to see my father's experiments and to ascertain the draft of carriages tried—talked of mechanics and dukes and politics and my father forbid me to go on writing. Then came Lord Somerville who sat and talked very agreeably and invited us to his country house . . . but still it did not forward my letter—I c^d never touch the forbidden pen—Then came Lady Darnley and various cards and notes and in short till two this went on—

Papa then walked off with Lord Somerville and we gave
orders that no one should be admitted so we only heard
vain thunders and I got on half a page—but then poor Peggy
Langan and her we admitted. She is in an excellent place
with Mrs. Haldeman . . . and she, Peggy, sat and talked of
how happy she was and how good her mistress is for half an
hour and I liked her simplicity and warm heart, but still as
I said before this did not further my letter—Coach at the
door. "Put on your hat this minute Maria and come out
and pay visits for we shall meet some of these people
tonight or tomorrow."

'To save myself trouble I send a list of the visits we made
just as my mother marked them on the card by which we
steered—God knows how I should steer without her.' Only
three of the ladies were at home, Lady Milbanke whose
mathematically-minded daughter Annabella, Maria liked
exceedingly, Lady Wellington and Mrs. Weddell—an agreeable old lady who had lived in the Sir Joshua Reynolds set
'and has the last century at her fingers' ends'.

While Maria was dressing to dine at Lady Levinge's, a
'long note from Miss Berry sent by her own maid to apolo-
gize for a mistake of her servant who had said *not at home* to
us—entreat we would *look in* this evening—Much hurried
dressing—Lady Levinge's dinner (which was not on table
till eight o'clock) very entertaining because quite a new set
of people . . . Called in the evening at Miss Berry's—
Without any comparison the most agreeable I have seen in
Town—quite like French society. Met there persons innumerable—among them Augustus Foster—Henry P(akenham) and Ld Caledon from Ireland—had a great deal of
conversation with Lady C Lindsay who is as agreeable as
all the Norths are said to be . . . *Mrs. Scott of Kilkenny here*
and flirting finely.

'Went shamefully late to Mrs. Sneyd's—then home found

my father in bed—stood at the foot and heard his account of his dinner at Sir Sam¹ Romilly: with Dr. Parr, Dumont, Malthus, etc. Very entertaining but I have not time to tell you more—I have been standing in my dressing-gown writing on the top of a chest of drawers and now my mother will positively not let me write any more—I must dress for a breakfast at Lady Davy's where we are to meet Lord Byron and nobody else to be admitted—

'I *must* just say that half an hour we spent with Lady Wellington yesterday was by far the most agreeable part of the day ... Lady W. diverted us by an account of the serious and friendly counsels she has had from many not to neglect her dress—

' "My dear Lady W.," said one lady, "how many times a day do you think of your dress?"

' "Why three times—morning, evening and night besides CASUALTIES."

' "But this won't do, you must *think* of it seriously at other times and when you go into the country always dress to keep up the habit, my dear Lady W."

'Sir W. Farquhar told Lady W. that the Dutchess of Rutland every day at home and when sure of seeing no creature, is dressed at all points to keep up the habit—he saw her one day *alone* at breakfast with her little son dressed as if for company and the same care which the conscious sylphs would have paid to the drapery and ringlets—her Grace going to the glass to arrange the ringlets and looking back over her shoulder at the effect behind—Good-bye, I must go and do likewise.'

Maria has left no account of this breakfast, the 'high intellectual banquet' Lady Davy looked forward to, with Maria's good sense, Lord Byron's imagination, and the genius of her 'own Treasure' happily mingling. All we know is from Byron who took an instant dislike to Edge-

5. THE DUCHESS OF WELLINGTON
(From a drawing by Sir Thomas Lawrence, P.R.A.)

worth, and hard it would be to find two more opposite
characters than the robust, loquacious old moralist whose
opinions were buttressed by a lifetime of practical usefulness, and the passionate, restless young poet. 'I thought him',
wrote Byron, 'a very tiresome coarse old Irish half and half
gentleman and her a pleasant, reserved old woman' (Maria
was forty-six). But after enjoying Edgeworth's *Memoirs* his
opinion of him mellowed.

'I thought Edgeworth a fine old fellow, of a clarety,
elderly, red complexion, but active, brisk and endless. He
was seventy, but did not look fifty—no, nor forty-eight
even. . . . Edgeworth bounced about, and talked loud and
long; but he seemed neither weakly nor decrepit, and hardly
old. He began by telling "that he had given Dr. Parr a
dressing, who had taken him for an Irish bogtrotter," '—a
long story that can scarcely have contributed to the intellectual banquet.

'He was not much admired in London . . . the fact was
everybody cared more about *her*. She was a nice little un-
assuming "Jeannie Deans-looking body" as we Scotch say
—and, if not handsome, not ill-looking. Her conversation
was as quiet as herself. One would never have guessed she
could write *her name*; whereas her father talked, *not* as if he
could write nothing else, but as if nothing else were worth
writing . . . Altogether they were an excellent cage of the
kind, and succeeded for two months till the landing of
Madame de Staël.'

Among Maria's new acquaintances were several of the
galaxy that shone at Holland House and Bowood; Sir
Samuel Romilly the great legal reformer and his beautiful
wife; Sir James Mackintosh renowned for the quality and
range of his conversation, who had just resigned the Re-
cordership of Bombay; Francis Horner the politician. All
were influenced by Dugald Stewart who as Mackintosh said

'breathed the love of virtue into whole generations of pupils' and to some extent at least were disciples of Jeremy Bentham and his utilitarian doctrines. To Bentham's service Etienne Dumont was dedicated, sacrificing his own talents to edit his manuscripts and translate them for publication in France. Maria spent a day at the Romilly's country house at Clapham, a red-letter day for the Romilly children who after living on her stories found themselves actually playing with the authoress; years later Maria recalled 'the child with whom I eat sillabub under the cow at Clapham'. She made friends as well with several of the pleasant little circle at Hampstead; the Carrs at Maryon Hall and Joanna Baillie whose now forgotten plays were extravagantly praised and said to reflect 'the genuine spirit of Shakespeare'.

'I have found Miss Edgeworth', wrote Joanna Baillie to Walter Scott, 'a frank, animated, sensible and amusing woman, entirely free from affectation of any kind, and of a confiding, affectionate and friendly disposition that has really gained upon my heart . . . She has been received by everybody, the first in literature and the first in rank, with the most gratifying eagerness and respect, and has delighted them all. She is cheerful and talks easily and fluently, seems interested in every subject that comes into play, and tells her little anecdote or story (when her father does not take it out of her mouth) very pleasantly. . . . You would have been amused if you had seen with what eagerness people crowded to get a sight of Miss E.—who is very short—peeping over shoulders and between curled *têtes* to get but one look. She said herself at a party where I met her that the crowd closed over her. She did indeed cause a strange commotion.'

The commotion showed no signs of abating when they left London in the middle of June, travelling to the West Country to visit the Kings at Clifton and thence to Malvern to stay with Anna Beddoes. In spite of the applause and all the adulation and attentions heaped upon her, Maria never lost her level-headed detachment. From the flash and thunder of that dazzling summer storm she emerged quite composed, indivisibly part of the triangle which glowed with mutual esteem and vibrated with her father's vigour. 'I return home loving my own friends and my own mode of life preferably to all others after comparison with all that is fine and gay and rich and rare.'

They were staying near Ross-on-Wye when they heard that Sneyd, who practised at the bar in Dublin, was engaged to Henrica Broadhurst, a young lady with means of her own who lived with her brother at Foston Hall near Derby. They had met her quite by chance when they stayed at Derby with the Strutts on the way to London and now they decided to go back there at once to meet her again. Maria in a whirl of excitement did not grudge the delay: 'Dear Sneyd I hope he will be as happy as love and fortune can make him.'

Chapter Seven

———————————◦◦◦◦———————————

1813-1817

At the end of June they were home again, back with the
aunts and Honora and six excited children—children
loved by Maria with almost maternal tenderness
which never crossed currents with their mother's claims.
To comfort her long ago after that winter in Paris, her
devoted stepmother promised that henceforth they should
share her children whom she brought up to love and admire
their famous sister. In their eyes Maria was always a delightful combination of fairy godmother and second mother.
'How kind you always were to us Maria, when we were
children,' Harriet said years later, reminding her how once
she gave up the entire afternoon to walking up and down a
little path, keeping watch while Fanny and Harriet, perched
in a tree, cooked themselves a meal in a kitchen rigged up
among the branches. But it was Fanny who belonged to her
specially, sometimes even being called 'Maria's daughter'.
No girl of fourteen, thought Maria this summer, ever gave
greater promise of beauty than did Fanny with her glossy
fair hair, regular features and pretty blue eyes. She was
clever, too; her father thought highly of her capacities, her
naturally logical mind and taste for science. Loving and
revering him just as Maria did, Fanny was the same obedient,
industrious pupil.

Maria came home famished, she said, for reading. Books old and new never lost their absorbing excitement; to waken at dawn to read—to sit up at midnight with a candle reading—best of all the readings aloud by the library fire. She longed as well to get on with her writing, to begin a second series of *Early Lessons* which mothers in London had begged for, besides preparing her long novel *Patronage* for the press. Hardly had they settled down however than large, aristocratic coach-loads of London acquaintances came rolling across the bogs to stay with them. Lord Carrington, happily described by Wraxall as 'without reproach and his fortune ample', brought his son, the tutor and a decrepit-looking son-in-law Lord Gardner, 'spindle-shanked by the gouty rheumatism', who when he was not twingeing and suffering made himself very pleasant. How they did talk in the intervals of being bustled about the country sightseeing, telling endless anecdotes that now fall dreadfully flat, Maria picking up all sorts of curious information such as that the hereditary Prince of Naples always kept a hog in a room close to his 'to be killed by the Prince whose delight it was to make hog puddings with his own royal hands'. Best of all Lord Gardner was 'charmed with little Francis—he has a boy of the same age of whom he seems doatingly fond. He said today, pointing him out to his brother-in-law, "There now, Bob, look at that boy running out on the grass, he has no woman, no maid *daddling* after him—That's as it should be —that will be a fine brave boy." '

When Lord Lansdowne and his engagingly sensible wife came in August they brought a large party, Sir George Stanton, Mr. Strangways and several others. As Lady Lansdowne loved walking, all that week they wandered through the fields, an animated bevy of ladies in fluttering tippets and muslins and dandy gentlemen, laughing and talking as they went along, the soft air carrying across the swamps and peat-stacks echoes of great events and famous names.

Almost all that went on in the world was known at Edgeworthstown; what visitors did not bring was retailed in long letters by Maria's correspondents. All this summer the great interest was Madame de Staël and whether or not she was *taking* in society. Reports on the whole were favourable. 'All agree that Madame de Staël is frankness itself and has an excellent heart . . . My father has now so far softened towards her that he says he shall like to see her here provided his younger daughters are out of the house.' She did not, however, extend her travels to Ireland. The autumn brought long accounts of the wonderful fortnight at Bowood which Maria had refused, where the Lansdownes assembled such a brilliant concourse of the witty and learned to meet her that 'if it had not been for chess-playing, music and dancing between times poor human nature never could have borned the fatigue of attention and of admiration—I am glad I was not there as I am sure I shd. have been worn to an atomy'. Dumont wrote to tell that she carried away from Bowood 'le Castle of rackrent. She is charmed with *Ennui* and *Manœuvring*—you are worthy of enthusiasm, but the rest of us are lost in this sad utilitarianism'.

A whole cargo of French translations arrived, visible proof of Maria's popularity in France. *Patronage* was being printed to earn her fresh laurels and £2,100—twice what she got for the second series of *Fashionable Tales*, and she was busy with her children's stories, writing them in close collaboration with her father. The evenings were enlivened by him trying out the simple experiments that Maria described, practical demonstrations that played an important part in his educational system though many scoffed at it and called him eccentric. 'In trying some experiments for Harry and Lucy a few nights ago, my father when setting fire to some tow and turpentine suddenly stopped and exclaimed, "How kind that dear Sister Ruxton of mine always was to me!—I remember thirty, yes forty years ago, plaguing her with trying these very experiments and she indulged me dear soul! and bore with all my fancies!"'

The war with France was now in its eleventh year. Outwardly at Edgeworthstown its effects were imperceptible. Maria scarcely mentioned it in her letters except sometimes to pass on news of Edward and Hercules Pakenham who were winning honours and renown in the Peninsula serving under Lord Wellington, or to describe Lady Wellington after Salamanca 'running as fast as she could to Lord Bury at Lord Bathurst's when he alighted, to learn the first news of her husband'. Once, indeed, news of one of Wellington's victories was carried hot-foot to Edgeworthstown where Lady Longford was staying. Maria from her corner in the library watched the old lady intently as she opened and read aloud the letter, almost more interested in her reactions than in the tidings. Overcome by emotion and unaware that sharp eyes followed her, Lady Longford laid it aside and hurrying into a window recess, with clasped hands, 'God keep him humble!' she cried aloud. Her voice and expression were unforgettable, charged with a vehemence which betrayed a facet of her formidable son-in-law's character new to Maria.

Yet the war had dealt them a heavy blow, a grievous trial even to Edgeworth's stoicism. Nothing mitigated the wretched circumstances of Lovell's captivity; not a spark or echo of the fury and flame, the gallantry and glory of the battlefield raised it to an heroic level. Caught like rabbits, he and many other civilians were shut up within the reeking walls of Verdun whence disquieting reports were brought home by the lucky few who managed to escape. The commissioners in charge of the internees were unscrupulous blackguards who encouraged them in drinking and gambling for their own profit. A worse environment for one of Lovell's temperament could scarcely be thought of, though how with his delicate constitution he survived the six years he stayed there was a miracle. His father never relaxed in his efforts to get him exchanged or sent to Switzerland, but the only amelioration in his lot was when he was transferred to Paris where a more interesting existence was possible and Maria's friends were ready to welcome him. His health was so bad that in the summer of 1812 he wrote urging his father to pass him over, 'a prisoner and in precarious health', and to make his next brother heir. This generous and unselfish gesture impressed them all: 'If he has suffered he has at least had an opportunity of shewing what he is,' said Maria.

At last, early in 1814, the end was in sight as the tide of victory swept across the Pyrenees and into France. As the Allied armies drew closer to Paris the internees were rounded up for removal to another camp. Lovell, warned of his danger by a poor shoe-black he befriended and educated, was striving to get a permit to remain where he was, when with spectacular suddenness, the war came to an end. As the Bonapartists left their offices and council-chambers behind them and fled from the city, the amazing truth suddenly dawned on him that no further efforts were necessary as he was a prisoner no longer.

At Edgeworthstown these momentous happenings passed almost unobserved, the whole household cast down in despair by its master's dangerous illness. All through April, racked with pain, he lay between life and death, suffering from what the doctors diagnosed as inflammation of the stomach. It had attacked him before, in the autumn of 1809, and he was still far from well when he was invited to serve on a commission for examining the nature and extent of the Irish bogs. Seeing it as a golden opportunity for giving William his first practical lessons in surveying and engineering, and protesting that as he could only die once he would sooner die doing something useful, he immediately took charge of 35,000 acres that had to be surveyed, levelled and bored to the hard ground. All that winter he was out from daybreak till dusk, wading through swamps and crossing wastes where the natives feared to venture, his health improving wonderfully under the rigorous discipline, bearing out his belief that the mind can sustain the body.

He was five years older now and his illness was proportionately harder to fight against. Maria almost demented by the harrowing uncertainty, was quite unable to think of anything else. Even when a letter from Lovell written at Johnson's bookshop, arrived early in May, it made little impression on her numbed heart: 'the arrival of the Angel Gabriel . . . could not make me either feel happy or look happy while my father was so ill and all my thoughts were absorbed in the single question—will he recover?'

But the knowledge that his son was safe and hurrying with all possible speed to Ireland was like a new lease of life to the sick man, his impatience to see him, to welcome him with joy, glowing in his heart, sending forth rays that revived his emaciated frame. Though still terribly weak he was mending steadily by May 10th, the day Lovell was expected to arrive.

At a late hour that night he still had not come, and the little party waiting anxiously in the library were almost giving up hope. At last Mrs. Edgeworth and Fanny went upstairs to put the invalid to bed, the two aunts retired to their dressing-room and only Maria, Honora, William and Harriet sat on by the fire downstairs, reading and sewing, their ears strained to the rustling night outside. Recollections of a spring day twelve years earlier when Lovell, young and sanguine had departed from this very room, must have flitted like chilly shades through Maria's mind. It fretted her to remember how at times he even seemed to dislike her, though why he should harbour such thoughts she could not tell. Any suggestion of dislike or disapproval upset her still as much as ever and with all her heart she hoped that the traces of the old misunderstanding had faded away.

Not an echo of clopping hooves and scraping wheels warned them before John the manservant burst into the room exclaiming, 'Mr. Lovell is come!' A moment later he was crossing the threshold, a slight, short man with auburn locks waving back from his well-developed forehead, his high Sneyd nose emphasizing the weakness of his wide mouth and small, receding chin. Maria sprang up, flying towards him and embracing him and as the rest clustered round critical Honora could not help feeling a little disappointed. Something in his voice upset her and the way he talked and gesticulated like a Frenchman. Later, however, she was touched by the patient good-humour with which he bore his father's withering comments upon these foreign mannerisms, the way he tripped about holding up the skirts of his coat and making great play with his hands, for all the world, Edgeworth declared, like some affected woman. Though nothing of this detracted from his delight at having Lovell with him; it was simply that like the Lord he chastened those he loved for their own good.

'My father's contentment at Lovell's return has done him more good than all the advice of the surgeons, I do believe, now that the danger is over,' Maria wrote to her aunt and to their old friend Mrs. O'Beirne, wife of the Bishop of Meath, she spoke of his pleasure at finding Lovell's 'character, heart and disposition every thing he could wish them to be . . . Lovell is particularly alive to kindness—he has learned its value in the school of adversity, which has a

wonderful power of softening the heart to the very core—
and at the same time bracing the character'.

The relentless ring in her words is chilling and catches the
ear again and again in her references to Lovell this summer.
Having disciplined herself from an early age, driven herself
on, bridled her impulses, ignored her aches and pains, until
now she could write spirited prose or tot up accounts while
raging toothache tormented her day after day, she could not
make allowances for weakness in others. Grateful though
she was for Lovell's unreserved friendliness to her, it shocked
her that he seemed to have no aim in life. While admitting
that he looked wretchedly ill, she thought that he fussed
too much about himself; while he fretted over his ailments
their indomitable father was daily recovering his energy and
high spirits. He on the contrary, proud and pleased with his
son, agreed that his health must be re-established before
anything else was thought about.

Fearing the effects of an Irish winter, Lovell, that autumn,
went to London. 'Since he has to leave us,' wrote Maria, 'it
is at least some comfort that he leaves home with such kind
feelings and agreeable associations with all his friends at
home—A more patient, amiable creature I never saw—But
his has been a melancholy lot in life hitherto.'

Very different from hers! As she told Sophy Ruxton,
each year seemed richer and happier than the last. Rich too
in money earned by her books though much of it slipped
away in charities or buying expensive presents for her
friends. In vain did her father expostulate, urging her to
curb the impulses that led to such improvidence. Though
generally a shrewd and excellent business-woman, where
her own money was concerned Maria's heart always got
the better of her head.

She was equally generous in the praise and encourage-
ment she gave to other writers. When she enjoyed a book

she almost always wrote to the author and many a diffident novice must have been cheered by a kind letter from the great Miss Edgeworth. In 1813 on the way to London *Pride and Prejudice* had amused them for several evenings. Probably Maria wrote to the anonymous author as this year she received a copy of *Mansfield Park* 'With the Authoress's compliments'. She thought it 'was like real life and very interesting'.

The great literary sensation of 1814 was the anonymously published *Waverley* which appeared in July. The run on it was so great that the three little volumes were almost impossible to obtain. Literary friends wrote from London enthusiastically praising it, country neighbours who were lucky enough to have it talked of nothing else. At last a kind friend lent the Edgeworths a set though only on the condition that each volume was returned the moment it was read. At the evening readings the whole party listened with rapt attention: 'I wish the author could have witnessed the impression it made—the strong hold it seized on the feelings of both old and young.' They were completely carried away by the romantic story, the noble chieftains and their clansmen, and the splendid background of wild and rugged scenery. 'Aut Scotus aut Diabolus', exclaimed Edgeworth as the last words of the last volume were read and his wife closed the book. Maria, rushing to her desk to pour out her praises and thanks to the Great Unknown, headed her letter with her father's words. She was feverishly writing when Mrs. Edgeworth opened the book again and said: 'There is a postscript by way of a preface.'

'Believe me, I have not nor can I convey to you the full idea of the pleasure, the delight we have had in reading *Waverley*, nor of the feeling of sorrow with which we came to the end of the history of persons whose presence had so filled our minds—we felt that we must return to the *flat realities* of life, that our stimulus was gone, and we were little disposed to read the "Postscript, which should have been a Preface".

' "Well, let us hear it," said my father, and Mrs. Edgeworth read on.

'Oh! my dear sir, how much pleasure would my father, my mother, my whole family, as well as myself have lost if we had not read to the last page! And the pleasure came upon us so unexpectedly—we had been so completely absorbed that every thought of ourselves, our own authorship, was far, far away.

'Thank you for the honour you have done us, and for the pleasure you have given us . . . and believe me, every opinion I have in this letter expressed, was formed before any individual in the family had peeped to the end of the book, or knew how much we owed you.'

His ambition, said the author, was 'to emulate the admirable Irish portraits drawn by Miss Edgeworth'.

Though her letter remained unacknowledged and the mystery unsolved through the long succession of novels that followed, from the first Maria suspected it was Walter Scott whose poems she admired so inordinately. This conviction added immeasurably to the value of his tribute and the excitement of that memorable evening, which seen from this distance of time marked a turning point. After that life was never quite the same, almost always harassed by the haunting apprehension of an unimaginable calamity. Not only was her father's sight failing rapidly but attacks of illness were recurring with alarming frequency. His will-power alone had escaped the ravages of old age. He still kept his family going with all the old vigour though rather more asperity, himself going steadfastly on just as usual. All winter he was busy with experiments for improving wheeled vehicles which he had promised to demonstrate to the

Dublin Society. Although he was far from well in January 1815 he insisted on taking his family to Dublin for three months while he gave his demonstrations; an exacting, exhausting undertaking which nearly killed him. Nothing could make him give in or alter any of his plans; he was 'wretchedly ill' throughout the second night of a two days' visit they paid to old Lady Louisa Conolly at magnificent Castletown on the journey home.

Life went on as usual that summer, friends coming to stay and morning callers by the score, letters from London bringing the latest news to amuse or to horrify. Much was horrifying, like nice, clever Miss Milbanke's marriage 'to that fiend Lord Byron' and all the scandalous talk about Lady Frances Webster and the Duke. 'For the Duchess of Wellington', wrote Maria to Lady Romilly, 'we feel all the deep and tender interest which her sweet disposition must inspire in all who know her as well as we do—Her 12 years constancy, her refusal of that amiable hero General Cole who was desperately in love with her, her refusal of the innumerable admirers who were at her feet during her reign as a beauty in Dublin has been ill rewarded by this Duke.' The Davy's matrimonial differences afforded only amusement. 'This was a lady who married for celebrity— carried home a scientific Punch and found he was not so diverting in private as in public.'

Pouring herself out in letters relieved for a while the leaden load on her heart. With her father dangerously ill off and on all summer, her state of mind was such that it was quite impossible to do as he directed and start work on a novel. Her recalcitrance shocked and disappointed him. Had he not taught her how essential it is to work steadily on, whatever the circumstances, for the benefit of others as well as herself? As he lay awake through the dreadful nights he must often have asked himself what would become of her when he was no longer there to urge her on. She who of all his children was the most shining example of his training, had still not conquered her fatal procrastination, letting valuable time slip away while her powers ran to seed.

Determined to make her rise superior to it, he did not spare her. 'My father says I am spoilt and that I think of nothing but my Aunt R. etc. and many heart-cutting things which it is no comfort to me to say to myself arise only from his illness.' But with honest self-contempt she knew there was truth in his accusations. 'I am, as my father says, grown good for nothing.' As humbly she submitted to his reproaches she struggled with herself to such good effect that soon she was telling Sophy that she was writing again. All was well and her father smiling and satisfied. Maria, working away at her novel was contributing to the stream of usefulness that had flowed there for so long. And now to his delight a fair promise of its continuance was being given by Lovell whose interest in educating the young showed signs of fructifying. Grown stronger now, he had spent the summer travelling about England seeing what was being done at the Bell and Lancaster and other free schools with a view to opening one in the village. Edgeworth was delighted with the idea and the kindness of heart that prompted it. Maria too was satisfied. 'The enthusiasm he feels about these schools seems to have quite cured all his complaints and to have inspired him both with new body and new soul.'

Though as a rule Maria wrote quickly, *Harrington*, a short one-volume novel was not finished until November 1816. By the time it was done she was quite at the end of her tether, broken down by the long-drawn-out agony of watching her father slowly wasting away. No amount of pain however could shake his self-possession. He was using all his influence to get William, an almost fully-fledged civil engineer, nominated for the new post of County Surveyor and he was helping him as well with the designs for a bridge he was to build. Every morning he gave little Francis a Latin lesson, preparing him for school, and was busy all day with manifold tasks; this winter he was composing an educational manual for Lovell's school and amusing himself by putting some old fables into verse.

His epic struggle made him particularly harsh with Maria, once more relapsed into that idle drifting, giving in to all the destructive emotions against which he had warned her time and time again. She made no attempt to carry out his suggestion that she should immediately start on a pendant volume to *Harrington*. Even when he ordered her out of his sight, her adoration and loyalty never faltered. All he said was just and right; she, weak, inadequate wretch, was to blame. The sight of her during these gloomy weeks, her usually brisk little figure transformed into a grey, sorrow-stricken ghost, filled all their hearts with pity. Gratefully she remembered how kind they were and Lovell above all. 'His kindness and sympathy to me in particular when I wanted them much, when I was in deep adversity with my father, . . . have left an indelible impression of affection and gratitude in my heart.'

Only her father ignored her plight, making no concessions. When Mr. Knox, 'a wit', stayed for two nights in January, each evening he made her read one of her plays aloud. Her spirited readings were always a great success but this time the strain was so great that she was blind to everything but the book in her hand. Nevertheless her battle was nearly over and when at the end of the month she took up an old sketch of a novel, unsuspected reserves of energy came to her aid. The moment he saw she was in earnest the

6. SHEEP-SHEARING AT EDGEWORTHSTOWN

John Langan, with Harriet and Sophy Edgeworth, looking on

(From a sketch by Charlotte Edgeworth)

happy relationship with her father was restored. For the next two months, he ordained *nothing*, no letter-writing even, must distract her from this book, the very last as he knew full well they would ever write together.

One important point had to be settled as one of the characters, her famous King Corny, was inspired by her Uncle Ruxton's eccentric brother-in-law James Corry of Shantonagh, Co. Monaghan. Over and over again she had listened to her aunt's stories about this extraordinary individual who flew into such rages with his own tangled hair that family and servants would fly from the house and who once without warning when the house was packed with visitors, blasted out of the rock upon which it was built half a kitchen. 'The chances are that Mr. Corry himself would never read the thing unless he were put on the scent but my Uncle Ruxton and Letty R.[1] certainly would—So my dear aunt hold a bed of justice directly with Sophy and . . . write me word post-haste how far I may go.'

By February 16th the first chapter of *Ormond* was finished and Maria read it out to her father as they drove to Pakenham Hall to make a wedding-call on Lord Longford whose marriage to Lady Georgiana Lygon had just taken place. Delighted by the opening scenes he at once took the book to his heart and never was their association more complete. 'I never saw nor could I have conceived anything equal to the energy and exertions of my father in correcting and recorrecting this story over and over again, sometimes hearing it read and dictating corrections for 4 or 5 hours together—between the fits of deadly sickness and often to the point of actual exhaustion—It was a proof of perseverance and energetic affection such as only he could give.' When she ran dry he took up the tale, dictating long passages that blend in too perfectly to be detected. By the

[1] James Corry's daughter Letty Rothwell.

end of April Maria with inflamed, half-blinded eyes from the long hours of toil, finished it and on May 31st, his birthday, she brought to his bedside the 160 printed pages.

In spite of a terrible night his voice was strong and cheerful. ' "Call Sneyd directly" he said, and swallowed some stirabout and said he felt renovated. Sneyd was seated at the foot of his bed. "Now, Maria, dip anywhere, read on." I began "King Corny recovered". Then he said, "I must tell Sneyd the story up to this."

'And most eloquently, most beautifully did he tell the story. No mortal could ever have guessed that he was an invalid, if they had only *heard* him *speak*.

'Just as I had here stopped writing my father came out of his room, looking wretchedly, but ordered the carriage and said he would go to Longford to see Mr. Fallon about materials for William's bridge. He took with him his three sons and "Maria to read *Ormond*"—great delight to me. He was much pleased, and this wonderful father of mine drove all the way to Longford; forced our way through the tumult of the most crowded market I ever saw—his voice heard clear all the way down the street—stayed half an hour in the carriage on the bridge talking to Mr. Fallon; and we were not home till half-past six. He could not dine with us, but after dinner he sent for us all into the library. He sat in the armchair by the fire; my mother in the opposite armchair, Pakenham in the chair behind her, Francis on a stool at her feet, Maria beside them; William next, Lucy, Sneyd; on the sofa opposite the fire . . . Honora, Fanny, Harriet and Sophy; my aunts next to my father and Lovell between them and the sofa. He was much pleased at Lovell and Sneyd's coming down for this day.'

Only a very little while was left now and as he lay awake at night he was driven nearly distracted by his anxiety for Maria, with her gudgeon-like capacity for swallowing anything and as heedlessly impetuous as her own child character Rosamond with whom it amused her to identify herself. Throwing her money away with reckless generosity, she would very soon be destitute. Fretted beyond all bearing by this fearful picture, early one dawn he summoned her to his bedside. As she stood by him he addressed her solemnly on the subject of extravagance, ordering her to call Fanny who duly came and took her place beside her. Graphically he described all the temptations that might induce Maria to part with her capital, the innumerable eventualities that were inevitable in such a large family. Finally as she knelt before him in tears he made her promise never on any account to squander away her property, adding that she was the only one of his children of whom he had anything to beg. Lovell was wise and economical; Fanny was prudence itself; his wife . . . but anything he could say of her would weaken the impression. Four days later, on 13th June 1817, he died.

A night or two afterwards as Maria sat weeping in her bedroom, tears that cut her weak and aching eyes like knives, Honora came in with a letter. Maria never forgot the kind look on her sister's face as she sat on the little stool by the fire watching Maria as she read it and then collapsed in 'utter helpless despair'. In this letter her father bequeathed to his beloved daughter the care of his posthumous character, adjuring her to fulfil her promise and last duty to him by completing and publishing the memoirs which he began in 1809 and never finished.

Chapter Eight

1817-1818

'Though I have lost more than ever daughter lost before I have still *much* left in the world. I am grateful to Providence and do my best to be happy and to be all that he, could he look down upon me, would approve,' Maria was able late that winter to write to her stepmother. The family had scattered in different directions at the end of the summer, the two aunts departing for good to go to their brother in Staffordshire and Maria taking refuge at Black Castle. There, helped by her aunt, she managed at last to subdue the grief which at one time she believed she could never get over. Besides having all her dear family still, she thanked God for giving her 'good animal spirits—and some portion of HIS elasticity of mind'. And early in the New Year, 1818, when they all met at home again, it was Maria brimming over with plans and purposes, who kept them going as they groped about in the shadows picking up the threads.

From the first Lovell had insisted that Edgeworthstown must still be their home; his kindness and consideration for them all were such that contrary to what their father willed, they appointed him their sole trustee to look after the funds that yielded their annuities. He was proving to be a good magistrate and a generous landlord though his heart was really wrapped up in his school which now that he had money to spend was expanding far beyond its humble beginnings. New schoolrooms were building in the village and a boarding-house for the sons of gentlemen and superior farmers, who for £40 a year would be educated side by side with the village boys—a daring educational experiment that he carried out successfully for a number of years. During these first forlorn months the school was a godsend to his sisters, giving them plenty to do and to think about, compiling little primers and manufacturing all kinds of necessary objects.

The old pattern of life was adhered to, their evening readings starting off with Jane Austen's two latest productions. *Northanger Abbey* seemed to Maria 'the most stupid nonsensical fiction' she ever read and the General's behaviour 'in packing the young lady off without a servant or the common civilities . . . outrageously out of drawing'. *Persuasion*, apart from the first fifty pages of family history, was 'exceedingly interesting and natural—The love and lover admirably well drawn so that we feel it quite real. Don't you see Capⁿ Wentworth or rather don't you in her place feel him taking the boisterous child off her back as she kneels by the sick boy on the sofa? And the overheard conversation about the nut—and—But I must stop. We have got no farther than the disaster of Miss Musgrave jumping off the steps.'

Trouble continued to dog the house. Now it was William whose health was causing anxiety. Heart-broken at losing his father and over-wrought and anxious about his work, he had been alone in the house all winter as he was employed in the district. Early in the year he collapsed completely, presenting 'a most deplorable spectacle . . . a ruin', said Maria, who was sure that if only he would make the effort he could pull himself together. In the throes of what now would be recognized as a nervous breakdown, William was incapable of any sort of effort and in March his kind step-mother carried him off to Cheltenham for medical advice, taking Fanny to nurse him.

Maria who had given up her agency work and account-keeping, devoted most of her time to the *Memoirs*. With Honora as her secretary and reader, she was revising the 400 pages her father had written, carrying on the account of his life from where it broke off in 1782. This sacred trust was causing her the most intense uneasiness. Always the most reticent of women, it horrified her to think of delivering up her father's frank and freely expressed account of his early difficulties and three marriages, to the callous mercies of the critics. The qualities that make his book entertaining, inspired her with dread. Though her mother and aunt agreed with her that it ought not to be published, no one thought of disobeying his wishes. But when it was finished Maria was determined to show it to two men who knew him intimately and to abide by what they said: Dumont, with whom he had many ideas in common and his brother-in-law Francis Beaufort, a captain in the Navy, who spent many of his leaves at Edgeworthstown and when he was on half-pay in 1803–4 almost lived there, helping to set up the telegraph between Dublin and Galway.

In the middle of the summer when Mrs. Edgeworth brought William home looking very much better, Maria was able to proceed with the plans she was making to go to England to meet her critics. Ever since 1814 and the restoration of Geneva's independence, Dumont had been living there, one of the most active and influential members of the *Conseil Municipal* and engrossed in reforming the laws of the canton. Hardly a year passed without his visiting England and this September he was due at Bowood where Lady Lansdowne insisted that Maria's meeting with him must take place. Maria made her arrangements accordingly. She was very comfortably off, with £500 a year from her father besides her very considerable earnings, and being, as she said, 'a luxurious little animal' she believed in doing things well. She was determined that Honora, who with her small, dark head and tall, slight figure had the Sneyd air of distinction, should be as well turned out as any fashionable young lady they might meet. That his womenfolk were well and suitably dressed, was always insisted upon by her father, and Maria, who was meticulously neat and fresh-looking, intended to carry on the good habit. Excellent milliners and dressmakers were to be had at Bath where she decided to spend a fortnight with her sister Anna while they indulged in an orgy of shopping. For the journey she hired 'a good creditable looking carriage' and Lovell insisted on sending their old manservant George Bristow, respectably clad 'in a new greatcoat and handsome suit of clothes out of livery', to look after them.

When they left home in August neither was feeling very cheerful, the *Memoirs* weighing heavily on Maria who wondered what Dumont was thinking; the manuscript of her father's volume had already been sent for him to read before they met. As for Honora, she confessed to Sneyd that the 'journey held very few charms for her', travelling in 'Maria's train and picking up the crumbs'. Protesting that she was not at all clever, the thought of Bowood, the haunt of politicians and all the intelligentsia, filled her with forebodings. But far worse trouble was to come. At Dublin while they waited for a favourable wind the shocking news arrived that William, bridge-building at Castle Forbes, had gone off his head. Lovell had fetched him home and with unexpected kindness Lady Granard sent for the two little boys, with Fanny and Harriet to look after them, to stay at Castle Forbes until proper arrangements for William could be made. Mrs. Edgeworth urged Maria to go on to England as she could do no good by returning and after agonies of indecision, with heavy hearts she and Honora embarked.

After the first they seldom spoke of it, doing their best to follow their stepmother's injunction 'to seize and enjoy the present'. All the same William's illness overshadowed the autumn and winter, a recurring nightmare which raised its grisly head when letters came and prodded them with icy fingers at unexpected moments. Maria concerned herself with the whole business, imploring her mother and Lovell for everyone's sake to send him away, his 'likeness to poor Henry made her tremble'. When Lovell at last agreed, it was Maria who arranged for him to go to Dr. Mayo's well-known mental hospital at Tonbridge and who begged to be allowed to defray the heavy expenses with the large sum she had received from her publishers. 'Pray, pray use it. I never intended to spend one farthing of the income of that *Harrington* and *Ormond* dreadfully earned money—I always meant to spend it on something for the family. . . . Can it be used better or as my father would more approve could he—Thank God most fervently that he was spared the knowledge or even the foreboding of this calamity.'

When late in the afternoon of September 7th their carriage bowled through the park at Bowood, Maria's only thought was Dumont, her only wish 'to rest my mind by going to my work again'. They were feeling better after a fortnight at Bath with warm-hearted, affectionate Anna and a letter from Dumont, whose taste was indisputable, had already reassured Maria. He was enthusiastic about her father's book which he thought very interesting and any doubts he had entertained about publishing it were completely wiped out. His words came like a reprieve: 'I never have felt one moment of so much pleasure as that which I experienced in reading his words.' And somewhere within that vast range of classical magnificence created by Robert Adam for Lord Lansdowne's father, they were received with the greatest cordiality, Lady Lansdowne 'so kind in her manner to Honora' who looked very pretty. But above all there was Dumont himself, portly as ever in his customary black suit, his great snuff-box dangling from its chain, to prove to her by word and look that everything he had written was heartfelt.

They settled down for a stay of several weeks: 'our own rooms opening one into the other are only too handsome and luxurious for us': fitting easily into the quiet daily routine. At 9.30 they met in the breakfast-room where they were waited upon by a silent, dexterous Milanese servant who 'salvered' them with tea and coffee and plied them with 'meat, sweetmeats—honey—cakes—buns—rolls, etc.' and when they had eaten their fill they wandered off into the library to settle when they should meet again for walking. 'Then Lady L. goes to her dear dressing-room and dear children—Dumont to his attic—Lord Lansdowne to his out of door works and we to our elegant dressing-room. Between one and two luncheon—then walk—happy time! Lady L. is so chearful and polite and easy—just as she was in her walks at Edgeworthstown—but very different walks are these—most various and delightful, from dressed flower knots, shrubbery and park walks to fields with inviting paths—wide downs—shady winding lanes—happy cottages ... The women in their blue bodices and black flat hats look as if they were picturesque decorations of the lanes.' The three little Fitzmaurices went with them, 'natural lively happy children walking skipping running along with us calling to Mamma at every yard ... Light little Lady Louisa flying about with her green persian sash floating and her long reed whip bending in her hand and her thick auburn curls over her face.' There never was a more delightful family or 'a happier wife or woman altogether . . . she and Lord Lansdowne are so fond of one another and shew it and do *not shew* it in a most agreeable manner'. Better still they convinced Maria (Lord Lansdowne 'in a most polite and delicate manner') of how much they liked her.

In the evening after dinner they sat round a table in the library, the ladies sewing clothes for the poor people, Lord Lansdowne reading or talking unless Dumont read a French play aloud—a pastime that occasionally led him into difficulties. It was impossible, he complained, 'to read Molière without a quicker eye than he had pour de certains propos', and off he would go to hunt about the shelves to find something that could cause him no anxiety.

During the fortnight he was there, no one could have taken greater trouble than Dumont did, going twice through Maria's voluminous manuscript, cutting and pencilling it just as her father used to and discussing it with her in long *tête-à-têtes*. This shared absorption in her work inevitably led Maria into confidences and admissions most unusual to her; her dependence, her need for guidance, were never so great. Yet the moment their task was laid aside the warm intimacy dissolved in cold, clear air; *Le vieux Célibataire* as she took to calling him behind his back, turned out strangely cold and inhuman, a curiously disappointing friend. The hope of an even closer relationship may not have been entirely absent from her thoughts when she reached Bowood, from what she afterwards wrote to her stepmother. 'Mr. Dumont left at Hunters for me his last translation of Bentham Tactique des Assemblees, etc.—on the first page wrote "Miss Maria Edgeworth de la part de son sincère et inaltérable ami—E. Dumont."—and yet either from monkish or philosophical principles never did man or

monk part with a friend with less appearance of feeling—
sincère I believe and *inaltérable* I am sure—and clear I am we
are not suited to each other except as author and critic—I
am most grateful for his criticism.'

Presently company began to arrive. One evening as Maria
was dressing for dinner Lord Grenville's coach and four
drove up to the door and a few minutes later she heard his
'ministerial foot treading grand in the corridor'. Easily
upset as she was by the faintest hint of disapproval, she
secretly dreaded meeting the former Prime Minister knowing that at a large dinner at his London house he had loudly
ridiculed certain incidents in *Patronage*. Matters were made
worse by neither she nor Honora hearing the bell. 'The
footman with his terrible knock at our door came with
"Dinner Ma'am all sat down" and we had to march into
that vast dining-room and take our seats.' In her confusion
it was some time before she could look about her and when
she did Lady Grenville 'with her fear or aversion' to Maria,
and her taciturn lord, did not soothe her feelings. 'Lady
Grenville was superbly dressed at all points—a fat little
woman—rosy good humoured unmeaning little face—Except for the quantity of Mechlin lace you might have taken
her for anybody's housekeeper . . . Lord Grenville with his
dark eyes and huge eyebrows was like an iron mask . . .
After dinner at coffee-time—sitting on the bed of roses
before a nice blaze of wood—Lady Grenville began to
chatter away about where is my Lord this and my Lady
that . . . when *les Messieurs* arrived the silence recurred—
It was hard heavy work when Lord Grenville took his seat
in the chair by the fire and all took their seats—Political
Economy and the law of evidence, Lord L. tried upon him
in vain—Dumont I saw from the first disliked him and sat
with his mouth shut up—Deadly heavy evening.'

Though she never felt at her ease with them the Grenvilles at least afforded her great amusement, Lady Grenville taking the air on the downs, dressed superbly in Valenciennes lace 'did not walk under less than 200 guineas—and the drollest trit-trot little walk, turning at short angles to be brisk and airy', while the wind caught her pelisse and blew her great white crape bonnet 'into all manner of strange shapes'. As for Lord Grenville, 'whenever he did let anything out it was very correct, deep and strong, in a slow—low House of Lords voice and his eyes always directed to Lord Lansdowne'. But only one of his pronouncements could she recall: 'Baffins Bay!—that is a curious conclusion My Lord they have drawn about Baffin's—Because Baffin in his journal writes "I have examined this bay and find no passage further" some have concluded that no such bay exists and would proceed to erase it from the charts.' And when after three days they departed, Maria 'never heard a sound more joyous than their parting wheels', a relief shared by Dumont. As they walked ahead of the others that afternoon his smouldering dislike of the Grenvilles exploded: 'Diable cet homme! C'est un homme de glace, de fer—Et la femme—The first time I did see her I did think he had married somebody out of his house—She is no better than somebody's housekeeper—sister of Lord Camelford too! Bon! Bah!'

Among the many who came and went were two young bachelors, Sir William Hort and his brother, the baronet pleasing Maria by the attention he paid to Honora though that critical young lady found both brothers 'far from agreeable and unsuited to this society'. Mr. Gally Knight, 'a rich amateur with a great deal of anecdote' came for a few days and fashionable Sir Henry Bunbury who amused Maria 'by telling things out of my line—when the Duke of Clarence first saw his wife he turned about and observed "Not so damned ugly as I expected".' And she was interested to meet the Secretary for War, Lord Bathurst, who brought his dark imperious little wife and two daughters.

'Lord Bathurst is a chearful formalist with smiling usage of the world sufficient to be an agreeable diplomatist—flat but not stiff backed—dry-faced—of the old school . . . Lady Bathurst is a very well-bred, well-drest, well-rouged affable without being offensively affable woman of the world and of the court—talking with a happy ease of all that is great and fine in this world in a low *proper* voice—never going beyond her own sofa-table talk and seated on a bed of roses at the round table all evening with a low candle to herself nets and spangles with great diligence a purse which will never be *used* by any mortal. She is remarkably obliging to me . . . We have many subjects in common. Her brother the Duke of Richmond and all Ireland. Her aunt Lady L. Conolly and Miss Emily Napier, all the Pakenhams and the Duchess of Wellington. Very communicative and confidential on that last subject and I am very sorry . . . to be convinced that the duchess has been more hurt by her friends than by her enemies and more by herself than by both put together—but still if she does not quite wash out his affections with tears they will be hers during the long autumn of life. He lately said to Mrs. Poole "After all home you know is what we must look to at the last."

'Lady Georgina Bathurst is a very pretty and I need hardly say fashionable looking lady of about 22 . . . She has been in Paris—speaks French well and enough French air and French flowers—not too much. The simplicity of their dress indeed struck us particularly after all the turmoil the Bath ladies and Bath dressmakers make in vain about this business —plain French silk frocks with a plain short full sleeve and plaited blond round the neck and a blond flounce—and that's all—a crescent of white gillyflowers or scarlet carnations on the head—Morning dresses more shewy—young ladies with profusion of flowers in straw bonnets and matrons with blond caps and crape bonnets and profusion of lace more than anything my poor countrified imagination could have conceived. Lady L.'s taste—brilliant in white cleanliness—finest materials, muslin or lace and work, white as the driven snow. But I am sure there must be a warehouse of morning gowns to supply her—for I never saw her in the same twice . . . We do very well—Honora always looks elegant and talks agreeable to all.'

They left Bowood at the end of September, rather sooner than was planned. The Dugald Stewarts were due to arrive there later in the autumn (it was in Dugald Stewart's classroom that Lord Lansdowne's political opinions were formed), and though Maria could not do as they suggested and stay on until then, she promised to come back again. A few days before they left 'Lady L. came to my room and paid me half an hour's visit. She brought back my father's m^{ss} in its Solander . . . She was exceedingly interested in it —She observed that his leading taste for mechanism had governed his destiny—she says it is not only entertaining and interesting but useful in shewing how such a character is formed and in encouraging others to hope that without early favorable circumstances they may distinguish themselves. "When he was settled after his first marriage at Hare Hatch he seemed then as much out of fortune's way as man could be and yet he found occupations that led to distinction and he formed that friendship for Mr. Day which was so honorable to both." She admires and loves Mr. Day as much as Dumont dislikes him—Had she seen him she would not have endured his manners however 24 hours.'

From Bowood they went straight to The Grove, Epping, a pretty country box on the edge of the forest where Captain Beaufort and his wife Alicia were living with her parents who just then were away at Brighton. Captain Wilson, a coarse, unlettered old merchant-captain who made his fortune in the Indian trade, in addition to The Grove had a house in Harley Street and a wife, two sons and several daughters all as unpolished and hospitable as himself. Aunt Ruxton spoke truly when she once remarked: 'Maria dislikes vulgarity more than vice.' Both she and her father, when they visited The Grove in 1813, had found it hard to bear with this simple, spontaneous family who never attempted to disguise their thoughts and impulses with any false veneer. Alicia, the soul of good-nature, always upset Maria by fussing and gushing and saying 'Oy' instead of 'I', though her faults were mild compared with her unmarried sisters'. And now she had a special reason to scrutinize them anxiously while struggling to preserve an open mind. Earlier in the summer when Mrs. Edgeworth took Fanny to stay at The Grove the elder son, Lestock, a plain, tongue-tied young man of eight and twenty whose tastes were centred on dogs and horses, had fallen desperately in love with her and she more than a little with him. There for the present matters rested, a close secret not to be breathed even to Francis Beaufort. For her 'sweet, pretty, feminine Fanny', endowed with such excellent qualities and capacities, only the best the world could give was good enough. Maria, like her father, considered birth and good-breeding indispensable assets, except when a man, through strength of character and high ideals, succeeded in raising himself from humble beginnings to a place in the world. Unfortunately for him the shy, unambitious young merchant fitted in with neither category, and as Maria's gaze rested upon him she felt quite certain he would never do. And that evening when she went to her room to dress, she was dismayed to find laid out upon the bed three beautiful feather capes which in a flash she saw were meant for herself, Honora and Fanny. Panic-stricken at the thought of compromising her little sister she bundled them up in her arms, and rushing along the passage to Alicia's room, pushed them on to her, insisting that she could never dream of accepting them and Alicia must explain. . . .

Captain Beaufort, a short, blunt-featured man, industrious and able, who already had devised a means of indicating the strength of the wind which is still known as the Beaufort Scale; with his zeal for improving wherever he could, had taken The Grove in hand, arranging the rooms and making paths and plantations outside. As he took Maria into an indoor workshop he explained that he hoped it might lead Lestock 'from the employment of the hands to the exercise of the mind'. While he studied the *Memoirs* and took charge of her worries over William's removal to Tonbridge and little Francis's admission to Charterhouse, Maria drove about the country in Lestock's gig through the 'chearful villages and heaths and pretty by-roads' she had known as a child when Thomas Day lived in the neighbourhood. As they spanked along the love-lorn, bashful young man sighed as he pointed out the different places where he and Fanny used to ride together. Beneath his plain, dark, impassive exterior Lestock Wilson hid a heart of gold. All through this month there was nothing he would not do for Maria, placing 31 Harley Street at her disposal whenever she wished to be in London, procuring posthorses, welcoming her back to The Grove between visits, but although she admitted that no one could be 'more usefully obliging' she did not take to him at all. When she and Honora went on to Hampstead to stay with the Baillies he drove them the whole way through country that startled her by the way it was being built over, becoming 'what you might call a citizen's paradise, such a variety of little snuggeries and such green trellices and bowers'. As for the

'Cockney Castles' at Hampstead, their towers and battle-
ments surpassed even the wildest dreams of Milton or
Walter Scott!

'Joanna Baillie and her sister—the most kind cordial
warm-hearted creatures—came running down their little
flagged walk to welcome us . . . They have a great deal of
agreeable and new conversation—not old trumpery literature
over and over again . . . Domestic affectionate creatures—
good to live with.' She thoroughly enjoyed the society she
met at their house when she was not away on her own
errands, carrying her father's *Memoirs* round to his old
friends, to show them what he had to say about them in
case they objected. And at the Baillies she heard about quite
a new set of people very different from any she knew:
'Mrs. Fry the Quaker who goes to reform the people at
Newgate . . . a delicate Madonna-looking woman—married
to a man who adores her and what is much more to the
purpose supplies her with money and lets her follow her
benevolent *courses* (I did not say *whims*) as she pleases.' And
the merchant-bankers, Samuel Hoare and Fowell Buxton,
who 'by their own munificence and by devoting their whole
time to managing the contributions of others, saved from
famine or rising in rebellion from want of food *twenty
thousand of the weavers of London* . . . But pray don't think
that the Miss Baillie's conversation is all about *stupid good*
people—They have a great variety I assure you.'

Gossip about the Byrons was on every tongue. A 'really
romantic' Miss Hamilton, an intimate friend of the Mil-
bankes, described how after the wedding when old Sir
Ralph handed his daughter into the carriage, Byron swore
a terrible oath at him and as they drove off, turned to his
bride and asked her 'how she *dared*, how she could ever
venture to marry a man she had refused'. At Maryon Hall,
Sarah Carr had plenty to tell as she travelled in England with

Lady Byron the year her husband left her. 'Went with her to the very place where Lady B had been married—She gave us a most *touching* account of Lady B's conduct—of her struggle to repress her feelings—of the absurd conclusion some people drew from her calm manner and composed countenance that she did *not feel* . . . of Lady B's coming as if in her sleep into Miss Carr's room that night [at Seaham], in the dead of night, and sitting on the side of her bed wishing *to be able to cry.*'

Delightful though it was she could not stay long at Hampstead. Business awaited her in London, a dentist must be found for Honora and the sights must be shown her. Her own self-reliance, the way she organized her days, astonished her: 'Could I four years ago have believed if it had been prophecied to me, that I, poor little i, should this day have been driving about London with Honora alone.' Though she limited herself to a few quiet breakfasts and afternoon visits on her excursions to the capital, it was not altogether easy; she was still a lioness whom people clamoured to meet. Even the haughty, exclusive Lavinia, Lady Spencer came hurrying from Althorpe to receive her at Wimbledon Park.

On the way to Wimbledon they spent a night at Grove House, Kensington Gore with Lady Elizabeth Whitbread, Lord Grey's daughter and widow of the rich brewer and politician who committed suicide in 1815. The country roads were a little confusing and they had difficulty in finding the house which was like 'any good-looking house in Kensington', though it struck Maria as a terrible comedown after the splendid establishment in Dover Street where they dined several times with the Whitbreads in 1813. They were shown into a long low library with french windows opening into a very pretty garden with lawns and trees. 'Lady Elizabeth after a time came in

. . . she was in second mourning. I used to think her rather plain but her countenance had been so softened by grief and has such an interesting charming expression that she is quite handsome— . . . She came to me and pressed me in her arms in the most affectionate manner.' More affecting still, Maria discovered that 'she had gone out of her own bed-chamber for us and nooked herself into some little den of a room'. A few mutual friends came in the evening, yet how different it all was, Maria could not help thinking, from the old days. 'Everything at dinner so elegant and yet so simple and proper—*brought down* to her present circumstances— with a kind of dignified humility and resigned chearfulness and sweetness in her whole manner—The most touching I ever saw.' Moreover she 'shewed such a distinguished liking for Honora' whose capitulation carries a faintly wist-ful note: 'What helps me to feel the love I actually do for her—she took a fancy to me.' All the same things were turning out much better than Honora expected, Maria being received everywhere 'with a kindness which is most gratifying not only as an authoress but as a *woman*' which made it easy and comfortable for both.

Walking in the grounds and listening to Lady Spencer were the amusements at Wimbledon where they spent three days, her ladyship as she talked and snuffed, laughing unrestrainedly at her own sallies. She talked brilliantly. Maria thought her 'by far the cleverest woman—I may say person—I have seen since I came to England'. But though she was dazzled by the wit and sparkle of Lady Spencer's far-flung recollections and opinions, and though she was 'amazingly condescending', there was an essential coldness, something haughty but coarse about her, that prevented Maria from feeling 'the slightest symptom of affection'.

The return to 'dear Bowood' at the beginning of November was saddened by Lady Romilly's death on October 29th. For the last five years she and Maria had kept up a lively correspondence while the Romillys' intimacy with the Lansdownes was almost lifelong. At Bowood in 1795 the successful young lawyer fell in love with Anne Garbett, and the following year with his staunch friend Dumont, he met her there again—this time to make the final arrangements for their wedding. Last September Dumont went straight from Bowood to East Cowes Castle where she lay at death's door to support her heart-broken husband. Dugald Stewart too had known and loved Romilly for forty years. No one could think or speak of anything but the devastating effect her loss must have on him. Next day, November 4th, they were stunned to hear of his suicide.

'The newspapers have told you the dreadful catastrophe, the death and the manner of the death of that great and good man Sir Samuel Romilly. My dearest mother, there seems no end of horrible calamities—There is no telling how this has been felt in this house.' Dugald Stewart, recovering from a stroke, wandered about indoors 'leaning on his daughter, a melancholy spectacle'; Lord Lansdowne, unable to sleep, looked wretched and could hardly mention it without tears 'notwithstanding all his efforts'. One evening Tom Moore who was living in a cottage near by came to dinner, sitting between Lady Lansdowne and Miss Edgeworth, 'both in their different ways very delightful'. Afterwards he sang his wild, sweet Irish melodies with a melting pathos that proved altogether too much for their overladen hearts. Tears stood in Dugald Stewart's eyes and Maria too 'seemed much affected'. Elated by the effect he produced, when he got home that night he wrote in his diary: 'This is a delightful triumph to touch these higher spirits.'

Chapter Nine

———————————➤◉◄———————————

1818-1819

Determined that her sisters should have the opportunities her father desired for them, Maria spent the winter with the Sneyds at Byrkley Lodge, their house on the Staffordshire border, not far from Derby. Edward Sneyd who inherited his family's good looks and an ample fortune, had a wife as amiably indolent as himself and an only child Emma, a 'marble beauty', the same age as her cousin Honora Edgeworth. Leisure was the keynote of that comfortable, well-fed, well-warmed household and after living in its feather-bed atmosphere for over a year Aunt Charlotte and Aunt Mary were so changed that Maria was quite shocked. With nothing to do with themselves, no 'motive' as she said, the lively interest they used to take in what went on was quenched by the lassitude of age and petty ailments. However, there was plenty of young society. Lord Vernon's two sons often rode over from Sudbury with their friend Brooke Boothby, 'a merry jesting young man of fashion'; coming in the morning to sing romantic ditties and to play the flute and violoncello to Emma's harp and Honora's piano, and in the evening to dine and dance quadrilles. They danced every evening, practising for the Christmas balls, Maria and Mrs. Sneyd 'dancing posts' and Mr. Sneyd too until he was 'seized with the cramp in his leg' and thereafter had to content himself with playing the fiddle.

Maria settled down contentedly, revising the *Memoirs* for hours every day in her room, talking and reading with the aunts and joining in the family's interests. Always cheerful and ready to fall in with any plans, with a flow of good talk and good stories and boundless sympathy for the confidences and problems she seemed to attract, laughter and tears ever ready to spring to the surface of her impregnable detachment, she was everywhere a great acquisition. She was much amused at this glimpse of life in a sporting neighbourhood, the foxhunting squires she sometimes sat next to at dinner being 'quite another style of character'. The informal coming and going was just what she wanted for Honora and when it was suggested that Fanny should also join the party Maria was overjoyed. Mrs. Edgeworth, who wanted Fanny, who was now nineteen, to see something more of the world before she decided whether or not to marry Lestock Wilson, was equally pleased. The Sneyds' kindness was repaid by Maria somehow getting all three of them invited as well when she and her sisters were asked to stay with Lord and Lady Stafford at Trentham, a great place built to resemble Buckingham House which held itself proudly aloof from the general run of Staffordshire society. The invitation created quite a commotion. The Sneyds had 'never been to Trentham before except for one morning vis'.

It was in 1813 that Maria became acquainted with Elizabeth, Marchioness of Stafford, who in her own right was Countess of Sutherland; a strong, vivid personality and a talented water-colourist, married to a dull husband. Regally gracious, reducing the boldest to shame with a dart from her bright brown eyes, this plump little woman who was only five feet tall had much impressed Edgeworth. Maria was delighted that Fanny should have the chance of seeing her. Lovell, who was on his way to Charterhouse with little Francis, brought her as far as Lichfield and there at the George, Maria met them and they spent the evening, 'the children of four different marriages all united and happy together'. Afterwards they went their different ways, Maria driving off with her charges through the frosty January dusk to Trentham, talking excitedly as they rattled along and reaching their destination by moonlight, just seeing the 'outlines of woods and hills—silver light upon the broad water and chearful lights in the front of a large house and wide open hall door. Nothing could be more polite and cordial than the reception given us by Lady Stafford and her good-natured nobleman-like lord.'

Lady Stafford won her heart by complimenting her on Fanny, 'whispering in my wide open ear—"she looks very pretty. She has a very intelligent, interesting countenance"' and later on Lord Stafford 'compared her to some of our most admired beauties'. The lovely young daughter of the house, Lady Elizabeth Leveson-Gower, took such a fancy to both the girls that Maria was asked to stay on for several days after the Sneyds went home. From this very exalted level Fanny obtained her first view of the world. One day looking pale, when everyone else went walking 'Miss Fanny in Lady Stafford's coach and four with two outriders was driven through these superb grounds', and in the mornings she rode with Lady Elizabeth while in the library Lady Stafford taught Honora 'her own method of drawing in water colors'. The 'magnificence of the whole establishment' was very impressive: '10 livery servants and four servants out of livery—in black. These last only appear in the sitting-rooms—or stand in the hall and ante chambers *con – tin – u – ally*—But the magnificence does not interfere with the comfort.' Among the grandees who were staying she met yet another new type, Mr. Standish, 'one of the exquisites', whose toilette was all gilt plate, 'and such dressing-boxes and essences and apparatus as make the ladies' maids and gentleman's gentlemen bless themselves . . . He has a very nice patch on his lip and such gales of perfume blow from him and his cambric is so exquisite . . .' Despite his scented elegance he was mad about fox-hunting. 'In speaking of this passion and deprecating my contempt he said, "I know it's all folly—I tell myself so—but in short, C'est plus fort que moi".'

At Byrkley Lodge when Maria 'mad with joy' brought Fanny back there, the music mornings and dancing evenings, the visits to Sudbury and a ball at Derby, assumed a special value as part of Fanny's education. For the Sneyd's, however, it was Maria's company that made the four months she stayed with them such happy ones that when the last morning came they could hardly bear to part with her. 'Mr. Sneyd with all his cold manner has the most tender heart like Aunt Mary's . . . When I got up from the breakfast table to stop his thanks by mine he took me in his arms and squeezed me so tight that I felt as flat as a pancake and then he ran out of the room absolutely crying. N.B. Mrs. Sneyd was by and sobbing like a child and the tears rolled down Emma's marble face.'

They were bound for Kensington Gore, to make a long stay at Grove House, the five days on the road crammed with calls and sightseeing. That Fanny might see 'a fair specimen of what a mercantile husband can make himself' they stayed at Smethwick Grove, on the outskirts of Birmingham, with the daughter of their father's old friend James Keir the chemist, who was married to a Swiss banker, M. Moilliet, who also had interests in the iron trade. Their 'mode of life—mercantile and literary and domestic' afforded a complete contrast to Trentham or Byrkley Lodge. But as soon as they reached the environs of London all three were swept into the vortex of entertaining that Maria's presence excited among the fashionable and learned. As Lady Elizabeth Whitbread only went out to her relations and seldom descended the staircase till dinner-time, Maria made it a rule to stay at home in the evenings. They attended breakfasts and luncheons innumerable, nearly everywhere meeting the 'Dead Dandy', Samuel Rogers, who 'bestowed upon Fanny many of his death-like smiles'. On St. Patrick's Day they went to Apsley House to see the Duchess of Wellington: 'nothing could be more like Kitty Pakenham former youth and beauty only excepted. There was a plate of shamrocks on the table—she presented a bunch of shamrock to me as she came forward to meet me and pressing my hand as she gave it to me said in a low voice with a sweet smile, "Vous en êtes digne".'

At a morning party at Lady Harrowby's Maria met the great Duke without realizing who he was, 'nor did I know till I got into the carriage . . . He looks so old and wrinkled I never sh^d have known him from likeness to bust and picture. His manner very agreeable, perfectly simple and dignified—He said only a few words but listened to some literary conversation that was going on as if he felt amused, laughing once heartily. It was lucky for me that I did not know who he was for the very fear of falling on dangerous subjects about husbands and wives in various novels we discussed w^d have inevitably brought me into some scrape had I known who he was.'

Her chief concern during these weeks was Fanny's love-affair. Privately she was worried to death about it, but though Fanny sat up half the night talking and arguing, she refused to express an opinion. Fanny did not know what to do. When she came to England on her own admission she was very much attached to Lestock, 'for his honorable character, active habits and steady clear good sense', and she was aware too that he loved her more than anyone ever might again. But the dazzling week at Trentham turned all her ideas topsy-turvy; never had she dreamed of such charming, accomplished society; never could she be happy 'with one who has not such tastes'. But the moment she saw her lover again his unfaltering devotion melted her heart. All the same it was difficult not to compare him unfavourably with the assured young men she met in society, while she soon saw for herself what a sorry figure he cut among clever people. Maria, bent on giving him every chance, took into her confidence her friend the learned Mrs. Marcet, authoress of the famous *Conversations on Chemistry* which inspired young Michael Faraday. Mrs. Marcet lost no time in arranging a series of breakfasts at her house in Hanover Square, where the young people could meet in the pleasantest possible manner, a few old friends making up an agreeable party. What struck Maria as a singularly happy arrangement was sheerest torture to poor Lestock, rendered hot and speechless by the savants and scientists around him. After his third ordeal he spoke strongly to Captain Beaufort, complaining he was being ill-used and made a fool of; try as he would at these 'nice breakfasts' he could not get his words out. Francis Beaufort, much in favour of the marriage, tackled Maria who in her turn appealed to Lady Elizabeth. Lestock was at once invited to dinner, but 'struck with something strange and ill-bred in his manner' Lady Elizabeth took an immediate dislike to him which, after the fashion of great ladies, she doubtless did not conceal. It must have been a dreadful evening for Fanny, her poor blundering lover doing nothing to mend matters. Whatever he did threw an even worse light on him. Next day when Maria and Fanny dined at Harley Street the old Wilsons sent their

carriage to fetch them and take them back at night. Prompted
by the honest wish to be polite and attentive, as they were
about to depart Lestock prepared to accompany them,
greatly to Maria's indignation making 'an attempt to get
into the carriage. I begged he w<u>d</u> not—"quite unnecessary"
—"Get you over to the other side", quoth he, attempting
to push in—but I put my knee and arm across and from fear
growing bold and strong as a lioness resisted—saying it must
not be. "If you say it must not I must submit—" "I *do* say
so, Sir—It must not be." He got down much discomfitted
and shut up the step . . . I consulted Lady E. W. next day
and asked if I had been too severe or exact in point of
propriety. "Good God, no. You could not have done
otherwise without committing her for ever. To be sure
you did right—I w<u>d</u> no more let a man go home with a
daughter of mine in the same circumstances! You know
what c<u>d</u> the motive be! Two miles out of town and back
to see ladies home!" '

'Very strongly by tone and look' did her ladyship express her disapproval of the young merchant, insisting not
only to Maria but also to Fanny that he was 'quite unpre-
sentable'. Not altogether surpising, every day Fanny felt
more certain that she did not love him after all.

She still hesitated, however, to make the final break, to
turn her back on such adoration that some instinct told her
she would never again arouse; morning after morning she
and Lestock paced up and down the paths at Grove House
in endless unhappy altercation. Though Lady Elizabeth,
whom no one would have dreamed of contradicting, per-
sisted in abusing him, as soon as she saw his case was
hopeless she veered right round in his favour. His self
command and honourable conduct to Fanny were most
praiseworthy, she declared, and on the last evening of the
Edgeworths' visit when he came to dinner, 'far from being

vulgar he was really quite gentlemanlike and interesting'.

At the Carr's house at Hampstead early one April morning the lovers met for the last time, he comporting himself with such dignified restraint that heartily glad though Maria was to see the last of him, she could not but admire his self-control. 'I then shook hands with him and said—Mr. Wilson, at parting from you I can truly say you have my perfect good will.' Little can he have cared about that, as he made her his bow and turned and went out of the room and out of the house and into the wilderness of a world without Fanny. Fanny's instinct proved quite right. No man ever loved her as Lestock Wilson did, with a love that never diminished and kept his world a wilderness for nearly ten years.

On the way to the Carrs at Frognall they stayed with the Hopes at Duchess Street, the enormous house that was bought for the collections of sculpture, furniture, pictures, Thomas Hope had amassed during years of travelling all over Europe and the East. Maria quite untouched by the symmetry and grace of inanimate objects, thought it was like living in a museum as she tripped through the vast, painted chambers decorated with classical and Oriental frescoes by her talented host. This rather forlorn impression was stressed by the sad state the Hopes were in, both recovering from severe illnesses and the loss of one of their children. A large dinner was given in Maria's honour to which some great people came with alacrity to renew their acquaintance with her—the Duke and Duchess of Bedford, Lord and Lady Jersey, Lord Palmerston and the Darnleys. Throughout the four days she was there a steady succession of fashionable carriages drew up at the door and in one of the large gilt drawing-rooms that was placed at her disposal she received her admirers. Though never counting it as more than a passing show, she certainly enjoyed her position and observing the great world from within it. Fine ladies were never in her eyes really human—self-absorbed, helpless creatures behind their glittering façades. She was much more in her element at Hampstead in the Baillie's frugal home or at Maryon Hall with the kindly Carrs—Thomas Carr was solicitor to the excise. It was from his house that she wrote on April 2nd:

'Here we are this delicious spring day in the midst of spring delights and in the midst of the far greater delight of a family happy as our own once was. Mr. Carr! Oh mother, I almost envy these dear good girls the happiness and affection they have for their father. If you could see them all running to meet him as he rides home on his white horse!—He is one of the happiest men I ever saw—working hard all day usefully and honorably and coming home every evening to such a happy, cultivated united family.' But the fortnight there was spoilt by Fanny, who emotionally exhausted, collapsed with a feverish illness from which she recovered only just in time for them to pay their promised visit to the Hopes at Deepdene, near Dorking.

As they drove there through the Surrey lanes one lovely afternoon, their coachman lost his way and daylight was waning when at last they beheld 'the red brick house which has set the valley on fire . . . Our friend the housekeeper and several footmen standing in the arched doorway watching in the dusk waiting for our arrival, and the first words in answer to mine of "Is it dinner time?" "Yes, Ma'am dinner has been waiting this hour" increased my uncomfortable feeling. To complete her discomfiture she was told that the fashionable London diner-out, 'Conversation' Sharp had brought a party of gentlemen over from Fredley Farm, his little retreat at Mickleham. 'We dressed in the utmost hurry skurry in less than five minutes I am sure and made our appearance in the drawing-room where luckily the circle were sitting and standing by dim fire light and any guilty faces could scarcely be seen.' No harm was done by the delay: an agreeable party, an admirable dinner 'and Conversation Sharp with his fund of good stories was *in great force* that day'.

She stayed ten days at Deepdene. Though Mrs. Hope 'in her way' was much kinder than the majority of fine ladies, there was very little inside her beautiful head and she had nothing really to occupy her. With her erudite host, the fair, florid, heavy-featured descendant of a long line of Scottish merchants and their Dutch wives, Maria had much to talk about. His taste, she considered 'the worst part of his mind' and his house 'scarcely handsome, grotesque and confused among trees in no one particular taste and besides flaring in red brick instead of stone or marble—Mr. Hope assures me that many churches in Lombardy, in particular that famous church in Milan, Santa Maria della Grazia, is of red brick and I am sorry for it ... The house is magnificently furnished but to my taste much too fine for a country house —There is too much Egyptian ornament, Egyptian hieroglyphic figures, bronze and gilt but all hideous. In one room called the Egyptian room there is a sofa bed broad enough for two aldermen, embossed gold hieroglyphic *frights* all pointing with their hands distorted backwards at an Osiris or a long-armed monster of some sort who sits after their fashion on her hams and heels and hath the likeness of a globe of gold on her lappeted, scaly lappeted head', and she never became reconciled to 'the frightful monsters in bronze or stone or plaister' that abounded in the halls and passages.

They drove about the country, to 'Norbury Park, Mr. Lock's place' and to 'Wootton with all its traditions' where they were received by 'an old thin stupid wizzen looking Mr. Evelyn who knew nothing about his ancestors or their pictures by which he was surrounded'. As Maria with her thoughts on the scholarly author of *Sylva*, glanced up at the choice old books mouldering on the library shelves 'the oaf said—"Ay here are more books here than I shall ever read I'm sure—and there are some up there that never were down I daresay since they were put up." ' As she walked about the park and woods at Deepdene with Thomas Hope, he confided to her 'the whole history of his love, courtship and marriage and moreover of Miss Berry's courtship of him—disappointment—anger and quarrel with Mrs. Hope'. And one morning her hostess 'came softly stealing into the little room where we were all three writing and in her hand she held a superb Malachite necklace and cross with gold chains—Oh mother, I admired a piece of malachite in a marble table the other day and Mr. Hope explained that there is only one mine of it in the world in Russia. And Mrs. Hope has given me this necklace! And I could not refuse, her lips trembled so and she was in such agitation about it.'

At Deepdene Fanny went riding 'on a stumbling pony' with little Henry Hope but no sooner were they back at Grove House where their last ten days were spent, than 'clad in a new brown habit that fits to admiration', every morning she was to be seen cantering in Hyde Park beside young Samuel Whitbread. This tall, handsome younger son of Lady Elizabeth though much addicted to horses and hunting had abilities that later made him a useful Member of Parliament and a Fellow of the Royal Society. He was very much taken with pretty Fanny Edgeworth, mounting her on his beautiful horses and greatly to Maria's satisfaction escorting her everywhere; 'Mr. Whitbread has become Fanny's gentleman in waiting'. When the last morning came and Maria and Honora drove off in the open carriage on the first stage of their journey, to sleep at Lord Carring-

ton's place, Wycombe Abbey, Sam Whitbread and Fanny
rode along beside them for the first seven miles or so. On
that lovely May morning the world and the future must
have looked very bright to Maria, and the road ahead a
joyful progress from one set of warmly-welcoming friends
to another.

Like her father Maria loved nothing better than a large
family party all together under the same roof and no one
rejoiced more than she did when towards the end of this
year, 1819, Aunt Charlotte and Aunt Mary came back to
end their days at their 'hearts' home'. While they were
taking off their bonnets in their own old rooms Maria
hastened to announce the glad tidings to Mrs. Ruxton.

'I wish you could have seen and *heard* their arrival here—
The poor people in this village and for many miles round
had assembled for a mile and a half from the town—there
was a line of children on each side of the road, from Lovell's
school. They met the carriage with the bugle horn and fifes
and bag pipes and all such music and such greeting as the
poor could give met them—Molly Bristow's house was the
first they saw illuminated. But what was really touching a
wretched little hovel in the ditch by the road where some
one lived whom the "good ladies" had served, had its rush
lights in the window. The crowd wanted to take the horses
from the carriage but this was forbidden. Lovell had a few
flambeaux which lighted the road completely and fortunately the horses were very steady—such popping of guns!
such huzzaing—such shouting! such bonfires! Lovell walked
to meet them, got on the barouche seat and came in with
them. They were received with warm hearts within the
house and they were much affected. The whole village is
illuminated to the poorest house—Every window has this
day been cleaned.' And after dinner the whole party walked

through the village, Aunt Mary leaning on Lovell's arm at the head, fiddlers, pipers, horns playing a march preceded them, and a large schoolroom was 'lighted up for the people that they might have a dance'.

Chapter Ten

1820-1821

As she intended, when her father's *Memoirs* were published in May 1820 Maria was 'far, far away', on the other side of the English Channel. With Fanny and Harriet she was at Paris, comfortably installed in an apartment in the Faubourg St. Germain.

Paris under the Bourbons was far gayer than it was in the days of the Consulate, and several important Irish families had houses there. Among them were the Granards and Lady de Ros—a fine lady whose persevering labours at her easel raised her above her kind; and Henrietta Foster, niece of their old friend John Foster, Lord Oriel, last Speaker of the Irish House of Commons, lately married to the elderly Count de Salis, was one of the leaders of fashion. The young Countess at once piloted the Edgeworths round the shops, Maria laying out twenty guineas on pretty trifles for her sisters who should lack no adornment when she launched them in society. The best dancing-master was engaged to give them lessons and Fanny was to go riding with Lady de Ros in the King's Riding-house three times a week. Though clever, animated Harriet's features were not classical like Fanny's, she had pretty pink cheeks, curly fair hair and great vitality. No one was ever more proud of their pair of young swans than Maria: 'I am told by everybody that my sisters are *lovely* in English and charmante in French.'

They made their début at Lady Granard's, dressed to perfection as everyone agreed in 'white lace gowns made up
by the *best* dressmaker, with simple rouleaus of satin . . .
M. Hippolite the best hairdresser in Paris and the Prince of
Coxcombs dressed their hair in dear kind Madame de Salis'
dressing-room. Harriet's was cut a little and combed into
curls—Fanny's like *la belle Hamilton* with pomegranates
(new) and white rose and small white lilies very well put
in.' Maria was besieged on all sides, every distinguished man
in the room seeking an introduction. Alexandre Humboldt
the naturalist, 'held me by the ear and I flatter myself I had
hold of a piece of his ear when Lady Granard dragged us
asunder to present me to a Polish Countess Ortoska, who
was full of Early Lessons, Frank, Rosamond and Practical
Education'. The following evening she went alone to a very
splendid, ultra-royal dinner at the de Salis' and an invitation
arrived for a party at 'the English Embassadors Sᵣ C. Stuart.
The day after I had sent my letter of introduction from Lady
Harrowby and my card Madame Maria Edgeworth et
Mesdemoiselles Edgeworth ses sœurs (which I was told was
the proper thing) came an invitation to Madame and
Mdˢᵉˡˡᵉˢ ses sœurs. . . . It is so very odd to me to be Madame
and keep house and go about in this way that I often feel
I was acting a part in a dream.' Another acquaintance, Mr.
Chenevix, was settled there with his wife the Comtesse de
Riou and her friend Lady Sebright; he as 'agreeable kind
and *malin* as usual and the Comtesse a fine woman and fine
lady on a large scale—and I don't like her.'

'Sunday morning—sermon—St. Sulpice—We went with
la Comtesse de Salis, le comte and le Baron, a batchelor and
kind of Cisisbeo man—N.B. le comte de S. is very heavy
and not firm on his legs ever—I am always afraid of pushing
him down and he always draws back himself as if he was

afraid of it whenever one comes near him . . . Many introductions and compliments on the numerous steps of the
church—then all down on their knees upon chairs in the
church—Then up again buzzing like so many bees . . .
After church—morning visit to Madame de Pastoret—Oh!
my dear mother think of my finding her in that very
boudoir! every thing the same . . . She is but little changed
except in being very tidy and clean in the morning. Sunday
night, what ever you may think of it we went to a bal
d'enfants at the charming Countess Ortowska's' where
Maria was besieged by Duchesses, Princesses, Ladies-in-
Waiting and the English governess who 'made a Panegyric
upon Professional Education which she says is most highly
esteemed in France and Germany—If this *could* have been
heard sooner!'

Maria who had been summoned to a reception later that
evening at the Duchesse d'Escars who received for the King,
went with the de Salis: 'Comtesse, Baronne, Comte and I
whirled away to the Tuileries . . . Mounted a staircase of I
believe 200 and forty steps—I thought the Comte's knees
must have failed as I leaned on his arm. The long gallery
passage lighted well, opened into little low suites of apartments—most beautifully hung—some with silk some with
cachemire shawl drapery in tents at each end, one end over
ottomans the other over recesses with windows looking out
into gardens of Tuileries—moonlight and lamps in profusion. N.B. recesses and tents very convenient for les dames
de palais etc.—In these rooms with busts of kings and
pictures of princes swarmed dukes and duchesses and old
nobility with historic names and stars on their coats and red
ribbons with silver bells at their button-holes and ladies in
little white satin hats and toques with profusion of ostrich
feathers *or* still better because more expensive, *marabous* viz.
powder puff feathers—and the roofs were too low for such

lofty heads—literally I thought some touched—and I am clear that if some of the tallest dukes had *looked* up and if there had been any cobwebs these must have touched their mouths.'

One evening they drove out to Passy to dine with Madame Gautier, all the remaining members of the Delessert family assembling to meet them: 'the *air*, the feeling of domestic happiness, was the charm of charms'. Another time, at Madame de Pastoret's, they met Madame de Staël's daughter Albertine, Duchesse de Broglie, 'a very handsome little woman with large soft dark eyes—in a mob gauze cap, simply dressed—not only gracious but quite *tendre* for me—engaged me to dine next day—and sisters for evening'. Since the collapse of her husband's bank, Madame Récamier lived in rooms at a convent though 'only because it is cheap and respectable'. One night after dining at the English Embassy they climbed up seventy-eight stairs at the Abbaye aux Bois to call on her. 'All came up with asthma—elegant room and she as elegant as ever—Matthieu de Montmorenci—Queen of Sweden—Madame de Boigne, a charming woman ready to devour us. Madame la Maréchale Moreau, a battered beauty beautifully dressed —smelling of garlic and screeching in vain to pass for a wit.' In the course of the evening, according to Harriet, 'a man bawled out a poem in the most barbarous manner'.

The old French nobility, though shockingly superstitious and always talking of dreams and portents, were still the most agreeable to be with: 'We live much too much with these *wrong thinking* people—but their manners are decidedly superior to any of the other party that we have seen.' A much simpler hospitality prevailed in the homes of professors and scientists. One night they visited the great naturalist, Cuvier, in his rooms in the Collège de France, an expedition 'which in truth I thought we should never accomplish alive—Such streets, such turns, in the old old parts of the city . . . Once diverted Harriet by crying out "Ah mon *cher* cocher arrêtez!"—Like Madame du Barri— "Un moment *Monsieur* le Bourreau—" . . . M. Cuvier came down a desperate flight of stairs to the very carriage door to receive us. Face pitted with small pox, with keen, benevolent full grey eyes and hair that looks as if it never had been cut and seldom combed but often powdered and the powder half blown, half scratched out. We were shewn up narrow stairs where many ladies and gentlemen of the most distinguished names and talents were assembled. M. de Proney is as like an honest water-dog as ever—Biot[1] has grown into a fat little double volume of himself . . . When he began to converse his superior abilities were immediately apparent, even in the ease frankness and simplicity of his conversation . . .'

This agreeable conversation was broken off abruptly by 'a blackish grave important looking' Polish Prince Czartowrinski monopolizing her and 'many compliments passed about works on education. And then we went to a table to look at Prince Maximilian de Neufville's journey to Brazil magnificently printed in Germany—So when we were round the little marble table with a lamp and a book all tongues began to clatter and it became wondrous agreeable —and behind me I heard English well spoken and this was by Mr. Trelawney—heard from him a panegyric on the Abbé Edgeworth—he knew him well . . . Shambling servant—tea and supper altogether, odd but very agreeable— Only 2/3 of the company could sit round the table but all the behind back ranks were very happy and wondrous loud and talkative—Science literature politics nonsense in happy proportions—Biot sat behind Fanny's back with his per-

[1] Biot, Jean-Baptiste (1774–1862), astronomer, mathematician and chemist.

spiring head at times nearly in her mouth—I like him desperately but *the smell* nearly made me sick when I was talking or listening—I could have wished that every man in the room (Mr. Trelawney and Czartowrinski excepted) had been plunged into a bath—Proney with his hair nearly in my plate was telling me most entertaining anecdotes of Buonaparte and Cuvier's head nearly meeting him across me each talking as hard as he could—but not at all striving to shew wit or learning . . . Harriet's intelligent animated eyes and bright colored cheek I saw every now and then appearing on the off side of Cuvier's shoulder and every now and then he turned to her in the midst of his anecdotes and made her one of us—I could have kissed him for it if he had been washed.'

'Indeed,' wrote Harriet, 'Maria well deserves all the attention she receives for well as I knew her I did not know the extent of all her talents: the extent of her modesty I was well acquainted with. . . . After displaying all that is most brilliant to Princesses and Peers or after the deepest arguments with the most scientific and learned, she goes to order our gowns or to contrive a new habit skirt or to talk nonsense or sense with us—how astonished some of her solemn admirers would be if they were to see her rolling with laughter at some egregious folly.'

Early in June they went to stay with Maria's old friends M. Morel de Vindé, *pair de France* and a former Minister, and his wife, at their romantic château, La Celle, twenty miles out of Paris. Once a royal hunting-box it became 'wonderfully changed and enlarged, the residence of Madame de Pompadour. I now write to you in her very apartments in which Lewis the 15th and she revelled'. The large white-walled bedchamber where Maria sat writing, with long windows opening on to a garden ablaze with rose-acacias and rhododendrons all in full beauty, was still furnished with some of the Pompadour's pieces, 'her immense marble slab dressing table and her best chest of drawers, painted in blue and grey birds and branches with tarnished gilt ornaments'. A pretty dressing-room adjoined the bedroom and a cabinet painted with flowers and fruit, had a glass door leading into the garden. 'To each room there are exquisitely contrived private exits and little dens of closets and antechambers which must have seen many strange exits and entrances in their day—and in their nights . . . Our washing closet was I am sure Madame de Pompadour's favourite retreat. The white wainscoat, now very yellow is painted with grey pictures of monkeys in men's and women's clothes in groups in compartments—The most grotesque figures you can imagine—Many of them are not only grotesque but dirty—for instance monkeys in old men and old women's clothes administering and receiving clysters—This favourite subject with the French is here represented à plusieurs reprises—I have some notion of having read somewhere of this cabinet of monkeys and of having heard that the principal monkey who figures in it was some real person.'

Every afternoon they 'drove out to see places in the neighbourhood' and one day it was Malmaison. Though still belonging to the de Beauharnais family, it was empty except for a steward, the solitude and silence filling Maria with melancholy though the flowers in the well-kept gardens were in their June glory and nightingales sang in the groves. Many pictures and other treasures had been removed, great holes gaping in the parquet floors where statues had been dragged out, as the steward explained 'for the Emperor of Russia'; his mysterious whisperings about 'my master' and 'the armies' reminding Maria of the way old John Langan used to whisper about 'the rubbels'. At St. Germains, lately used as barracks by the English, they were taken round by an 'exceedingly clever and well-informed female guide . . . Lewis the 14$\underline{\text{th}}$ and Madame de la Vallière seemed to have been her very intimate acquaintances.—She was in all their secrets . . . She shewed us Madame de la Vallière's room—poor soul all *gilt*—the gilding of her woe! In the high gilt dome of this little room the guide shewed us the trap door through which Lewis the 14$\underline{\text{th}}$ used to come down—How they managed it I don't well understand for it must have been a perilous operation the room is so high—But my guide who I am clear saw him do it assured me his Majesty came down very easily let down in his own arm chair.'

'Sunday we went to mass early in the morning in the chapel belonging to this house—and such mummery! Then dear Proney took us to see a belier hydraulique which he has made for M. de V which supplies the house with water. He explained it admirably, much to Fanny's satisfaction. The preceding day a crowd of black and grey-headed men and boys had arrived—an uncle of Madame de V's "mon oncle François" et puis a monstrous paunched homme de confiance with her 3 nephews who are at achool in Paris . . . Then there were various men not worth naming very like different kinds of monkeys. Billiards—Backgammon— and a huge cup and ball as large as a nine-pin ball besides ivory tiring-irons supplied for men, women and boys amusement this Sunday and at night Loto in M. de V's room—Poor man he has taken it into his hypochondriacal pate that there is a smell of paint in the salon which was painted 3 months ago . . . he dare not enter it except with a handkerchief stuffed into his mouth in which plight and with his black silk cap on his head, he comes to hand me into dinner every day and he is in such a hurry to get in and out that I wonder we have not both come down on the slippery parquetted floor.'

Soon after they got back to Paris, wrote Fanny, 'we went to Neuilly and were presented by the Dame d'honneur, Maria's devoted admirer M<u>me</u> Dolomien to S. A. S. le Duc d'Orléans[1]—And much was I disappointed with his appearance—rather English in his manner but not high bred—or the least dignified—short and fat. The Duchess daughter to the King of Sicily thin and pulled looking—just got out something about "vos ouvrages et le plaisir de vous voir" when M<u>me</u> Montjoye, M<u>me</u> Dolomien's sister, took us round them outside of the circle to M<u>lle</u>[2] her particular charge. She found three chairs for us . . . M<u>me</u> d'Orglande and one of the two sisters kept continually talking to Maria and the rest of the circle of ladies looked critically at each other and dolefully at themselves, except the immediate neighbours of the Princess and M<u>lle</u>. At 10 o'clock everybody seemed struck with panic and took leave. M<u>lle</u> came and said some words to Maria. They look as if they had suffered much.'

Soon afterwards Maria was again invited to Neuilly to spend an evening quietly with the Duke and Duchess, the Duke showing her pictures of himself as an exile teaching at a school in America and both he and his sister Mademoiselle d'Orléans insisting how admirably they were taught in their youth by Madame de Genlis. Maria's interest in her was as strong as ever, her curiosity to find out more about her carrying her beyond the bounds of tact. When she dined with the Dowager Duchess,[3] widow of Philippe Egalité, at her little court at Ivry, she could not help questioning this dignified old lady who 'moved with the air of a

---

[1] Louis-Philippe, Duc d'Orléans, afterwards King of France (1773–1850).

[2] His sister, Louise Marie Adélaide, Mlle d'Orléans (1777–1847).

[3] Louise Marie Adélaide de Bourbon, daughter of the Duc de Penthièvre, married Louis Philippe Joseph (Philippe Egalité) Duc d'Orléans (1747–1793).

princess' but met with short shrift. 'C'est une personne', replied the Duchess, 'qui m'a causée tant de peines que je ne voudrais jamais la nommer.'

In the middle of July when they were about to depart on their way to Geneva, Maria reflected with satisfaction that in the past three months no people could have seen a greater variety 'of characters and manners and being behind the scenes of life in many societies and families.' A wide range, from the Orléans' court and the *petits comités* (private parties) at the Tuileries to which English people were seldom invited, to political breakfasts at Degérando's and Camille Jordan's and the studio of Madame Vigée le Brun—'better worth seeing than her pictures'. At Degérando's they met the Marquise de Villette, 'Voltaire's Belle et Bonne', who took them back to her house where he always stayed when he came to Paris. She showed them, among other relics, 'the laced waistcoat and fine robe de chambre in which he appeared for the last time' and from one of the plaster hands of his statue dangled 'the crown of bays, the brown withered leaves of that crown of bays, which was placed on his head when he appeared for the last time at the Théâtre Français'. At Camille Jordan's Maria sat next to Benjamin Constant the politician who for twelve years was Madame de Staël's indispensable, though not always willing, appendage, and took an immediate dislike to him. 'He is a fair *whithky*-looking man, very near sighted with spectacles which seem to pinch his nose. He pokes out his chin to keep the spectacles on and yet looks over the top of his spectacles, *squinching* up his eyes so that you cannot see your way into his mind.'

To enumerate the hundreds they met would fill a volume; when they were not driving out to be entertained or instructed an incessant ringing of the door-bell kept their manservant Rudolphe on the run. A persistent morning caller was 'Mr. Chenevix and his cane' who seemed to like them prodigiously. But Maria complained that although he talked delightfully 'he never considers that anything is to be thought of but *talk* and I really sit on thorns sometimes when I know how time is going—he all the time holding a magnifying glass over every French character shewing us horrible things where we thought all was delightful'.

The Moilliet's who were spending the summer at their beautiful Château de Pregny on the shores of the lake close to Geneva, welcomed Maria there at the end of July. These kind friends could not do too much for them, giving them a suite of rooms and insisting that they should use Pregny as their home during their ten weeks' stay in Switzerland, coming and going just as they liked. The views were of such breath-taking loveliness that Maria was quite carried away: 'I did not think it possible that I should feel so much pleasure from the sight of the beauties of nature . . . the first moment when I saw Mont Blanc will remain long an era in my life—a new idea—a new feeling standing alone and above all others in the mind.'

Pregny at once became the rallying point of everyone with any pretensions at social or intellectual distinction—Dumont, Pictet, Dr. and Mrs. Marcet, M. de Candolle the old botanist by far the brightest lights. A few days after they arrived when Maria and her sisters escorted by M. Moilliet set out on a little excursion to Chamonix their old friend Pictet insisted on going too. 'It was impossible to see this country to more advantage than with Pictet—wherever we stopped [the people] flocked round him with joy and cordial gratitude in their faces . . . We were for his sake received by these good people as if we had been Swiss—the great difficulty was to make them take payment from us.' Riding a mule along precipitous paths; scaling a mountain with the aid of an Alpenstock and an intelligent, well-informed guide; gazing at glaciers and caverns and talking to patient, industrious peasants—these were but a few of Maria's memorable experiences. No sooner were they back again than invitations and crowds began pouring in; dinners at the houses of the different members of the great Pictet clan— Pictets, Prévosts, Vernets, Rilliets—and evening gatherings on the lawns sloping down to the lake.

'The chief difference I observe between the Parisian and Genevese *society* is, the stiffness and uniformity of the manners and if you except half a dozen distinguished persons such as Pictet, Dumont, Decandolle, Prévost, etc., the men are all mere husbands. The women are far far superior to the men in appearance, information and conversation. They have all accomplishments, many in a high degree, especially music and drawing, but they have something prim and stiff and *apprêté* in their manners which I cannot bear . . . they stand in a room like dolls with their legs tied and their backs are too flat . . . They are very good and kind and I am ashamed of feeling that *manner* influences me so much— To do them justice they do not roar all at once about politics as the Parisians do.

'The conversation of such men as I have named must be always sufficient to please and instruct—and this would be delightful if we could have it without *the others.* (N.B. Amazing good cakes piled in profusion.) Enter 3 English ladies over-dressed in silks blonde and flowers—"Ah c'est ainsi que les Anglaises tuent nos petites Réunions." Enter a man in a sword and bag—looking very fond of his sword but not much used to it nor to its jangling chain—I asked Dumont who he was? Dumont with his satirical joyous smile answered "*One of our Kings,* one of our syndics— M. Turretin." . . . Dumont is much more agreeable and less cold and *stickish* than he was at Bowood—very kind and cordial—He seems to enjoy his universal consideration here exceedingly and he loves Mont-Blanc next to Bentham, above all created things—I had no idea till I saw him here how much he loved the beauties of nature and the fresh air ... Dumont spoke to me in the kindest, in the most tender and affectionate manner of our *Memoirs*—He says he hears from England and from all who have read them that they have produced the effect that he wished, that he hoped—in short he spoke as we felt and as if he had been one of our own selves.'

Maria thoroughly enjoyed her wonderful reception at Geneva and the fuss made of her sisters who arrayed in pretty sprigged muslins and ribbons, with floppy straw hats shading their delicate complexions and glossy ringlets, were greatly admired by sundry dark-eyed youths who lay at their feet on the sunny sward and plied them with ices and cakes at the moonlit festivals. This did not turn her from her intention of seeing the country. Most of August was taken up by a three weeks' tour they made with the Moilliets of the Cantons as far as Interlaken. Though the inns where they put up were often exceedingly primitive, however bad the conditions might be, declared Harriet, Maria always made them laugh: 'even when the soup is full of soot, the room full of geese and the fish swimming in oil, and with herself and her own two companions never fails, even when the smell of the dung-hill enters at every window and fleas at every fold of the blanket'.

The third and pleasantest excursion occupied six days in the middle of September when they drove round the Lake of Geneva with Dumont who turned out the easiest and most delightful of fellow-travellers. 'Never from early morning to late in the evening, eating or fasting, was he out of humour ... the gayest of the party and Maria and he exactly like people on the stage.' Stout and unwieldy though he was, at dusk when they came to a halt for the night in some over-crowded town he 'toiled up and down the stairs to find beds for us without any groaning or grumbling'. In his bag were four little volumes of French plays and each evening he read one aloud 'incomparably well'.

Though Maria's newly awakened taste for scenery exacted so many exclamations as to be quite fatiguing, it was still the human scene that interested her most. She paid her first visit to Coppet when they breakfasted there with Baron de Staël on the first stage of the journey round the Cantons; it was exactly three years since Madame de Staël's coffin was laid in the mausoleum in a corner of the park. 'From some misapprehension they had not expected us and had breakfasted—but M. de Staël is remarkably well-bred, easy and obliging in his manners and this did not *put him out at all.* While breakfast was preparing he took us to see some pictures and busts of Madame de Staël and M. Necker. These were in M. de Staël's apartment and in going to it we saw almost all the house—all the rooms which she had inhabited and of which we could not think of as of common rooms. They have a classical power over the mind and this was much heightened by the strong attachment and respect for her memory shewn in every word and look and *silence* by her son and her friend Miss Randal who walked with us through these rooms—She is a fat coarsish looking woman but with a delicate tenderness of mind and strong feeling.' Maria soon found a chance to question her privately about Benjamin Constant. Miss Randall's opinion was harsh: 'I always felt when he was beside me as if I had a toad or some cold-blooded venomous animal—There is no creature I ever disliked more.' They strolled under the fine old trees in the park, rowed upon the lake and afterwards rested in Madame de Staël's own cabinet, Maria brooding over the past, on the impetuous, unbridled passions that once had rocked these walls, on the 'gold-dust' of Corinne's small-talk shimmering in the air and upon all that was silenced for ever. 'How much eloquence and such as can never more be heard has been heard here.'

Other visits followed. She liked and got on well with Auguste de Staël 'who is in general under valued', and charming Albertine de Broglie who was beloved by all who knew her. At the end of September the Edgeworths spent four days at Coppet, one of the other guests being Charles de Bonstetten 'a most entertaining butterfly of 72' whose youthful charm and high spirits fifty years earlier at Cambridge created such emotional havoc in elderly Thomas Gray. 'Yesterday evening', wrote Maria, 'as I was sitting in the armchair on the right of the fire M. de Bonstettin whispered "You are now in the exact spot in the very chair in which Madame de Staël used to sit." Her friends were excessively attached to her. This old man of seventy talked of her with tears in his eyes . . . There is something inexpressibly melancholy and awful in this house, in these rooms, where the thought continually recurs "Here genius *was*!—Here *was* ambition!—Love!—All the struggles of all the fury passions! Here was Madame de Staël." That night the historian Sismondi who accompanied Madame de Staël to Italy and several others dined there. When at last the guests went home and their chairs were pushed away it was enchanting "to see the closing circle round the fire, when Madame de Broglie, the duke, M. de Staël, Miss Randal, Dumont and Bonstettin all joining comfortably told witty or comic or interesting anecdotes and talked on till eleven o'clock, all manner of good nonsense".'

Maria's popularity with the social and intellectual coteries living along the shores of the lake kept the days humming with events and encounters until nearly the end of October. 'She is a wonderful creature,' wrote Harriet, 'and though

I talk of peace at Geneva I never saw her so surrounded or so adoringly attended to—Rows of four deep encircle her chair and Fanny and I are scolded [*sic*] from her orbit.'

On the return journey to Paris they made a pious pilgrimage to Lyons where half a century earlier their father spent nearly two years. After the acclamations that usually hailed Maria's arrival this unheralded visit must have been a melancholy experience: 'Lyons! where his active spirit once reigned and where now scarce a trace, a memory of him remains,' though its streets and buildings were painfully familiar to all three from 'the prints in the great portfolio'. And so they went on their way to Paris and an apartment in Rue St. Honoré, life shaping again much as it was in the summer.

When they left Switzerland nothing had been lacking in the affectionate emotion of Dumont's farewell and in November when a scurrilous review of the *Memoirs* was published in the *Quarterly* he wrote Maria the kindest of letters, entreating her never to read 'this infamous article'. With great strength of mind, following his advice, she refused to be upset by it. During this month among several would-be translators of her books she met a charming young Mademoiselle Swanton of Irish descent to whom she entrusted the task. It was the beginning of a long association between Maria and the girl who soon afterwards became Madame Hilaire Belloc and the grandmother of two distinguished English writers.

They might have remained in Paris indefinitely had it not been for the wonderful news that William had made such an excellent recovery that he was expected back at Edgeworthstown within the next three months. All the family of course must be there to welcome him and as Maria's progress across England was always exceedingly protracted, they decided to leave at once. A short while in London, a week at Clifton, another week at Bowood, a few days at Easton Grey with the Thomas Smiths where Maria met and made friends with the political economist David Ricardo, were only a few of the divagations on the road to Holyhead. Charades were all the rage and at Bowood one wet day as Maria and Lord Lansdowne sat by the fire, he speaking 'very seriously of Windham's life and death', with a great burst of noise 'a tribe of gentlemen neighing like horses' rushed into the room and out again, returning a moment later on all fours grunting like pigs. 'You never saw a man look more surprised than Lord Lansdowne.'

She caught cold on the journey and by the time she reached Holyhead she was suffering from erysipelas. The doctor advised her in spite of it to cross to Dublin with the result that she was seriously ill there for several days. As soon as she could travel her sisters took her to Black Castle but she managed all the same to get back to Edgeworthstown in plenty of time for William's arrival.

Chapter Eleven

————————————>•€————————————

1821-1822

When she heard of people complaining that the damp Irish climate was unwholesome and bad for their health, Maria's invariable comment was that if only they had enough to do they would not even notice the weather. As soon as she got home she set to work on a sequel to *Frank* in accordance with her promise to her father to write continuations to her children's stories. The sequel to *Rosamond* soon to be published she actually completed at Pregny: 'it is by no means necessary for me to be at home or in any particular place to invent and write'. Family affairs too engulfed her; and Lucy, news of whose serious illness reached them while they were abroad, was now and for many years to come a helpless invalid, to be amused and read to. What with everyone's requirements and her own work and letter-writing there was ample to do indoors; many a letter did she write on behalf of good causes and good people—soliciting a favour for a deserving acquaintance or an opening for a promising lad. Outside, there was her garden, the plot below her bedroom window where generations of scarlet-cloaked children weeded and raked for sister Maria to whom flowers were a delight all her life; and the village which afforded plenty of scope for her ingenuity and benevolence. If she had not time to notice the weather, months of pitiless rain nevertheless brought terrible sufferings on the poor. Without interfering with Lovell's estate affairs, she carried on her father's practice of finding work for the workless. 'What do you think is my employment out of doors at this moment—making a gutter, a sewer and a pathway in the street of Edgeworths Town and I do declare I am as much interested about it as I ever was in writing anything in my life . . . I find that making said gutter and pathway will employ 20 men for a fortnight or 3 weeks and feed them well with a meal—with Mrs. E's assistance my gutter goes on famously.'

With the head of the family virtually a schoolmaster, Edgeworthstown was no longer at the hub of county affairs; few interesting people came nowadays and the neighbourhood generally had changed, with the Granards rarely at Castle Forbes and young Lady Longford far from forthcoming to her neighbours. There were few opportunities for attractive, intelligent girls like Fanny and Harriet (though Harriet loved the wet Irish landscape and wrote of it nostalgically when she was away). Maria was bombarded by invitations to stay with her friends in England; and with her little sisters as her excuse she thoroughly enjoyed moving on from one country house to another. And so after a bare eight months at home they set out again on their travels, leaving Edgeworthstown in October to winter in England.

Maria's ever-youthful interest in the most trifling everyday happenings which always threw a spell over children, had woven close bonds between her and her young sisters. Their enjoyment was all that mattered to her, and as they drove through North Wales and the industrial Midlands on the way to Smethwick Grove, she revelled in seeing it anew through their eyes. 'The drive last night from 6 till 9 through the *land of flames* was most sublime. I cannot decide which struck Harriet most, this or the slate quarry. The *blast*

which we heard and felt when we were in the dark sub-
terranean passage of the Welch giants causeway was most
sublime.'

For the next two months as they wandered from one big
country house to the next, Maria's insatiable appetite for
seeing, hearing and drawing comparisons found plenty to
satisfy it. From Wycombe Abbey where the 'fine lady' wife
and daughters of her valued friend Lord Carrington,
fashionably apparelled rested perpetually on sofas or sat
about with books pretending to read, never stirring except
for an airing in the carriage, to Gatcomb Park where the
plebeian Ricardos compensated 'for want of manner and
loud voices, etc.' by their energy, benevolence and warm
family affections. At Bowood where everything was always
delightful she again met the Bathursts and accepted an invitation to stay at Cirencester Park—'an antient house with
modern furniture and comfortable luxuries'. She still considered Lady Bathurst to be a perfect example of a great
lady and pondered upon the 'striking difference between the
ease of motion—manner and conversation of the high-born
fashionables compared to others'. Fanny and Harriet fitted
in admirably, looking, she thought, so well in the evenings
'in their muslin gowns over white satin, the tulle all freshly
crimped', and Fanny's equestrian prowess when she rode in
the mornings with Lord Bathurst and his party was praised
by the gentlemen who were 'unanimously charmed with her
manner of riding'. From these social heights and on the way
to a very grand house-party and ball at Deepdene, they
descended to the modest home in Salisbury of Dr. Fowler,
learned in archaeology, geology and physic, whose pleasure
in literary talk and *ideas* and eager pursuit of knowledge,
awakened poignant memories of her father.

New Year's Day found them at Maryon Hall, Hampstead, where the Carr's newly-married daughter Sarah and

her husband, the able lawyer Stephen Lushington, were also staying. January 1st, the anniversary of Thomas Carr's wedding day as well as Maria's birthday, was celebrated, wrote Fanny, 'in a most glorious manner ... The two Miss Baillies—Mr. Burrell, Mr. Carr's earliest friend and school-fellow—Dr. Holland and old Mrs. Mulso[1] (whom Honora no doubt remembers by her more common appellation of *Goody*) came as necessary ingredients of the New Year's dinner. After the cloth was removed and the large punch bowl filled ... the happy day was drunk with three times three every one standing—after which Mrs. Mulso sang a song written in honor of the day—and of the persons present in which there was one stanza for Miss E. and one for the Lushingtons—the Dr. was moved to tears. The poetess laureate was then drunk with three times three and Auld Lang Syne—then Miss Edgeworth and various other songs with great spirit concluding with proper loyalty by God save the King in full chorus—Coffee and tea passed by placidly after which according to established custom Mrs. Carr and her eldest son led off followed by Mr. Carr and Miss J. Baillie in a country dance—after which a Scotch reel and a quadrille led the merry hours along till the Mrs Baillies went.' Then off they all rushed upstairs to don their disguises for 'a sort of masquerade', and no one's spirits were higher than Maria's who wrapped in a red cloak was an old Irish nurse come 'all the way from Killogensawce to look for my two childer that left me last year to go to foreign parts and was I heerd at Mistress Carr's.'

In mid-January they went straight from the unpretentious, home-loving Baillies ('To this day' said Harriet, 'Joanna Baillie would rather be hemming a table-cloth or making marmalade than reading any book whatever') to stay with the versatile, eccentric Sir John Sebright at Beech-

[1] Niece of Mrs. Chapone.

wood Park. 'Sir John who had galloped past us as we left St. Albans and who had taken a good stare into the carriage, met us at his park gate to welcome us with the most gracious countenance his eyebrows would permit.' Through the 'cold straggling large house with a front door to the north blowing through it', by a blazing fire in the library a choice little group awaited them: Mrs. Marcet, Mrs. Somerville, an attractive, fair-haired little Scottish woman whose modest demeanour would lead no one to suspect the extent of her learning or fame as a brilliant mathematician 'of whom La Place[1] said she was the only woman in England who could understand and *correct* his works'; and Dr. Wollaston the melancholy-looking Secretary of the Royal Society. A couple of sporting bachelors and 'six ugly odd-looking daughters' whose tall, lank, white-clad forms, creeping furtively about the house in obvious terror of their father, made Harriet think uncomfortably of ghosts, made up the party. At dinner that night Sir John at the top of his voice regaled Maria (who knew Lady Sebright in Paris) with a long account of his matrimonial misfortunes. His wife's departure, he declared, was entirely the doing of 'that infamous Madame de Riou' who misguidedly he had invited to Beechwood and 'who finished by turning me out of my own house'. It was there that Richard Chenevix first met her and although, said Sir John, 'he spoke of her first in the grossest terms' in the end 'he was possessed—I don't know how the devil it happened'.

'Sir John is one of the most entertaining characters I ever saw—He is very clever, very vain—very odd, full of fancies and paradoxes and with the abilities to defend them all . . . great variety and range of acquirements in literature and science—an excellent chemist—mineralogist—horseman—huntsman—breeder of horses and dogs and pigeons whom

[1] La Place, Marquis de, French mathematician, 1749-1827

he breeds and educates on philosophical principles . . . A lecture he gave me at breakfast, on breaking horses and throwing a horse on his haunches was worthy of the first lecturer in Christendom. His maxim is that no violence should be used to animals—that all we need do is to teach them by gentle degrees . . . Half the company including 2 of his daughters were sneering and suppressing smiles while he was lecturing with great ability upon horsemanship —But alas notwithstanding his philosophical tenderness principles about dogs and horses I am afraid he has been violent with his children—He has treated his daughters like dogs perhaps and his dogs like children. Certainly they all look under abject awe of him and scarcely speak above their breath when he is within hearing—I think my father would be struck with horror . . . Sir John, however, amused me incessantly—he is quite a new character—strong head and warm heart and oddity enough for ten.' Wollaston who 'let himself be worshipped too much by the Miss Sebrights' disappointed her: 'I cannot bear to see a great man living and loving to live among his inferiors—an intellectual giant appears mean and pitiful lording it among pigmies.'

From Beechwood Park they went on to Sir James Mackintosh's house Mardoaks, stopping as sightseers at Hatfield on the way. Hearing Maria was there, Lady Salisbury sent for her: 'So we went into the library where she was sitting. She is a lively good-humoured darkish faced looking woman —very alert and active—what do you think of her fox-hunting tho' past seventy—true as I am alive. An old groom goes out with her—rides a hunter a little better than her own—rides on always a little before her to shew her where she may go—turns to her every now and then and says "Come on—why the devil don't you leap" or "You must not go there—Why the devil do you go there?" etc.'

At Mardoaks where they were 'most cordially welcomed', for several days Maria revelled in her host's conversation, 'the most delightful I ever heard—It is superior to Dumont's in imagination and eloquence and almost equal in wit.' One morning at breakfast he told them no less than twelve new anecdotes. Well might the French 'exclaim in speaking of Mackintosh, *Quelle abondance!*'

At the end of the month they were at Grove House again, and nearly three years after that May morning when Maria drove away from its gates with Fanny and young Sam Whitbread trotting beside her carriage. Whatever Fanny's feelings may have been, Maria certainly cherished great hopes; he now sat in Parliament as Member for Middlesex and was exactly what she would have liked as a husband for Fanny. It was disappointing to find that he was away 'hunting—Lord knows where—Lady E. W. has written to say we are here. We shall see—what we shall see.'

Lady Elizabeth was in terrible trouble over her elder son's clandestine marriage to a woman of bad reputation, the bare thought of whom filled her with loathing. Although she talked of it endlessly, Lady Elizabeth 'never could name her—but still said *her* or "that person" '—a person, as she insisted, of the utmost vulgarity. Though vulgarity was not confined to this unwelcome daughter-in-law: 'Could you conceive that a rejected suitor of Lady E. W.'s a man of twenty thousand per Ann$^{\underline{m}}$ and of old family, could make use of such a vulgar expression as this, "When I come to see your Ladyship you know I have always my *sitting breeches* on." I saw this in a letter she received from the gentleman yesterday.'

Ten days went by. 'Sam is in disgrace—his mother is with reason enraged that he should absent himself from such a debate and not be *here* either.' When a week later he arrived, Maria's hopes fizzled out. 'Sam is to be here all this

week—very kind—all smooth—but my opinion is he has
no farther thought.' And though a day or two later Fanny
was to be seen cantering one of his horses 'in a circle *on the
lawn*' while he stood by exclaiming that he did not know
which enjoyed it most, the lady or the horse 'which went
snorting as it galloped almost at full speed', she failed to
rekindle the ardour of three years ago. One night he took
them to hear a debate at the House of Commons and after
that no more is heard of him.

At the beginning of March they moved into a furnished
house, 8 Holles Street, strategically placed midway between
the Marcets in Hanover Square and the Somervilles in
Harley Street. At these two houses Dr. Wollaston and all
the scientists and men of learning might be met at the breakfasts and evening parties which the Edgeworths frequented
while they were in London. Maria's interests, however,
extended in all directions. Since she first heard Elizabeth Fry
spoken of, her scepticism had changed to admiration and she
was extremely anxious to see her and her work at close
quarters. Having obtained tickets for one of Mrs. Fry's
prayer meetings at Newgate, early one morning the three
little sisters were standing outside the prison. 'The private
door of the jailor opened and at sight of our tickets the great
doors and little doors . . . unbolted and unlocked and in we
went and on through dreary passages till we came to a room
where rows of empty benches fronted us, a table before
them on which a large Bible lay, chairs before the table for
Mrs. Fry and her sisters—chairs and benches on each side
for company auditors . . . Enter Mrs. Fry in drab coloured
silk cloak and plain borderless quaker cap—a most benevolent countenance—a Guido Madonna face—calm, benign. "I
must make an enquiry. Is Maria Edgeworth here and
where?" I went forward and shewed her where my sisters
were sitting—She told me that the benches were for the

convicts and bid us come and sit beside her. Her first smile as she looked upon me I never can forget—The prisoners came in and in an orderly manner ranged themselves on the benches—all quite clean . . . On a very low bench in front . . . little children placed themselves and were *settled* by their mothers. . . .

'She opened the Bible and read in the most sweetly solemn, sedate voice I ever heard—slowly and distinctly without any thing in the manner that could distract attention from the matter. Sometimes she paused to explain which she did with great judgement . . . They were very attentive—unaffectedly interested I thought in all she said and touched by her manner. . . . I studied their countenances carefully but I could not see any which I should have decided was *bad*. Yet Mrs. Fry assured me that all these women had been of the worst sort. Mrs. F. often says a prayer extempore—but this day she was quite silent while she covered her face with her hand for some minutes—They were perfectly silent with their eyes fixed on her, impatient to hear her, not to go—When she said "*You may go*" they all went away slowly. . . .

'We went through the female wards with Mrs. F. and saw the women at various works—knitting—rug-making, etc.—They have done a great quantity of needlework, some of it is most neatly executed and some very ingenious— When I expressed my foolish wonder at this Mrs. Fry's sister (who by the by appears as sensible and active as herself) replied, "We have to do, recollect Ma'am, not with fools but rogues." The profit of their industry is all theirs— The actual good done by employing these people and keeping them from mischief and keeping them tolerably happy during their period of imprisonment is great . . . at all events she has effected much good. . . .

'We emerged again from the thick dark silent walls of

Newgate to the bustling city and thence to the elegant part of the town—And before we had time to arrange our ideas and while the mild quaker face and voice, wonderful resolution and successful exertions of this admirable woman was still in our minds, morning visitors flowed in and common life again went on. I only remember we ended that day with Lydia Whyte and that the contrast between her and Mrs. Fry in every point of appearance and reality struck me strongly—Her bead hat crowned with feathers—her haggard face—rouged and dying! Her life hanging by a thread over the brink of the grave and she turning and clinging to the gay world! that world which is forsaking and laughing at her.'

The world too which clamoured ceaselessly at Maria's door in Holles Street, bringing relays of visitors and showers of notes and cards. 'We know at least 5 or 6 totally independent sets—of scientific—literary—political—travelled—artist society and fine and fashionable of various shades . . . I forgot to mention the *theatrical blues*. Through Lydia Whyte we have become more acquainted with Mrs. Siddons than I ever expected to be. Invited us to a private reading party at her own house made for our little selves.'

As the kaleidoscopic weeks flashed by even Maria's well-ordered mind grew confused. 'Many many dinners and evening parties have rolled over one another and are swept out of my memory by the tide of the last fortnight.' One night they went to Almack's, Fanny and Harriet wearing gowns of silk pattinet gauze embroidered with crystals, their heads dressed by Lady Lansdowne's French hairdresser who entwined in Harriet's curls a wreath of French roses lent by Mrs. Hope who had taken a great deal of trouble to get their tickets. Though everyone assured Maria that both girls looked delightful, Fanny 'the most elegant-looking young woman in the room', the sad fact remains that they did not dance once the whole evening. Henry Wellesley, 'a most fashionable fine one', it is true asked Fanny to waltz with him, but she 'very properly refused' and though Maria pointedly said that her sister danced only quadrilles he bowed and went on his way. It was Maria who attracted the gentlemen—Captain Waldegrave who came and talked and presently went off to fetch the exclusive Mr. Bootle-Wilbraham who, protesting that he was her most devoted humble servant, declared he was ready whenever she pleased to show her the Milbank penitentiary. 'He is a grand man and presently returned with a grander—the grandest in the room—the Marquis of Londonderry—who *by his own account* had been dying for some time with impatience to be introduced to us. Talked much of Castle Rackrent, etc. and of Ireland . . . He introduced us to jolly fat Lady Londonderry who was vastly gracious and invited us to one of the 4 grand parties she gives every season—*and* it surprised me very much to perceive the rapidity with which a minister's having talked to a person for a few minutes spread through the room.'

Even Almack's and a night or two later the 'well-bred crowd at Lady Londonderry's' and 'the prodigious satisfaction of feeling ourselves at such a height of fashion' gave them nothing they seriously valued. The gorgeous throng drifting through rooms scintillating with candle-light and jewels, the soft strains of music and the sweetness of swinging garlands and banks of exotics, slid by them like a dream. None of it stirred their souls or afforded exhilarating glimpses into the labyrinths of the mind. From feasting and frivolity they turned away with relief to the pursuit of knowledge and the rich rewards of enlightening and instructive talk. Maria who always enjoyed introducing her friends to other kindred spirits, often took Francis Beaufort with them to the literary and scientific gatherings that suited his tastes as much as theirs. At Mr. Ricardo's breakfast-table political economy was invariably discussed and when M. de Staël and his sister paid a brief visit to London Maria introduced them there and at other interesting houses.

At Captain Kater's, an army officer who sold his commission in order to devote himself to science, Maria got to know young Herschel whom she recognized at once as 'a man of great abilities and noble character'; one night she drove nine miles into Essex to dine with Joseph and Elizabeth Fry at Plashet; at the Lushingtons they met Lady Byron whom Maria found 'cold and dull and a flat-dog looking face' though Harriet thought 'her eyes looked nearly cried out of her head'; at a musical party at Devonshire House, 'as select as four or five hundred garters, stars and coronets could be' they met Sydney Smith, the witty Rector of Foston-le-Clay who looked just like a modified Punchinello; he was making one of his brief descents upon London from the Yorkshire moors. Maria, prejudiced against him and somewhat afraid of him too, was not anxious to make his acquaintance; he had stolen ideas from her father, she said, and 'then turned them to ridicule'. In the course of the next ten days, however, they met him wherever they went, and all they had to complain of, said Harriet, 'was that our jaws ached a little with too much laughing. He is very agreeable and his conversation and Maria's suit remarkably well.'

One night to their surprise they found him at Lady Jersey's. 'We had left him established to amuse the whole company at Miss White's, not an hour before, and here he was now established as happily with Lady Jersey. When Maria came up to him he said with wonderful impudence —for Heaven knows he says twenty for every word of any body else, when Maria cried, "Here, at it again, what power of lungs you must have"—"I, indeed! you know Miss Edgeworth, you say five words for every one I utter."

Maria demurred at this and he said, "Yes, you utter five for each of mine and each of yours is worth ten of mine." To this no answer could be made and Maria retreated.'

At the end of eight weeks Maria gave up her house and accompanied by Francis Beaufort, with little Francis from Charterhouse tucked up on the barouche seat beside him, they drove into Hampshire to see the naval dockyard at Portsmouth and to explore the Isle of Wight before they returned to Ireland.

Chapter Twelve

—————————————— ❧❋❧ ——————————————

1823

One wet windy day at the end of May 1823, Maria's travelling carriage was lashed securely to the deck of the steam-packet bound for Glasgow. Inside it she lay with closed eyes and a throbbing head, all her fortitude required to bear the tossing as the little ship lurched and rolled among the waves. Out in the open Harriet and Sophy lay prone among the mast ropes, faintly rejecting the overtures of several 'forward' gentlemen who paused to cast commiserating glances at the pretty sufferers and to recommend brandy and water. When in the early hours of next day they reached their inn at Glasgow, they felt more dead than alive though Maria with her usual capacity for making light of adversity was soon writing home of their 'good passage in steam boat'.

She had long wished to revisit Scotland and to meet in the flesh her correspondent of many years' standing, Sir Walter Scott. Her arrival in Glasgow was acclaimed with all the usual excitement and three days' lionizing ensued, professors and lawyers flocking to meet her at the house of her friends the Bannatynes in Carleton Place. Harriet and Sophy took great delight in the reverent solemnity with which 'Maria's devoted lovers' sat round her, praising her works and hanging on her utterances, the 'apostolic face' of one Mr. Graham being particularly comical. Three crowded days, sightseeing and visiting factories, wherever they went encouraging signs of the strides made by material progress meeting their eyes; muslin was being embroidered by machinery and new buildings lighted by gas.

On the way to stay with the Dugald Stewarts at Kinneil House, overlooking the Firth of Forth, they made a three days' tour in the Lowlands. As the carriage lurched along the fearful roads and crawled up the hills Harriet read *Rob Roy* aloud 'whenever the country would let us read'. Wild and mournful though the hills appeared through the ceaseless drifting rain, they glowed for Maria with the romance and magic of Scott's poems and novels that had fired her imagination for so long. But it was her interest in educational experiments that brought them on the first night to Lanark to see Robert Owen's famous school. 'All the children of the village go to the school before they are 10 and learn what they can before they go into the cotton-spinning manufactory which they cannot enter before that age— afterwards they can attend the schools only after 8 o'clock in the evening when work ceases—Young manufacturers of all ages then go to the school *if they like it*—Nothing upon compulsion.' That evening as she inspected different classes of pupils learning their lessons after fourteen hours in the mills, she noticed how the feet and ankles of those dancing reels were deformed from treadling. As this was inevitable, the recollection did not mar their enjoyment of next day's sightseeing when at Clackmannan Tower Maria's wrath waxed fierce against 'that vile robber Lord Elgin who after having plundered the temples at Athens has carried off Bruce's sword'.

Late on the third evening they reached the 'whitewashed castle-mansion' where the old philosopher, paralysed and inarticulate, had retired with his wife and daughter to end

N   193

his days. At the end of many odd passages and staircases in a fire-lit, candle-lit drawing-room they found their hostess, a woman of noted charm, whom Sophy saw as 'a very large person with a plain face—small blue eyes and projecting lips and a fat face with purplish color—her voice very soft and low'. But she welcomed them with open arms, asking after all the family as she gathered them round her on the sofa by the fire, telling them to feel at home, 'which' wrote Maria, 'we did'.

'This house which was the dower-house of the beautiful (Gunning) Duchess of Hamilton, is a fine strange wild old place . . . There are plenty of ghosts at our service, one in particular the Lady Lilburn who was said to be in her lifetime no better than she should be and is seen often all in white as a ghost should be, stretching her white garments and white wings fluttering from the top of the castle from whence she leaps into the sea—a prodigious leap of 3 or 400 yards—but nothing for a well-bred ghost. At other times she wears boots and stumps up and down stairs and across the passages and through bedchambers at dead of night frightening ladies' maids and others—we have not heard her yet.' Far more annoying was the unexpected appearance in the flesh of Lord Minto's unmarried daughter Lady Anna Maria Elliot, 'a travelled chatterer' who settled herself down to out-stay the Edgeworths. She talked incessantly of 'lords and ladies, dukes and duchesses, ministers, princes, powers and potentates dead and alive', ruining the comfortable fireside confidences Maria was enjoying with her hostess while the young ones amused themselves scrambling about on the rocks and searching the hillsides for ferns. Mrs. Stewart's ill-natured remarks about the Scotts can be traced back to Sir Walter's student days when although he was one of Dugald Stewart's pupils he was never as impressed by him as others were. She gossiped about his unpopularity with the literary clique in Edinburgh, his violence in politics, and scandalous accounts of Lady Scott's origin that were spread about by a 'cast mistress' of Lord Downshire's, to the effect that Madame Charpentier's daughter was fathered by his lordship and not by Jean Charpentier the Royalist refugee from Lyons. As she sat sewing in the panelled drawing-room Maria listened attentively though at Edinburgh she soon saw how unjustly he was criticized by those who were jealous of his spectacular rise to fame and prosperity.

The evening they arrived there, on returning to their lodgings in Abercromby Place after calling on some friends, Maria 'found a note from Sir Walter to tell us that *Staffa* alias McDonald alias Laird of Staffa had come to him this evening and brought one of the boatmen of his Island to sing some of their gaelic songs—the man was to return in the morning—Sir W took the liberty as he politely said of begging we would come if possible to hear what we might never happen on any other occasion—he said there was no party only their own family and two old friends. Ten o'clock struck while I read the note—We were tired— We were not fit to be seen—But I thought it best to accept of *Walter Scott's* cordial invitation—sent for a hackney coach and just as we were without dressing went—As the coach stopped we saw the hall lighted and the moment the door opened heard the joyous sounds of loud singing—Three servants in livery—"*The Miss Edgeworths*" sounded from hall to landing place and as I paused just in the anti-room to give a moment's time I heard the first sound of Walter Scott's kind voice "The Miss Edgeworths COME!" The room was lighted only by one globe lamp—A circle were singing loud and beating time—all stopped in an instant and Walter Scott in the most cordial courteous manner stepped forward to welcome us—"Miss Edgeworth, this is so kind of you!"

'My first impression was that he was neither so large nor so heavy in appearance as I had been led to expect by description, prints, bust and picture—He is more lame than I expected, but not unwieldy—His countenance even by the uncertain light in which I first saw it pleased me much—benevolent and full of genius without the slightest *effort* at expression—delightfully natural—as—as if he did not know he was Walter Scott or the great Unknown of the North—as if he only thought of making others happy—After naming to us Lady Scott Staffa my daughter Lockhart, that is Sophia, another daughter Anne, my son—my son-in-law Lockhart just in the broken circle as they stood and shewing me that he had spoken truth that only his family and two old friends Mr. W$\underline{m}$ Clarke[1] and Mr. Sharpe[2] were present, he sat down for a minute on a low sofa beside me and upon my saying—"Do not let us interrupt what was going on" he immediately rose and begged *Staffa* to bid his boatman to strike up again, "Will you then join in the circle with us," he put the end of a silk handkerchief into my hand and others into my sisters . . . and the boatman began to roar out a Gaelic song to which they all stamped in time and repeated the chorus which as far as I could hear sounded like "*At am Vaun! At am Vaun!*" frequently repeated with prodigious enthusiasm . . . But the boatman's dark eyes were ready to start out of his head with rapture as he sung and he stamped and shook the handkerchiefs on each side and the circle imitated as if they were all delighted—All but Lady Scott who seemed to be quite out of place—a French woman much dressed with a cockatoo of scarlet feathers on one side in a scarlet turban—she repeated in broken English, "Scott, we had better have done with this now —I was just saying that if any body from the street had

[1] William Clerk, lawyer and a schoolfellow of Scott's.
[2] Charles Kirkpatrick Sharp, connoisseur and wit.

looked in upon us they must have thought us all mad I am sure."

'Lady Scott is so exactly what I had heard described that it seemed as if we had seen her before—She must have been very handsome—French dark large eyes—civil and good natured—Supper—at a round table a family supper with attention to us just sufficient and no more. The impression left on my mind this night was that Walter Scott is one of the best bred men I ever saw—with all the exquisite politeness which he knows so well to describe . . . As we rose to depart Scott settled that Lady S should call for us in the morning the moment that he was to be free from his duty in the Courts. . . .

'When we wakened in the morning the whole scene of the preceding night seemed like a dream—At 12 however the real Lady Scott in rouge and flowers and veil—resplendent—called—dressed out in this way to walk through dusty college library and old Castle and Holyrood House, etc.—We called for Scott who came out of the courts with joyous face as if he had nothing to do or think of in this world, but to shew us Edinburgh and seeming to enjoy it all as much as we could. He carried us to Parliament House —Library—Castle and Holyrood House—His conversation all the time better than anything we could see!—full of apropos anecdote—historic—serious or comic just as occasion called for it and all with a bonhomie and an ease that made us forget that it was any trouble even to his lameness to mount flights of eternal stairs. . . .

'Scott was delightful in Holyrood House when he came to Mary's apartments and to the little *banqueting room* vile corner closet where poor Mary and Rizzio supped—six persons how could they stow into such a place—He placed himself alternately in the places where Ruthven and the king and Mary sat and stood—describing as Robertson has described the ghastly man just risen from the bed of sickness to commit a murder.'

Next day they dined at his house in Castle Street: 'only his own family and his friend Skene[1] and wife and sister and Staffa (who is long-winded in highland stories) and Sir Henry Stewart—I sat beside Scott at dinner—His conversation all evening was delightful . . . more original than McIntosh's—His strong affection for his early friends and his country gives a power and charm to his conversation which cannot be given even by the polish of the London world or by the habit of literary conversation.'

Though his authorship of the novels was an open secret he kept up the old mystification, stubbornly refusing to acknowledge them. When he obliquely alluded to one of the characters that evening 'there was an arch simplicity in his look at which we could hardly forbear laughing—but we make it a point of good breeding never to PRONG him on this subject—He cannot bear to have any of his works talked of before him'. A copy of *Quentin Durward* was lying on the table and taking it up Mrs. Skene exclaimed, 'This is really too barefaced.' Anne Scott passed it off by saying something to Sophy about 'those works that are sent to Papa, you know'. Harriet told Fanny: 'Scott is very impudent about the books—he continually quotes songs out of them—repeats sentences that he has quoted in them, etc., etc. But always looking nohow and yet very droll but if ever he is asked and very often without being asked, he solemnly declares himself not to be the author.'

The week Maria intended to spend there was prolonged 'at Scott's urging' to a fortnight—a fortnight strewn with roses. Never was she made more welcome, never were her sisters prouder or more amused at the attentions lavished

[1] James Skene of Rubislaw, a lawyer and an intimate friend of Scott's.

on her and the callers who besieged their lodging at all
hours. Coming in late one afternoon, believing everyone
in the town to be at dinner and that they were safe from
being disturbed, they were hardly out of their cloaks before
young Professor Gautier from Geneva was shown in, to be
followed in rapid succession by Baron Hume the judge and
Jeffery of the *Edinburgh Review* 'as usual throwing his arms
about and humming a tune'. But all that really mattered to
Maria was that 'H and S please and are pleased so much
here'. It was pleasant to see the three together walking
about the windy streets, Maria's slight, neat figure moving
as lightly and gaily as the pretty girls' who, far from tall
themselves, nevertheless towered over her. Such warm
family affection, such eager intelligent pleasure in everything, when illumined by fame's magnetic beam became
irresistible. Though it was more than her fame and talents
that made Scott Maria's devoted friend. Something deeper,
a spiritual kinship, drew them together. Their philosophy
of life was very similar; both were essentially humble and
sternly disciplined. Life interested them more than art and
each was taken up by a variety of activities besides authorship. While they were in Edinburgh, he went everywhere
with them, driving about the country and calling at various
great houses. Sometimes they had him to themselves, sometimes one or two of his family came as well—Lady Scott,
crowned with full-blown roses and struggling with her
broken English as if she had that moment landed from
France, the oddest 'black-eyed brown-skinned and rouged
figure' Maria ever saw; Lockhart 'that perpendicular tower
of silence with its handsome head' whom she finally succeeded in melting: Sophia 'slight, elegant and very pleasing'; and Anne 'very handsome but I do not like her'.
Sophy thought Sir Walter showed far too much favouritism
to Sophia and said 'snubbing things' to Anne, 'and forces

her to sing—which she does very much out of tune and hates moreover. Otherwise Sir W. S. is a most amiable family man as well as agreeable in society—His poor old head is quite filled with old ballads and legends which he does remember in the most astonishing manner . . . He is very lame but very active and came running and scrambling after us wherever we went.'

Several younger ones too ran about after them, among them Lord Robert Kerr, 'a poor little spindle shank dragoon', who took them to see his beautiful ancestral home New-battle, belonging to his brother Lord Lothian. But as bad as his little nieces and the governess who were the only ones at home, he knew nothing whatsoever about the pictures or anything else. On these country drives when their cavaliers rode beside the carriage, and coming to some favourite beauty-spot or ruin they stopped and everyone alighted to explore, Sophy was invariably entreated to sing to them. Light-hearted, unlearned Sophy was very attrac-tive to the opposite sex and perching herself romantically on a grassy knoll or rock she would sing *Dear harp of my country* and other songs of Ireland very effectively and to loud applause. She sang too at Castle Street on the many even-ings they spent with the Scotts, when two or three of his familiar friends and legal associates such as Lord Meadow-bank, Adam Ferguson and Will Clerk, were generally of the party. Evenings when the charm of Sir Walter's conversa-tion and story-telling was Maria's delight, out of it flowing at last and inevitably the old Scots ballads and songs. Soon everyone in the room would be singing until according to time-honoured custom the evening was brought to an end with the Jacobite toast *Fill, fill your glasses high.*

The last of these occasions was ruined for Maria by the Halls, the future baronet of Dunglass, 'that odious Cale-donian bore and his wife', and his sailor brother Basil, who invited themselves. Though they met now for the first time, five years earlier Captain Basil Hall had dedicated to Maria his account of the Loochoo Islands, 'which' as he wrote to Mrs. Marcet, 'is like a common sailor scratching his name on Nelson's pillar'. But his gesture did nothing this evening to predispose Maria in his favour; though she thought him clever he was far too ready to show off: 'It puts me in a fever of irritation to sit near him.' Yet two years later when he went to America to collect material for his numerous travel books, she took endless trouble to give him literary advice and help in a correspondence that lasted for seventeen years and was only broken off by his death.

As soon as she left Edinburgh Scott wrote of Maria to Joanna Baillie: 'it is scarcely possible to say more of this very remarkable person than that she not only completely answered, but exceeded the expectations I had formed. I am particularly pleased with the naïvete and good-humoured ardour of mind which she united with such formidable powers of acute observation. In external appearance, she is quite the fairy of our nursery tale, the Whippety Stourie, if you remember such a sprite, who came flying through the window to work all sorts of marvels.'

Before the Edgeworths set off on their tour William joined them: he had been road-making in County Waterford with Nimmo the celebrated Scottish engineer who, under a government scheme, was reclaiming wastes in the west of Ireland. Maria was particularly anxious that he should see the great roads Telford had laid across the Highlands and the Caledonian Canal with all its locks and bridges. 'The chaise holds us four commodiously withinside whenever it rains,' two cushions on the floor making a seat just high enough for Maria—'What a happy thing it is on some occasions to be as little as i am.' At Fern Tower near

Crieff they were 'overwhelmed with civilities' by a gallant, one-armed old soldier Sir David Baird whose lady traced out on a map the best route for Maria to follow.

The *Lady of the Lake* threw such romantic glamour over the Trossachs that crowds of visitors flocked there from all over Britain longing to behold those scenes which the simple Highlanders were only too ready to point out with a matter-of-factness that heightened the effect. From Callendar near Loch Katrine, in the heart of this enchanted region, Maria wrote: 'where is the lake of our own or any other times that has such delightful power over the imagination by the recollections it raises—As we were rowed along our boatman named to us the points we most wished to see—quietly named them without being asked and seemingly with a full belief that he was telling us plain facts without any flowers of speech—Rowing sleepily on he said, "There's the place on that rock see yonder where the King blew his horn"—"And there is the place where the Lady of the Lake landed." . . . He landed us just at the spot where the lady

From underneath an aged oak
That slanted from the Islet rock

shot her little skiff to the silver strand on the opposite side . . . He seemed quite as clear of the existence of the lady of the lake and of all her adventures as of the existence of Benlady [Ben Ledi] and Benvenue, the Trossacs and the pass where Cromwell's soldiers drove up the cattle (as mentioned in Waverley). He shewed us the place on the mountain of Benvenue where formerly there was no means of ascent but by the ladder of broom and hazel twigs where the king climbed with footing nice—a far projecting precipice.'

As they travelled slowly northwards along Telford's roads 'beautifully winding over the hills and through the valleys', Maria's pleasure in 'the romantic wild scenes of the Highlands' far surpassed her expectations. They took long walks in the lovely weather, encountering many a charming Highlander ready to tell the legends of his land or to sing the songs of 'Ossian';[1] 'as to any real inconvenience at Highland inns we have met with none—always enough to eat—good fish—good eggs—good lamb—and good humor'. Fort William, Fort Augustus, Aviemore and Inverness; then as they made their way southwards again misfortune overtook them. Driving one windy day from Inverness to Elgin Maria caught cold and by the time they reached Forres was in the throes of her old enemy erysipelas. They were lucky in finding themselves in a comfortable inn with a good doctor at hand, but it was eleven days before she was fit to travel again and then they went no farther than a neighbouring country house, Bellevue, to spend a few days with 'Ossian's' son and daughter-in-law, while she rested and recuperated.

Though she stoutly refused to let her health interfere with her plans Maria was still very weak when they got back to Edinburgh and several exhausting days, friends and admirers clamouring to see her before she finally departed. At last late in the evening of July 27th they reached Abbotsford. The great work of transforming the simple cottage into an ornate Gothic castle was still in progress and as they drove up to an unfinished gateway in front of a huge pile of building they heard 'Sir Walter's kind voice welcoming us —he was surrounded by young men who were breathing tobacco smoke and whom we found to be the Cornet, little Walter[2] and his friend a Mr. Surtis. Young Scott was quite alert, shook hands as if he was glad to see us and took us

[1] J. Macpherson, 1736–1796

[2] 'The Cornet' was Sir Walter's elder son, Walter b. 1801, and 'little Walter' his nephew.

through heaps of stone and mortar which lay in every direction to a large room with an oak carved ceiling where were a heap of people—Lady Scott who is always civil, was very kind. Mrs. Lockhart has always the most welcoming manner and Miss Anne was civil in her way—Mr. Lockhart bent his tall form—and Scott then named the black people in the background—my son Charles—rather little—very young—handsome but he then looked awkward and rather cross but with fine clever eyes . . . Mr. Campbell of Glen something a melancholy little Highlander . . . and Mr. Constable the bookseller—very fat and paunchy with a very smooth well-shaven exceedingly clean face—rather sleeky and silky in his manner. Tea and supper came. They were all agreeable and we came up to our rooms which are small but very comfortable.'[1]

Maria was in her element in this happy family circle revolving round the massive figure of Sir Walter, garbed in his usual green shooting jacket, grey breeches and heavy shoes; his infectious geniality, as Lockhart[2] said, keeping his large house-party 'happy with him, with themselves, and with each other'. Each day had its special amusement, excursions to Melrose and Dryburgh, to Ettrick Forest and the ruins of Newark where, in its hall in olden times 'the ladies bent their necks of snow to hear the Lay of the Last Minstrel'. They often called at neighbouring houses on the way and enjoyed many an alfresco picnic at some such picturesque haunt as Thomas the Rhymer's waterfall; and once

---

[1] Harriet.

[2] Lockhart in a letter to John Wilson ('Christopher North'): 'Miss Edgeworth is at Abbotsford, and has been for some time; a little, dark, bearded, sharp, withered, active, laughing, talking, impudent, fearless, outspoken, honest, Whiggish, unchristian, good-tempered, kindly, ultra-Irish body. I like her one day and damn her to perdition the next. She is a very queer character . . .'

as daylight faded to star-lit dusk, they dined on the banks of St. Mary's Loch. At the end of the feast, Scott 'scrambled to gather bluebells and heath flowers, with which all the young ladies must twine their hair—and they sang, and he recited, until it was time to go home under the softest of harvest moons'.[1]

Lady Scott who always accused her husband of tiring out his guests with too much walking and talking, took great care of Maria who liked her better every day as she discovered the excellent qualities behind her odd manner. 'This Lady Scott has in my opinion been much belied and misrepresented.' The better she got to know Sir Walter, the more enthusiastic was she: 'The wonder grows every hour upon me how Scott finds time to do all he does—Look at his plantations, at the extent of woods and miles of walks through his plantations which he has made in this place in 12 years and you w$^{\underline{d}}$ think he c$^{\underline{d}}$ have done nothing but plant—Look at his buildings and you would think he c$^{\underline{d}}$ have done nothing but build—Everything carried on in the best manner and on the most liberal scale.' She admired his taste too—the thick stone walls and heavily embossed ceilings, the varnished yellow oak panelling and the sham antiquities outside: a well with an arch over it, with its weather-stains and weeds looked quite 200 years old and an ice-house built in the form of a tower compared most favourably with the towers of Melrose.

'All day long from the moment he sits down to breakfast (at which by the by he sits a comfortable time) till night when unwillingly we take our candles, he is conversing or walking with us or reading to us—WHEN has he time to write—He says "Oh I have plenty of time—people have always time enough if they would but use all they have—I rise early."—Early, how early—Only at seven o'clock—

[1] Lockhart. *Memoirs of the Life of Sir Walter Scott.* 1837.

And in the 3 hours from 7 till 10 he gets all this monstrous quantity of writing done—Lady Scott says that sometimes when they are alone on a rainy day he gets a quarter of a volume written off at once.'

'I never saw an author, less of an author in his habits,' Maria told her Uncle Ruxton. 'This I early observed, but I have been more struck with it in living with him longer.' What was more, he exploded one of her father's firmest convictions. 'After seeing and hearing Scott it is quite impossible to maintain that there is no such thing as original genius.'

As the fortnight they stayed at Abbotsford sped to its close, throughout the last two days Maria and her sisters, heartbroken at having to leave such a nice family, gave in to gusts of weeping that astonished the young Scots. As Sophy explained: 'We had all become so nicely intimate with each other.' 'There was a dreadful scene at parting, the great Maria nearly went into fits; she had taken such a fancy to us all,' Anne Scott wrote to her former governess.

Not only was it the last of Abbotsford, but also the last lap of their journey, with nothing more to look forward to than a short visit to Sir Samuel Romilly's daughter, Mrs. Kennedy, at Dalquharran Castle, and a few days with the Bannatynes in Glasgow. It seemed just like a melancholy dream to Harriet as they retraced their steps westwards, along the same road upon which they had joyously set out, passing once again through Hamilton and Lanark 'after two months of so much seeing and doing, enjoying and suffering'. Maria had quite made up her mind to come back again next year with Fanny, who this time unselfishly had insisted upon Sophy taking her place. Nothing ever appeased Maria's longing for her idolized sister-child, an all-pervading love that pierced right through her defences and was exalted by her respect for Fanny's superior qualities and crystal-clear mind. 'I cannot rest,' she wrote to her now from Scotland, 'until you have seen all I love and admire and feel grateful to—I feel as if I had but half enjoyed the whole. . . . As a companion nothing can ever be equal to you or replace you for me.'

Chapter Thirteen

1824-1829

Maria after all never took Fanny to Scotland. The pattern at home was changing. Early in 1824 Sophy became engaged to her soldier cousin Captain Barry Fox who fought as an ensign in the Peninsula and had seen active service in many other parts of the world since then. Having been left very comfortably off by his grandfather Lord Farnham, he sold his commission soon after the wedding in March to take his bride away for a year to Italy, and Fanny was invited to go with them. Could Maria spare her? That was the only objection: reading, writing, talking, walking, she and Fanny were always together. But though her heart ached at losing her 'tender love and bright intelligence', Maria's principles enabled her to let Fanny go without a word of protest, her infallible remedy, occupation, working its usual charm. She made plans. In the winter she would go to London to meet Anna Beddoes who was to return from Florence where she was living. But during the summer news came of Anna's sudden illness and death and Maria spent the winter at home after all. She was there to welcome Anna's two daughters and their good-looking young sailor brother Henry, who all found their way there and were kept and looked after until their plans for the future were settled. The elder boy Tom, who was to make his mark as a poet, was studying in Germany and did not appear; although he was said to be so clever, Maria never found him otherwise than dull and unresponsive and an undutiful son to 'poor Anna'.

So a younger generation came to augment the depleted family party, Aunt Mary since the death of her sister in 1822 its oldest member and invalid Lucy the youngest, with Mrs. Edgeworth 'the life and soul and conductor and provider of all things'. Always acting in unison, Maria never presuming to more than a daughter's status, these were the two who kept the household going as nearly as possible as formerly. Though Lovell was a kind and obliging brother he was never one of the family circle, leading his life apart with his affairs and friends, his comings and goings known to himself alone. Though Maria regretted that nearly all his time was given up to his school, in his fashion he carried on the torch. Many young men, thanks to him, were doing well in their careers and his methods never failed to make a good impression on all who visited the school. Literally hundreds of people including parties of 'carriage-folk' came to the theatre in the village to see the plays the boys staged and acted themselves. But indoors it was Mrs. Edgeworth's strong character and Maria's resourcefulness and manifold activities that were the mainspring behind the well-ordered family life. As time went on it was not always easy to maintain it. The annuities, hitherto paid most punctiliously, were beginning to fall into arrears. Money was short everywhere though Lovell did not seem unduly worried. But nothing, Maria declared, ever did worry him: even when the pinch was being felt 'everything at the school and all over the world is *couleur de rose* with him. He is one of the very happiest beings I ever saw.'

She went as often as ever to Black Castle, to the bowery cottage at the end of an avenue where 'that dear likeness to

o

my father' still lived with her old husband and two daughters. At close on eighty Mrs. Ruxton was just the same, vividly interested in everything that went on and reading the manuscripts of Maria's children's stories with all her old critical enthusiasm. She was the kindest, most benevolent of aunts, and warmed Maria's heart by exclaiming once after William had called on his way to Dublin: 'Really he is a very fine young man—and very agreeable too—I do assure you now Maria he is.' 'I never denied it,' said Maria.

At Black Castle she often met the scholarly Vicar of Trim, Richard Butler, whose parish was also within riding distance of Edgeworthstown. Maria became very attached to this shy cleric whose unhappy awareness of his own defects aroused her sympathy: 'Mr. Butler is rather melancholy and sensitive—he knows he is plain and awkward but he pretends to nothing.' Often too he wended his way to Edgeworthstown, his spirits fluctuating painfully under the stress of unrequited love. When Mrs. Ruxton getting wind of these frequent visits, asked him point blank which of her nieces he liked most, going scarlet with confusion he stammered out he preferred Miss Harriet. For a long while, however, Harriet, who besides nursing Lucy was busy with her girl's school in the village, did not encourage him and Maria took him under her wing, finding him singularly well-informed and agreeable. Edgeworthstown held many attractions for him; in a letter to a friend he declared it was the pleasantest house he knew, 'for everybody does in it just what he likes, and there is always there some generally interesting company. I am quite sure you would like Miss Edgeworth.'

He was among the privileged ones who were invited to meet Sir Walter Scott when he came to stay for a long week-end in August 1825, on his way to Killarney. His elder son and his well-dowered bride were living in Dublin where Captain Scott's regiment was stationed and Sir Walter who had with him Anne and Lockhart, picked them up and brought them along as well. Many a time he had been asked to Edgeworthstown and it is easy to picture the excitement with which he was greeted. On the first night the school band 'after dinner by moonlight' played Scottish tunes outside the windows and Sir Walter was delighted at seeing the schoolboys romping according to their wont upon the lawn, playing at leap-frog while their parents, strolling about under the trees, looked on. 'Next day we went to the school for a very short time and saw a little of everything and a most favourable impression was left. It being Saturday religious instruction was going on as we went in. Catholics with their priest in one room—Protestants with Mr. Keating in the other. More delightful conversation I have seldom in my life heard than we have been blessed with these three days. What a touch of sorrow must mix with the pleasures of all who have had great losses. Lovell, my mother and I at 12 o'clock at night joined in exclaiming, "How delightful! O! that he had lived to see and hear this." '

The pleasure of his company was prolonged for Maria and Harriet who travelled on with him to Killarney. On the way, wrote Lockhart, they were 'agreeably delayed by the hospitalities of Miss Edgeworth's old friends, and several of Sir Walter's new ones, at various mansions on our line of route'. A hospitality that was almost unparalleled, though Judge Moore of Lamberton near Maryborough surpassed everybody else by secretly packing up a hamper with 'a pickled salmon, a most lordly venison pasty and half a dozen bottles of champagne', which they only discovered when they reached the inn where they dined. At Tralee William, who was laying out the road to Glengariff, joined them and the day they reached Dublin coincided with the return of the travellers from Italy, bringing Francis and Pakenham with them for their holidays. It was August 15th, Sir Walter's birthday, and when they all dined that night at his son's house in St. Stephen's Green they drank his health 'though with more feeling than gaiety'. Already the storm-clouds were piling up round him and though his courage was high his body was weary and ailing. Though he was not the only one there that night whose future would soon be a prey to hitherto unimagined perils. No one suspected it and least of all Maria whose regret at parting from that 'noblest and gentlest of lions' was mingled with her ecstasy at Fanny's safe return.

The portrait of Lovell Edgeworth to be seen at the National Gallery in Dublin was probably painted about this time, when he was approaching fifty; the auburn locks above his stupendous forehead are flecked with grey, his complexion clarety and elderly. Not a trace can be discerned of the optimism Maria speaks of. What the painter saw and emphasized was the suffering in his small, deep-set blue eyes and the furrows scored on his mild, irresolute countenance. The dissipated tastes he had acquired during his eleven years' internment, though kept hidden from his family, had never lost their hold, involving him in extravagances that allied with his feckless generosity and general financial incompetence, plunged him ever deeper into debt. Then sooner than admit that the trust fund yielded too little to pay the full amount of his brothers' and sisters' annuities, he borrowed to supplement it, thereby increasing the welter of bills, notes and unpaid interests which finally completely overwhelmed him. In December 1825 his affairs reached a crisis, his creditors clamouring for their money and doing all they could to force him to mortgage or sell his property. Concealment was no longer possible and from Dublin he wrote to his family revealing the dreadful position he was in.

Mrs. Edgeworth and Maria upon whom the brunt of it fell, found themselves facing ruin without a soul to whom they could turn for help. Though Sneyd's kindness might be depended upon he had long ago abandoned his profession to lead an invalidish life, wandering from one watering-place to another with his equally hypochondriacal wife. It was Maria who undertook to shoulder the burden, backed up by the whole family. Lovell appointed her his agent, putting into her hands the whole miserable imbroglio by which he stood condemned. Magnificently she rose to the occasion, her business acumen as keen as ever, her resolution never deserting her as she crossed swords with attorneys and staved off a 'flock of kites' who were threatening to seize the house and furniture. As she unravelled the tangle it was seen that the debts far exceeded what was at first supposed. For two years the situation was often desperate though nothing would induce Maria to allow an inch of the property to go outside the family. Sneyd, William and Honora all had means of their own which they either lent her or invested in portions of the estate, and some of their neighbours lent her money. But what touched her more profoundly than anything else was the way their richer farmers rallied to her aid, out of gratitude for her father's kindness and consideration to them in the past, bringing her their savings to help his children. At whatever cost to herself, from the very first the interest on every loan was regularly paid.

The whole family looked up to Maria as their saviour, whose strength and skill alone preserved all they held dear from a cataclysm whose rumblings were uncomfortably close for years. Helped by a good agent, the management of the whole estate was once more in her hands; to her the tenants came with their troubles and requests and to her twice a year they paid their rent. She looked after the village herself, repairing and letting the houses and giving all the employment she could. The only responsibility left to Lovell was his school and for this he was always given full credit, Maria's illustrious guests—men like Herschel, Sir David Brewster the physicist and Dr. Robinson the astronomical professor at Armagh Observatory—at his invitation taking part in the lessons and putting the boys through their paces.

Even during the first precarious year life went on the same, friends and relations coming and going and in July the great Sir Humphry Davy who as Maria observed was 'always kind and constant in his friendship to us'. The President of the Royal Society's conversation, its scientific and worldly flavour nicely blended, was like a gush of life-giving air to Maria, wearied out as she was by 'odious accounts'. 'Travelling and his increased acquaintance with the world has enlarged the range without lowering the *pitch* of Sir Humphry's mind: an allusion I have borrowed from an entertaining essay on training hawks sent to me by Sir John Sebright.' As her father used to say 'things always come in bundles'; while Sir Humphry was with them their old friend Judge Foster (brother of Madame de Salis) arrived for the night on his way to Roscommon and he had scarcely departed before Nimmo in a very smart German barouche drove up to the door, 'and here sprang up fresh subjects of information'.

What brought happiness to them all was Harriet's marriage that summer to Richard Butler who was already like one of themselves. Though in dire straits for money Maria, horrified by the bareness of his rectory, was resolved that the little bride should find her new home properly equipped. It was, she said, 'the only private pleasure I have enjoyed—procuring some home comforts for Harriet'—a typical understatement. She furnished the Rectory at Trim from top to bottom as her wedding gift to her.

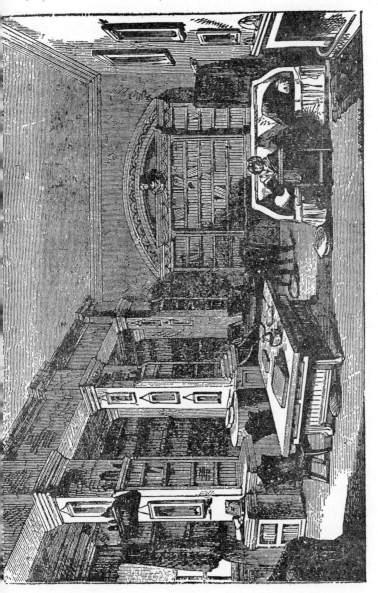

Maria writing at her desk in the library. (She was exceedingly annoyed when she found herself included in the picture)

At Christmas nearly all the family assembled at Edge-worthstown: Sophy and Barry Fox and their infant son—'the most charming little animal' Maria ever saw, and the Butlers came over two days later. Francis and Pakenham, home from school, decorated the rooms with holly and evergreens and Maria who was just back after three months at Black Castle pondered secretly over her Aunt Ruxton, resolving to cultivate the same magnanimity and tolerance. 'In you,' she wrote to her, 'there is a peculiar habit of allowing constantly for the *compensating* good qualities of all connected with you and never unjustly expecting impossible perfection. This which I have so often admired in you I have often determined to imitate and in this my 60th year to commence in a few days I will I am resolved make great progress. "Rosamond at 60" says Margaret.'

In the years that followed she often needed all the tolerance she could muster in her dealings with Lovell and when towards the close of 1828 the possibility of a new relationship suddenly loomed up and turned rapidly into a certainty, it became more essential than ever to rivet her mind on the '*compensating* good qualities'.

Captain Beaufort who was always particularly fond of his niece Fanny, enchanted Maria at the time of Harriet's wedding by 'talking most kindly of my dear F. How he does love her and how justly he says she is as near perfection as a woman can be.' Though she was the dearest of companions and far better able than any of her sisters to share Maria's intellectual interests and increasing passion for science and inventions, as time advanced Maria felt more and more worried. With all her gifts and graces Fanny for whom she once cherished such high hopes had somehow missed the mark. There was, it is said, a disappointment in Dublin—an admirer who loved and rode away. Life passed her by and as she watched it go and saw herself forlornly entering her thirtieth year, the discontented, disillusioned tone of her letters to her uncle caused him real distress. Writing to reprove her for giving in to such thoughts, he sugared his scolding: 'Youth, beauty and talent should not form a coalition with misanthropy.' That summer at Edgeworthstown and elsewhere he saw a great deal of his niece and all he saw and heard convinced him that Fanny ought to be married. Indeed she should have married years ago. There was poor Lestock Wilson close on forty and still a bachelor because of her. In the course of their confidential talks Fanny admitted that she too cherished tender memories of that time. When it was hinted that another meeting with Lestock might be managed she did not discourage it, in fact this little plot became 'the one subject of absorbing importance' between her and her uncle. At the end of October when he returned to England he lost no time in visiting his brother-in-law with the result that three weeks later Lestock Wilson appeared at Edgeworthstown, just as shy, silent and adoring as ever. In three days he and Fanny were engaged.

All Maria's self-command must have been needed to face with composure one whose presence inevitably conjured up such a variety of uncomfortable recollections. But to Sophy Ruxton to whom she had often confided her cares about Fanny, she staunchly insisted that she was 'perfectly satisfied . . . And now that my first wish my most ardent prayer to Heaven is granted and that my dear Fanny is going to be married to a man whom I think fully worthy of her by the nobleness of his heart and TRUTH manliness and tenderness of his nature, what have I more to ask—Have not I reason to be most happy, most grateful to God?—And so I am—But there is a deadly sickness comes across my joy when I think of the separating from her—It wrings—it writhes my heart—But this is selfishness and I just keep it *down* as well as I can.' But during the brief engagement (the wedding took place quietly on 1st January 1829, Maria's sixty-second birthday) her desolation was often acute as she saw Fanny slipping away from her. 'What a wonderful power Love is which severs and unites so despotically—and which can by its own magical power supply all that it insists upon its votaries sacrificing of previous felicity.' And she found it hard too as she brooded upon the Wilsons to reconcile herself to the conditions under which Fanny's married life was to begin in the house in Russell Place which Lestock shared with his brother and his wife. She need not have worried over it. When the time came Fanny settled down there very contentedly and the letters she wrote this winter as she sat by her own fireside snugly wrapped up in one of the same feather capes that Maria long ago had cast from her with contumely, proved without a shadow of doubt how happy she was.

Not so Maria. She knew too well that long must she feel her loss with 'anguish, selfish anguish'. Though business indoors and out took up most of her time there was no longer the consolation of the sympathetic companionship she yearned for. Mrs. Ruxton urged her to think about writing a novel. She had written nothing of the kind since *Ormond*; had vowed indeed she never would again—storytelling was altogether too intimately bound up with her father to be endurable or even possible without him. Yet as she turned the thought over it seemed that time miraculously had smoothed away the pain, leaving the fascination of inventing scenes and characters as potent as it used to be. 'The delightful warmth of creation' was coursing freely at every spare moment when she was called upon to face another and far crueller loss. Her affection for William was heightened by admiration for the way he tackled and overcame the prejudice and difficulties that beset his path after his return from Tonbridge, going doggedly and successfully on with his career. This spring he came home with a hacking cough which turned rapidly into galloping consumption. Doctors from Dublin and his stepmother's devoted nursing could not avert the end which with strange prescience he foretold to the very day. 'During William's illness he said to my mother, "I came home on the 7th of April, Charlotte died the 7th of April. Do not be surprised if I die the 7th of May"—it is extraordinary that he remembered she died on the 7th of April and still more that his own prediction should be accomplished. In ONE month from the time he came home to us dead and cold—all that was so much, so nobly, so energetically alive.'

For years she had cheerfully carried a burden of worries and responsibilities heavy enough to crush most people and the shock of William's death was the last straw. She fell ill and for many months was forced to lead an invalid life on the sofa, forbidden even to write. She amused herself by working out the plot of her novel and planning the market-house in the village she intended to 'help build' with the proceeds of some diamond ear-rings left to her by a distant cousin: 'I think her manes if wandering near her father's antient haunts would be gratified by this.'

At the end of September when Wordsworth called on her she was still not strong enough to talk to him for long though she did not regret it. 'I enjoyed the snatches I had of Mr. Wordsworth's conversation and I think I had quite as much as was good for me or for *him* in my opinion—He is sensible—but has an abundance, a superfluity of words—and he talks too much like a book and like one of his own books, neither prose nor poetry. . . . It is a rather soft slow proud humility tone—very prosing—as if he were always speaking *ex cathedra* for the instruction of the rising generation and never forgetting that he is MR. WORDSWORTH the author and one of the poets of the lake . . . He has contrived very comfortably to travel all over Europe with different rich travellers—I hope they were none of them so impatient as I am of long-winded speakers . . . Mr. Marshall and his son with whom he came here seem to doat.'

Yet another great grief this dolorous year had in store for her before its course was run. In November she heard of Dumont's sudden death at Milan six weeks earlier, struck down by a fatal stroke on his way back to Geneva after travelling in Lombardy. 'My dear,' Maria wrote to Fanny, 'it is an irreparable loss!—and so I have felt and must feel it.'

Chapter Fourteen

1830-1831

Maria did not see Fanny again until September 1830 when she came with her husband to spend a month at Edgeworthstown. This longed-for event was the one ray of light that lifted the gloom of a melancholy summer. Wherever she turned there was misery. To the peasants, nearly all in dire distress 'with neither food nor work', the big white house in the midst of its flowery garden and spreading 'lawn' must have seemed like a paradise in their desert. One, moreover, to which they did not look in vain for sustenance; Maria having procured large quantities of meal sold it to them at half-price to tide them over till the harvest. The prevailing sadness followed her in August when she went to stay at the little house near Dublin where her widowed Aunt Ruxton and her daughters were living. At eighty-five the old lady was visibly failing and Maria who planned to spend the winter in London with Fanny, knew that in all likelihood she would never see her again. She was used to standing back, relaxing her light hold and watching while what once seemed so fixed and permanent crumbled away or took on another shape, and beloved, familiar, *necessary* figures disappeared from her orbit. All the same it was with a heavy heart that she left her aunt at last to hasten home to welcome Fanny.

Maria's philosophic calm did not stem her lively, inexhaustible interest in all the miracles of invention that were coming to pass in the world, some of them like the electric telegraph and railways, experimented in by her father fifty years ago. How well she could remember his loaded farm wagons being hauled by the horses along rails laid across the rough fields! When she left Edgeworthstown at the beginning of October with a big party—Francis Beaufort, now hydrographer to the Royal Navy, and the Barry Foxes travelling to England with her and the Wilsons—she was all agog to see the new Liverpool and Manchester Railway, only just opened by the Duke of Wellington. Unfortunately the pomp and splendour of the day had been marred by one of the Members for Liverpool, Mr. Huskisson, descending from his carriage when the engine stopped to take in water, being knocked down and killed by a passing train. In Liverpool cemetery Maria gazed at his last resting-place: 'Poor Mr. Huskisson—there he lies—they have given him the space of 20 ignoble graves.'

Maria's magic name worked the usual wonders. 'We were invited by Mr. Hodgson . . . to go on the Liv. railway in the very carriage in which the Duke of W went. We ascended the step-ladder off which Huskisson fell and we got into a fine crimson velvet canopied car . . . stiff gilt tassels to look like solid gold all round the top and a stiff edge which is to look like drapery and which tears bonnets and knocks heads . . . In front of the Duke's car was an empty space in the *poop* into which Mr. Hodgson had chairs brought for us—viz. Fanny Lestock Capt B and Sophy . . . Our carriage was sent on to meet us about 13 miles from Liverpool at a place called The Viaduct . . . They sounded horns and at a signal given off we flew—The swiftness of the motion could be perceived only by the apparently swift *receding* of the objects we passed—and by the freshness of the

breeze we created—We went under a tunnel in darkness for
300 yards and were glad to come safe to light again—F. B.
was quite disappointed by not going at greater speed—
the utmost rate being some what short of 20 miles an
hour.'

Fanny's evident happiness was a great consolation and
though Maria could not help finding Lestock rather dull his
compensating good qualities brimmed over. He was 'so very
attentive and kind that it is delightful to travel with him—
as Fanny observes "He really has *a sort of good nature* that
makes him remember all one's little fancies".' The house in
Russell Place was given up soon after they got back and
they moved to Welbeck Street until Fanny's new home,
1 North Audley Street, was ready to go into.

During the eight years since Maria was last in London a
great tide of building had swept northwards: when she and
Fanny drove one day to Windmill Hill, Hampstead, to call
on the Baillies she was amazed at what she saw. 'Hampstead
and London are now almost joined—some of the plaister
streets are really magnificent when one forgets that they are
plaister. But there is ever some voice which cries Must fall!
must fall! Must fall! Must scale off—soon soon soon.' And
on the first Sunday when Lestock took her to see the new
Zoological Gardens she was 'properly surprised by the new
town that has been built in the Regent's Park—and indignant at plaister statues and horrid useless *domes* and pedi-
ments crowded with mock sculpture figures which damp
and smoke must destroy in a season or two. The Zoological
Gardens charmed me.' She fell asleep that night with 'the
vultures scream in my ears—and the feeling of the monkey
pulling my bonnet and shaking it with all his might; he
got his paw into one of the velvet bows when I turned my
back', Lestock and several other gentlemen rushing to rescue
her. A day or two later the news of her aunt's death called

forth this sad reflection: 'I thought my mind was prepared —we always deceive ourselves.'

Except for a fortnight in November when she went to Kent to stay with Sneyd and his wife who were living near Goudhurst, Maria spent the winter and following spring with Fanny, going every now and again to the Baillies at Hampstead for two or three days. 'They are so genuine and warm hearted that if they had not an ounce of literature between them I should nevertheless love them o'er and o'er —Too besides I am SURE they love me and with poor little me that goes I own a great way down into my heart.' She did not care much for some of their neighbours, the industrial and banking families whose handsome houses overlooked the Heath: 'Whole gangs of mighty rich well-dressed—most of them nauseously affected but for those who don't mind that very good people (whom I never desire to see again tho' they all worshipped me *quantum suff*).'

With undiminished popularity, Maria was much sought after. Lady Lansdowne was not long in giving 'quite a private really select, not London select party for me of their own family and most intimate friends who as Lady L politely said were all my old friends whom I had formerly known or seen in Town frequently'. Among them was old Conversation Sharp whose stories, Maria complained, were so staled by repetition that 'you smell them coming too plainly and too often'. She was often at Lansdowne House, fonder of Lady Lansdowne who was as sensible and simple as ever, than of anyone else in the fashionable and political set. She was always at her ease too with courteous, homely Lord Lansdowne and enjoyed sitting next him at their 'delightful dinners' while he talked away confidentially 'in his low voice in his snugs'. She was invited as a matter of

7. LOUISA, MARCHIONESS OF LANSDOWNE
(*Sir Thomas Lawrence, P.R.A.*)

course to every big evening party there and so were the Wilsons, Lady Lansdowne according Lestock 'a most gracious smile' when he was presented to her, that was like balm to Maria's heart.

It was Maria's great object this winter to launch Fanny and her husband successfully among her own friends, and although she let it be known that she kept out of 'all fine company and great parties and see only my friends' of these she had enough to fill up all and every day and as many evenings as she chose. In the daytime Fanny went everywhere with her, to Stafford House and Mrs. Hope's and to Lady Elizabeth Whitbread's Kensington retreat, and several times Rogers invited her as well when Maria breakfasted with him. 'Rogers who is not more yellow than ever nor more satirical for both are impossible has been very good natured to me,' wrote Maria. She saw a great deal of the learned and scientific set who attracted her most of all. Though Davy and Wollaston were dead, others like Dr. Holland, Mrs. Marcet and the Katers were still active and among the younger ones Herschel and Babbage were her friends: while the Lockharts, now established in London, provided a pleasant mixture of literature and happy domesticity. To see this younger generation in their homes, Dr. Holland with his 'fine happy-looking children—and he does so seem to enjoy them' and the Lockharts surrounded by theirs, always stirred up that peculiar, *touching* feeling of tenderness which the sight and sound of children evoked. Her awareness of each child as a distinct individual, a little person of importance, seems to have drawn them to her instinctively and she was in her element this Christmas at the Lockharts' children's party, eating iced plum cake and helping in Hunt the Slipper, declaring that if that delightful creature Sophia Lockhart 'had invented for ever she could not have found what would please me more'.

Late in January when Maria was laid up with a badly sprained ankle a letter was brought round to 1 North Audley Street from Apsley House, a pathetic little note echoing like a knell across far-away scenes of youthful happiness.

'I had resolved not to take any notice of her Grace this time, as she took no notice of me last time I was in London —But when I heard she was seriously ill my heart softened towards her ... Much to my delight came a little pencil note from the Duchess, begging me to come to Apsley House if I wished to give pleasure to an early friend who could never forget the kindness she had received at Edgeworthstown ... I was in or under my sprained ankle at the time but I resolved (as she said "*the sooner the better*") to go next day at the hour appointed 3 o'clock—I found it quite easy (with motive) to trample on impossibilities—especially with the help of Fanny's arm—There was no going up stairs at Apsley House—for the Duke has had apartments on the ground floor appropriated—a whole suite to the Duchess's use now that she is ill ... So leaning on Fanny's arm I had only to go through a long passage that led to something—a magnificent room—not from its size, height, length or breadth magnificent—but from its contents—the presents of cities —kingdoms and sovereigns. In the midst, on a narrow, high mattressed sofa like Lucy's all white—and paler than ever Lucy was, paler than marble—more delicate than life, lay— as if laid out a corpse—the Duchess of Wellington. Always little and delicate looking, she now looked a miniature figure of herself in wax work—As I entered I heard her voice before I saw her; before I could distinguish her features among the borders of her cap—only saw the place where her head lay on the huge raised pillow—The head moved, the head only, and the sweet voice of Kitty Pakenham exclaimed:

' "Oh Miss Edgeworth you are the truest of the true—

the kindest of the kind" and a delicate little deathlike white hand stretched itself out to me before I could reach the couch and when I got there I could not speak . . . But she with the most perfect composure—more than composure, cheerfulness of tone and look, went on speaking . . . As she spoke all the Kitty Pakenham expression appeared in that little shrunk face and the color of life, the eloquent blood, very faint color—spoke—and the smile of former times and the teeth pearly no more—but still and ladylike—tho' much larger in proportion appeared—And she raised herself more and more upon her elbow as she spoke—and spoke with more and more animation—in charming language with that peculiar grace and elegance of kindness—recollected so much of past times of my father most particularly—whose affection she convinced me had touched her deeply and whose admiration I more than ever felt had been deserved—

'Opposite to her couch there was a deep glass case such as is seen in museums—the whole side of the room—in 3 compartments—middle projecting. At the back of the middle hung the gold shield, in imitation of the shield of Achilles, with all the Duke of Wellington's victories em-embossed on the margin and in the centre the Duke and his staff on horseback—the group surrounded with blazing rays —This magnificent present was from the City of London. In the compartments on either side were the great candalabras belonging to the massive plateau given by Portugal . . . The figures and multitudinous ornaments belonging to this plateau lying on their backs in another glass case, filling half the opposite side of the room—At either end in deep glass cases from top to bottom ranged the services of Dresden china and of German presented by the Emperor of Austria and K of Prussia . . . While I looked at them the Duchess raising herself quite up exclaimed with weak-voiced strong-souled enthusiasm:

' "All tributes to merit—there is the value! and pure! *pure*, no corruption ever suspected even—Even of the Duke of Marlborough that could not be said so truly."

'The fresh UNTIRED enthusiasm she has for his character —for her own still youthful imagination of her hero—after all she has gone through is quite wonderful!—There she is fading away—living to the last still feeding, when she can feed on nothing else, on his glories and the perfume of his incense . . . I hope she will not outlive the pleasure she now feels, I am assured, in the Duke's returning kindness—I hope she will not last too long and tire out that easily tired pity of his.'

The Duchess having expressed a wish to see young Pakenham Edgeworth (her brother the late General Sir Edward Pakenham's godson) who was then in London getting ready to sail for India and the offices of the East India Company; Maria took him to Apsley House and presented him. But whatever thoughts and memories she carried away from that sofa where the dying Duchess lay enshrined among the Iron Duke's resplendent trophies, were swiftly dispersed by the diversity and interest of her own day by day experiences. Everything as it came was absorbing, from Fanny's new house and domestic arrangements to the characters and situations Maria came against as with gay good-humour and a seeing eye, she tripped in and out of her friends' houses; or soared far beyond material concerns, to the glorious realms of knowledge and discovery.

'Feb. 6ᵗʰ I am just come home after breakfasting with Sir James Mackintosh . . . My hand and my mind are both unsteadied, unfitted for business or sober thought after this intoxicating draught—Oh what it is to come again within the radiance of genius. Not only every object appears so radiant, so *couleur de rose*—But I feel myself so encreased in powers, in range of mind, with a *vue d'oiseau* of all things—

raised above the dun dim fog and bustle of life . . . How can anyone like to live with their inferiors—prefer this to the delight of being raised up by a superior to the bright regions of genius.'

'Feb 11<u>th</u> You must have seen in the papers the death of Mr. Hope . . . But it was scarcely possible that it could strike you so much as it did me—I who had seen him but a few days before, I who had been rallying him upon his being hypochondriac . . . I had forced Mrs. Hope to go up and say that he *must* see me—that an old friend who had such regard for him and for whom I knew he had a sincere regard must be admitted to see him even in *robe de chambre*—He sent me word to say that if I could bear to see a poor sick man in his night cap he begged I w<u>d</u> come up. So I did and followed Mrs. Hope through all the magnificent apartments and then up to their attics and through and through room after room till I got into his retreat—and then a feeble voice from an arm chair, "Oh my dear Miss Edgeworth—My kind friend to the last" and I saw a figure sunk like La Harpe—in figured silk *robe de chambre* and night cap—death in his pallid shrunk face—a gleam of affectionate pleasure lighted it up for an instant and straight it sunk again—He asked most kindly for my two sisters—faultered at their married names —But shewed he recollected them perfectly—"Tell them I am glad they are happy." . . . When I rallied him at parting on his low spirits and said "how much younger you are than I am" etc.

' "No no"—shaking his head "not in mind—not in the powers of life—God bless you—Goodbye."

'I told him I would only say *au revoir* . . . As I got up I told him laughing he was only ill of a plethora of happiness that he had everything this world could give, etc. and only wanted a little adversity. "Yes" said he, "I am happy Blest with such a wife and such a son!"

'He looked with feeble but most touching gratitude up to her—and she drew back without speaking. I wish to record this while fresh and full in my mind.'

'March 29th Old as I am and imaginative as I am thought to be I have really always found that the pleasures I have expected would be great have been actually greater in the enjoyment than in the anticipation (this is written you know in my 64th year)—The pleasure of being with Fanny has been far *far* greater than I expected—the pleasures of altogether, including the kindness of old friends and the civilities of acquaintances much greater than I had expected . . . But above all the long expected pleasure of our visit to Herschel has surpassed all my expectations. Mrs. Herschel who by the way is very pretty *which does no harm* is such a delightful person . . . She was extremely kind to Fanny whom she took to particularly and Mr. Herschel to Lestock—they invited F and L in the most cordial manner to come back again "and again—and again, any Saturday you know you can run down to us and go up again Monday morning as early as you please in time for Mr. Wilson's business". . . . This is above all delightful to me to feel that the seeds of so much happiness are sown and likely to grow and flourish when I am far away.'

Maria when she drove down alone on the Thursday to Observatory House, Slough, took with her her marked copy of Herschel's *Natural Philosophy* and for two whole days they went through it together, he 'patiently kindly and clearly explaining' all she had difficulty in grasping. On Saturday evening Fanny 'looking wondrous sprank' came bowling down in Lestock's green chaise just in time for a large and very agreeable dinner-party where Maria met 'the Provost of Eton in his wig, both facetious and learned' and Mrs. Gwatkin, a niece of Sir Joshua Reynolds. Next morning they went to Windsor chapel where the Royal Family

sat 'in separate compartments of their bay windowed seat
up aloft' and what with chanting and anthems and a sermon
the service went on for three hours. When at last it was over
'the tide flowed fast and strong to the door at which Royalty
was expected to go out and various beadle folk did what
they could to keep a proper space for the K and Q's exeunt
—But in vain. I was one of the foremost and a man begged
and prayed I would stand back and even twitched my sleeve
but I was deaf and at last whispered 'I'm a poor stranger and
never mind me! I MUST have a sight of the King and Queen
now or never.' So he smiled and let me stand and quite close
I saw her in her black bonnet like anybody else! Her
pictures had led me to expect something younger and hand-
somer—and above all with more of an air and a grace and
a shape and a face—I did not recognize in her the dignified
Queen of Lady Wellesley's idolatry—but a goodnatured
looking good sort of body. Went by particular desire to
Eton College to see the Provost and Mrs. Goodall . . . Good
luncheon including potted char.' And, by far the most
exhilarating, late that night '18 feet aloft on a little stage of
about 8 feet by 3' they each in turn looked through a
reflecting telescope twenty feet long at Saturn and his belts
and satellites, though it was the moon which particularly
'surprised and charmed' Maria.

Next morning on the way back to London, Maria and
Fanny called on Sir Joshua's 'obliging niece' to see her
collection of his pictures, many of which had blackened out
of all recognition, 'the sad results of Sir Joshua's experiments in colour'. Maria was much taken by a picture of a
child sitting on a bank with flowers in her lap, put there, Mrs.
Gwatkin told her, because 'some fool of a woman' gazing at
the child's interlaced fingers, had exclaimed 'How beautiful
and how natural the dish of prawns the dear little thing has
in her lap.' Sir Joshua 'threw flowers over the prawns'.

Mr. Gwatkin was 'one of the thin dried old race of true hunter and shooter men and roast beef of old England men, a true patriot loyal K and Konstitution man—I wean. He was wondrous rich—but has run through two large fortunes and is now scrubbing on upon a few thousands . . . I finished with a noble slice of "the roast beef of old England that was fed Ma'am" said Mr. Gwatkin pausing on the knife—"by his present Majesty, God bless him!—And what is your opinion pray Miss Edgeworth may I ask of this reform bill—for or against, Eh? And what wine do you take?" I gave him my opinion in a bumper toast "Reform without Revolution, if possible" with which he was quite satisfied.'

A few days later they dined at Lady Davy's in Park Street, the party consisting 'of 8 select—of Lady D. flanked by (2) Lord Ashburner—end of table—(3) Rogers right and (4) Maria next him—(5) Gally Knight at foot (6) L. Wilson beside him—(7) Lord Mahon (8) Mrs. Wilson.

'Well-sounding party—number right for table and Davy's fine plate and good dinner and champagne and all sorts of wines—and yet it did not do well. Rogers was cross and Lady Davy marked it and was cross to him when he would not eat fish—Then Lord Mahon who was pert after his fashion vexed Rogers more and more and then his Lordship blundered about something and Rogers had him down and coolly and spitefully trampled on him—And though they talked over all the beauties of art and nature all over the world afterwards yet still there was a leaven of malice that spoiled it all . . . The insincerity of this London life strikes me now more than when I was younger. At the last dinner where I met Rogers he and Mr. Hay were more than flirting disgustingly with Lady Lyndhurst[1]—This night he said to

[1] *Née* Sarah Garay Brunsden, widow of Colonel Thomas of the First Foot Guards. Married the celebrated judge and Lord Chancellor in 1819. d. 1834.

me "We have never met since we were in company with that *terrible woman*"—"Very terrible you seemed to think her when you were sitting beside her"—"Then I protest I told Hay as we were coming in that he *must* be the victim that night—Oh what can a man do, a gentleman, he can't go away when the woman begins—he can't leave her to herself you know. Besides she can *hate* as well as love. Oh she is an under-bred creature who is pushing herself forward." '

Maria was in some trepidation all the evening, Gally Knight having just published 'a stupid *jeu d'esprit* called *The Giantess*' which she found quite unreadable. 'All the time Gally K was near me I dreaded that something would come round of this Giantess—But luckily I escaped—the Dwarf came off safe.'

Her crowded days left little time for reading or even coherent letter-writing: 'If you knew all the notes about nothing I have to reply to.' At that moment on her table three authoress's books lay unread: *Old and New Irish Sketches* by Mrs. C. S. Hall, 'the 2$^{\underline{d}}$ volume dedicated to Miss E.'; a three-volume novel by Mrs. Eden 'with a preface with much about Miss E. in it'; and *Geraldine Desmond* 'a book of great pretension by Miss Crumpe, three volumes and long preface and Miss E. in it'. All requiring letters of thanks and the unknown Miss Crumpe insisting upon coming to see her as well as two young gentlemen sent by Babbage. It was the same, day after day, every moment of her time being scrambled for and snatched by someone.

On Monday, April 25th she drove to Apsley House to call on the Duchess 'without the slightest suspicion that she was worse than when I had last seen her—When I saw the gate only just opened enough to let out the porter's head and saw Smith parleying with him nothing occurred to me but that the man doubted whether I was a person who ought to be admitted—So I put out my card and Smith returning said:

"*Ma'am the Duchess of Wellington died on Saturday morn^g.*" '

Asking to see the Duchess's maid, 'after some minutes the gates opened softly and I went in to that melancholy house —that great silent hall—window shutters closed—not a creature to be seen or heard. One man servant appeared at last and as I moved towards the side of the house where I had formerly been "not that way Ma'am walk in here if you please" and then came that maid of whose attachment the Duchess the last time I saw her had spoken highly, and truly as I now saw—by the first look and words—

' "Too true Ma'am—She is gone from us!"

' "Was the Duke in Town?"

' "Yes Ma'am—BESIDE HER."

'Not a word more on that subject. But I was glad to have that *certain*— . . . They had no apprehension of her danger nor had she herself as the maid told me—till Friday morning when she was seized with violent pain (cancer I believe it was) and she continued in tortures till she died on Saturday morning "calm and resigned". The poor maid could hardly speak. She went in and brought me a lock of her mistress's hair—silver grey, all but a few light brown that just recalled the beautiful Kitty Pakenham formerly.' That night or the next, 'the night of the illuminations', the London crowds ran wild celebrating the passing of the Reform Bill which the Duke had resolutely opposed. Candles were hastily lighted in Fanny's drawing-room windows as 'a poor but numerous mob came from Grosvenor Square pouring about 12 o'clock, rushing and shouting Huzzas and Lights . . . After poking sticks in at the window of next door kitchen they passed on—Many women in straw bonnets and children running and shouting as they ran—an odious noise and I saw and heard no more after they died away at the end of the street. I went to bed and fast asleep—It is true that they began to break windows at Appesley House and were fired at by servants and stopped when policemen told them that the Duchess's corpse lay in the house.'

On May 6th nineteen-year-old Pakenham sat in Maria's dressing-room drinking an early cup of coffee with her: 'This is my last with Pakenham—But there is no use in mourning.' Later that day he embarked at Gravesend for India and an absence of eleven years. And one month later at an early stage of her homeward journey, Maria wrote: 'My last days in London crowned the whole in all that was entertaining and amusing—curious—gratifying and delightful to head and heart—I will fill up viva voce when I get amongst you once more my own dear dears.' One night it was the Opera with Lady Guilford and the next a French play 'Leontine Fay in *Une faute*—The most admirable actress I ever saw and in the most touching piece . . . 3 young men, S. Whitbread, Major Keppell and Lord Mahon separately told me the impression made on them by this actress in this piece was such that they could not sleep afterwards! I had no trial how this would be with me because we went off from the playhouse to Sir James South's to see the occulation of Jupiter—That was indeed a sublime reality! . . . Next morning St. Paul's—Moral sublime' and 'luncheon at the Bishop's—40 people. But now I come at the very last to what surprised and touched and gratified me more than ALL the rest—Lestock actually wept when he took leave of me and pressed me to his generous noble heart as if I was his own *own* sister—urging me to come back again . . . How exquisitely this touched and gratified me—All my future happiness with Fanny depending so much on his loving me.'

Chapter Fifteen

1831-1833

The inevitable aftermath of nine months away was an immense accumulation of business, stacks of correspondence and accounts which, however hard Maria worked, never seemed to get smaller. The amount she got through day after day was formidable and though at times the drudgery of it appeared to be almost too much for her strength, an unfailing reserve of vitality carried her on. Though the debts were reduced to manageable proportions, all her vigilance was needed to keep things going smoothly; while she carried out her duties as a landowner she worked and planned from one half-yearly rent day to the next. Every effort had to be strained to get the tenants to pay punctually, thereby enabling her to meet the interests due on the loans.

To the struggle of keeping the estate in the hands of the family and the house as their home every other consideration was sacrificed; accepting circumstances as they came she had no regrets. 'I should be very sorry if I were told this minute that I was never to see London again and yet I am wondrous contented and happy at home' she wrote this summer. There was so much to enjoy if only in hasty snatches; her garden for example where nearly every plant had its history, sprung from seeds sent by admirers from all parts of the globe or associated with friends, like her cherished peony tree from old Lord Oriel's garden at Collon. In the village where the market house was nearly built she had innumerable irons in the fire besides the benevolent interest she took in everyone's business; and always in her mind was her novel *Helen*, the history of a well-born, high-minded young lady, fortunately with many hospitable friends, who sacrificed her fortune to pay the debts of a beloved dead uncle. Written at odd moments, by fits and starts, it took several years to complete and sometimes drove her to the verge of despair. It was Harriet Butler and her literary-minded husband who brought her safely through it, his wise, discriminating advice bracing her to persevere to the end. The Rectory at Trim was taking the place of Black Castle as a haven where Maria was always welcome and where many a luxury and ornament were the visible proofs of her generosity. To Trim she carried chapter after chapter of *Helen* to be read aloud by Harriet while she and Mr. Butler 'cut and trimmed it to our taste'. She was never happier than when she was with them and we get a glimpse of her there this autumn from Fanny Wilson: 'not at all kilt by her exertions and today quite brilliant—making turbans and fichus and as happy and idle as a child', while Harriet read her 'a pamphlet about Tithes'.

Yet it cannot always have been easy to be cheerful and sanguine, 'bringing sunshine to shady places' as Richard Butler said. The turn of events was often singularly unfortunate, and never more so than this very autumn. For years the hopes of his mother and sisters were concentrated on Francis who, after Lovell and Sneyd, was the heir. In their indulgent eyes this small, fair, precociously-intelligent boy came very near perfection. But the high promise he gave at Charterhouse was not fulfilled at Cambridge which he left at nineteen to study philosophy at home. Now, three years later, he was staying in London on his way to pursue his studies in France and Germany. Without ambition or common sense to restrain him, before he was there many weeks the prospect of some day achieving a creditable academic career appealed to him infinitely less than his sudden desire to marry an attractive, penniless Spanish girl of sixteen, Rosa Florentina Eroles, the daughter of a refugee general. In spite of his family's protests married they were that December, shortly afterwards departing for Florence where Francis eked out his meagre patrimony by taking pupils. There was nothing there to inspire or reward Maria.

Then as time progressed, on her rounds of the village she cannot have failed to notice the steady downward trend in Lovell's school and scholars. Low-class young yahoos from Dublin might be seen in the evenings loafing outside their lodging in the public-houses, while the boarding-house boys became ever less deserving of being described as 'young gentlemen'. All his flair like his zeal had deserted him. At home he kept himself more and more to his own quarters, seldom seen except at dinner and sometimes he was ill and shut away for days on end. Though Maria tried to be tolerant she did not see how mortification was eating his heart out. Since 1826 his position at home in spite of their kindness was by no means an enviable one. The sight of his tiny, grey-haired, ageing sister manfully shouldering his burdens, taking his place, sacrificing her life, fame, art, to repair the havoc he had wrought must have taunted him perpetually. It is not astonishing that his weak will quailed and crumpled up, or that he sought forgetfulness in secret tippling. Through the mist that has gathered round Lovell's disintegration enough can be seen to suggest that by the spring of 1833, for a long while he must have caused his family great distress.

Though he was very unwell the doctors all agreed, Maria said, 'if only he would take better care of himself' he would quickly recover. It was by this time quite evident that the money-affairs of his school must be in a bad way and in May he went to Dublin to try and collect fees that were owed him. When Sneyd, escorting Fanny Wilson, arrived there later in the month they found him lying ill and in a great state of anxiety at the Commercial Hotel, Sackville Street. He confessed to them what he dared not tell Maria: he had broken the solemn promise he gave her never again to raise money without her knowledge. On his notes and bonds he had been borrowing and now with his creditors harrying him he was at his wits' end where to turn—in debt to the tune of £3,000.

Though Fanny wrote as gently as she could to break the news, Maria was not unprepared. 'The blow is one which I have long expected. I got your letter into my possession before my coffee (for how could I wait to know whether you were on Irish ground or not) yet still I *bored* it exceedingly well.' Yet coming just now when the old debts were reduced to less than half and for the first time Maria was feeling she could relax a little, made it peculiarly bitter. But resolutely she concentrated on the present good. Fanny was in Ireland! That was happiness enough and soon she and Sneyd were at Edgeworthstown to spend the entire summer there. And *Helen* was finished at last and while in London her friend Lockhart was arranging for Bentley to publish it and obtaining exceptionally good terms, every morning and evening the family met in the library to listen while Harriet read it aloud. Never was there an audience more attentive and appreciative or prouder of the authoress than they: old Aunt Mary's interest was such as to be 'quite delightful' and Sneyd who was literary in an amateurish way, declared that *Helen* was 'altogether in Maria's best style'. To Sneyd, bald, battered-looking and forty-seven, a prey to every nervous pang, the charm of his old home was still poignant; that atmosphere that no trials of time or calamity could ruffle. 'I am sure you would like the cheerful fusion of this home party,' he wrote to his wife: 'each star is worthy of separate observation for its serenity, brilliancy or magnitude; but it is as a constellation they claim most regard, linked together by strong attachment, and moving in harmony through their useful course . . . I am a stranger to any book but *Helen*.' One evening, he said, after the usual reading, 'Harriet and I walked round the lawn; the owls shrieking and flitting by in pursuit of bats: clouds in endless varieties in the unsettled heavens. The library, as we looked in at it through the windows, with all its walls and pictures lighted up by the lamps, looked beautiful. I thought how my father would have been touched to look in as we did on his assembled family.'

Harsh facts however had to be faced and soon Maria was at grips again with Lovell's bankrupt finances. At the root of his present trouble was the school, as in addition to long arrears of unpaid school fees, with easy-going generosity he was educating whole families of boys free of charge. Though it was Maria who went into it all and worked out ways and means, the whole family co-operated, Sneyd generously offering to buy up Lovell's life-interest in what remained of his estate provided Maria continued to act as agent.

Finally, in a long letter Maria put his position clearly in front of Lovell. She might, she said, be willing to pay these new debts and to continue to look after his interests but on one condition only—he must agree to leave Edgeworths-town for ever. No longer could she go on sharing a roof with one 'in whom notwithstanding his admirable temper, abilities and affectionate nature I cannot have confidence'. If Maria went all the others would go with her; though the

8. THE HONOURABLE MRS. HOPE
(*Sir Thomas Lawrence, P.R.A.*)

house still belonged to him, without them to pay rent and
to share the expenses he could not possibly have afforded
to stay on. With characteristic mildness he no doubt con-
sented to her terms and in the course of the summer
'retired to Liverpool'. There on the allowance Maria made
him he remained for several years, later moving to Ruthin
where he died in 1842. Apart from paying an occasional
visit to Edgeworthstown he never lived there again.

The rest of the summer Maria spent clearing up after him,
paying off the staff and closing the school, writing round to
collect what she could in fees and settling up years-old
debts in the local shops. By the end of it not a penny was
owing though her financial obligations were so much increased that for a long while to come the threat of a forced
sale flapped its wings round the house. What she was up
against was enough to dishearten and weary any old woman
approaching her sixty-seventh birthday who had not
Maria's astonishing resilience. At the end of September when
the summer visitors were gone and Mrs. Edgeworth took
delicate Lucy to Clifton, at Edgeworthstown she was delightedly welcoming new arrivals, her relish for seeing and
hearing new things and new people quite unimpaired.

Her visitors who gave her a good deal of secret amusement, were Sir Culling Smith, a baronet with 'large fortune
and small figure', who contrasted comically with his tall
young wife the former Isabella Carr. Travelling in style
with their infant and nurse, lady's maid and gentleman's
gentleman, they were on their way to Ballinasloe and
Connemara. Sir Culling, full of political and philanthropic
zeal, talked incessantly of his plans for improving Ireland to
his unimpressed hostess: 'his belief in his own power of
making an angel out of every Paddy he met led me to doubt
whether his head was as good as his heart'. His notions

moreover about the road he was proposing to take, seemed excessively vague. Nevertheless as Maria gave him road-books and maps to study, the wonderful stories her father used to tell about what went on in the wilds of Connemara came back in force, rekindling her longing to see it. Tales about its 'King', Richard Martin of Ballinahinch Castle, who ruled over his people 'with almost absolute power, with laws of his own and setting all other laws at defiance'; who fought more duels than any man of his 'Blue-blaze-devil' days and cared so much for the life of animals that he brought a bill into Parliament for making cruelty to them illegal, 'thenceforth changing his cognomen from "Hair-trigger Dick" to "Humanity Martin" '. Carried away by excitement, she quite forgot what a nervous traveller she was or how much she depended on having one of her own family with her. When she rashly exclaimed how much she would like to go too, Sir Culling and Isabella 'burst into delight . . . so it was all settled in a moment. Honora approved, Aunt Mary hoped it would all turn out to my satisfaction, and off we set with four horses mighty grand in Sir Culling's travelling carriage which was a summer friend, an open or half-open German britzka, which was heavy and made to hold five.' The baby was left in Honora's charge; Sir Culling sat on the box, Maria and Isabella inside and the lady's maid and valet behind.

At first all went well, the weather was fine and at every stage Maria met acquaintances who one and all were amazed at finding her embarked on such an excursion; nothing they could say persuading Sir Culling that his carriage was quite unsuited to the Connemara bogs. Every day had its interest—the fair at Ballinasloe, the ruins of Clonmacnoise Abbey on the banks of the Shannon, the old Spanish houses at Galway, and at Oughterard on Loch Corrib they rowed across the lake to see a remarkable underground cavern. As they stood in the fern-festooned gloaming, a dark stream flowing at their feet, the thrilling effect was completed by an old woman hailed as Madgy Burke, who came down the steps. 'She scrambled on a high jut of rock in the cavern; she had a bundle of straw under one arm, and a light flickering in the other hand, her grizzled locks streaming, her garments loose and tattered, all which suddenly became visible as she set fire to a great wisp of straw, and another and another she plucked from her bundle and lighted, and waved the light above and underneath. It was like a scene in a melodrama of Cavern and Witch—the best cavern scene I ever beheld.' But when they reascended the steep steps to the field above, Madgy Burke darting forth from some exit of her own among the rocks, 'turned into a regular old Irish beggar woman', flattering the quality and higgling with Sir Culling for another sixpence. 'She told heaps of lies about her high rent and her cruel landlord—all which Sir Culling sifted—for he is a great sifter—and found not a word of truth at the bottom . . . never could he in the least comprehend how people can tell so many lies about everything. To which they all with their hearts could answer "Very aisy".'

From Oughterard their objective was Clifden, thirty-six miles farther on and right across Connemara. The new road through the wastes and bogs where William worked with Nimmo, had long since been abandoned unfinished when the money ran out. There was no alternative than to follow the old one, along which, as they were warned, no carriage was ever known to pass. And a terrible road it proved, cut up by such appalling sloughs that each time the horses had to be unharnessed and the carriage dragged through it by the swarm of men and boys who came running down from the mountains and up from the fields, bawling at one another in Irish as they followed the lurching britzka.

When a quagmire was reached they 'dragged, pushed, carried and screamed' it over, while a great giant of a man picked up terrified little Maria and carried her to safety. The ladies soon considered it safer to walk, but after trudging along for a considerable distance Clifden was still ten miles off though Ballinahinch Castle was considerably closer. Backed up by her 'dear giant Ulick', Maria persuaded Sir Culling, who was inclined to be obstinate, to send a gossoon with her card to Mrs. Martin, begging for a night's shelter. 'Sure here's my own boy will run with the speed of light', said Ulick, and with the promise of half a crown from Maria 'how he did take to his heels'.

It was pitch dark and eighteen terrible sloughs lay behind them when at last they drove along Thomas Martin's good road running beside his lake. 'Humanity' Martin who had recently died at a great age in France, had years ago handed over his heavily encumbered estates to his son who lived at the Castle with his wife and only daughter. When the travellers were shown in to a large drawing-room lit by fire-light, tall, thin, distinguished-looking Mrs. Martin, attired in deep mourning, came forward to receive them, her accent immediately telling Maria that she was used to the best Dublin circles. While they were talking a young girl, also in black, came in: 'My daughter, Miss Martin.' With her head thrown back, advancing to the centre of the room she swept them a low, beautiful curtsy before she retired to a dark corner of the sofa. When Maria went across to speak to her, Mary Martin was so overcome by shyness that she could only twist her head from side to side like one in torture. Observing how anxiously her mother watched her, Maria feared the girl might be mad, an uncomfortable impression that was not alleviated by the mouldering, dilapidated state the house was in, as they saw when they followed their hostess up the stairs and along the rambling passages to their rooms. Ceilings and walls were blotched all over with damp, broken windows patched with slates and wood, while the bedrooms were of Spartan simplicity—no curtains to Maria's windows and an old trunk as part of the furnishing.

Downstairs they found their host, a large Connemara gentleman with a brogue 'and a sort of brusque cordiality and hospitality struggling against constitutional shyness and reserve'. Dinner was ready and as Maria on Sir Culling's arm entered the dining-room she beheld to her surprise a bald, red-whiskered, odd-looking youngish man, very ill-at-ease, standing there, attired in a long green coat, with a gaudy neckerchief and an equally objectionable waistcoat; whether servant or guest she could not make out. 'But Mr. Martin, turning abruptly called: "McHugh, where are you, man? McHugh, sit down man, here." And McHugh sat down. I presently found he was an essential person in the family . . . a half-gentleman, half-do-all in the house—not an agent, not a game-keeper, not a huntsman, but a smatch of all these, McHugh here, McHugh there, McHugh everywhere—very active and acute and ready and bashful and daredevil kind of man, that would ride and boat and shoot in any weather and at any moment hazard his life to save a fellow creature's—or even for the mere pleasure of danger.'

Opposite her, 'with the light of branches of wax candles full upon her', Maria saw how young seventeen-year-old Mary looked; a girl who reminded her of a painting by Leonardo with her profusion of fine red-gold hair, rather prominent blue-grey eyes and carnation-coloured cheeks. As for the dinner, 'London *bon vivants* might have blest themselves! Venison such as Sir Culling declared could not be found in England . . . salmon, lobsters, oysters, game, all well cooked and well served . . . wines such as I was not

worthy of ... champagne and all manner of French wines'.
But this succulent feast was eaten in a howling gale, the locks
on the three fine mahogany doors being broken and the wind
blowing in on their backs as they swung to and fro.

In spite of the storm and rattling windows Maria slept
soundly and the moment she awoke she jumped out of bed
with excitement to see where she was. As she gazed at the
magnificent view of the lake with the mountains beyond it,
she could hardly believe she was actually in the King of
Connemara's castle; when she was dressed she hurried
downstairs and out of doors to take a good look round.
What she saw was 'a whitewashed dilapidated mansion
with nothing of a castle about it excepting four pepper-
box-looking towers stuck on at each corner'; a low,
ruinous-looking place without garden or park, rising up
from the rough ground, 'with cow-house and pigsty and
dung-hill adjoining, and a litter indescribable in a sunk sort
of backyard'. The spirit which once provoked her to write
Castle Rackrent surged up while she gazed. Longing to see
more of this ramshackle fastness and its owners, she was
torn by her *wish* to stay, knowing she *ought* to go. The tour
was supposed to take just over a week, bringing her home
in good time for her rent day and a visit from her land
agent. Now more than ever it was essential for her to be
there; she could not waste time dawdling about the country.
Little, however, did she guess what was impending as she
went in to breakfast. When half-way through the meal the
Smiths at last appeared, handsome Isabella was almost un-
recognizable, obviously racked with pain though trying
hard to smile, as she hobbled in supported by her husband.
But when she attempted to sit down, she fell helplessly back
into his arms, and as he was far too little to carry her, Mr.
Martin had to lift her up and take her upstairs to bed. And
there she remained, stricken by an alarming illness; Maria's

wish to stay gratified by circumstances that filled her with secret despair. Never in all her life was she so lost and lonely, trapped in this remote castle, far from her loved ones, without a soul to advise her, and worried to death about her rents. As the days passed and Isabella's illness became desperate and no good doctor available, Mr. Martin and Mary who always prescribed for the peasants, rushed upstairs and down with their books and prescriptions, quite unable to make up their minds whether to treat their patient for rheumatism or gout. 'In short all was terror and confusion, and poor Sir Culling . . . stood in tears by her bedside, and after sitting up two nights with her, was seized by asthmatic spasms in his chest. In the midst of all this it was one of the worst nights you can possibly imagine —blowing a storm and raining cats and dogs,' and Lady Smith was so dangerously ill that there was nothing for it but to send a man on horseback to Oughterard for a doctor. While the gentlemen were knocking up one of the Galway postilions and Maria stood sadly alone by the drawing-room fire, 'in came McHugh and coming quite close up to me he said: "Them Galway boys will not know the way across the bogs as I would. I'd be at Oughterard in half the time. I will go if they will let me with all the pleasure in life." "Such a night as this? Oh no, Mr. McHugh." "Oh yes, why not?" said he. And this good-hearted wild creature would have gone that instant if we would have let him. However we would not and he gave his instructions to the Galway boy how to keep clear of the sloughs and bogs.' The poor lad whose life was of no account apparently, safely accomplished his hazardous journey and next day was back with a capable doctor who pronounced Isabella's complaint to be unsettled gout.

In the meantime Mrs. Martin, who turned out to be a niece of her father's old friend Mr. Kirwan, President of the

Royal Irish Academy, was Maria's only solace. Her kindly recollections of William who often used to come to Ballinahinch, was another great bond, and these family links were agreeably interlarded 'by her quantity of anecdotes and her knowledge of people of the world'. As they sat in the unpapered, unpainted, uncurtained drawing-room exchanging reminiscences, Mary lay on a sofa opposite, wrapped in some philosophical abstraction of her own, not hearing one word they said, her mother declared: 'the only thing that keeps her there is you as an authoress and celebrated person'. Unlike her parents, the girl was an insatiable reader and Maria soon discovered that her acquirements were quite extraordinary. 'She has more knowledge of books, both scientific and learned, than any female creature I ever saw or heard of at her age:—heraldry, metaphysics, painting and painters' lives and tactics. She had a course of tactics from a French officer, and of engineering from Nimmo. She understands Latin, Greek and Hebrew, and I don't know how many modern languages.' As her French was learned from the refugee officer it was marred by a *ton de garnison* and she had imbibed such admiration for Napoleon that when Sir Culling spoke against him her 'face grew carnation colour, and down to the tips of her fingers she blushed with indignation'.

Sir Culling who liked holding forth about the rotation of crops and fields of turnips, could not stand the way Mary Martin talked him down, boasting about her father's vast possessions, his sixty-mile avenue, and her own tastes and habits. One morning she took them to see the green marble quarries 'by which her father hopes to pay all his father's debts and live like an emperor sooner or later—several of the common people gathered round, while we were looking at the huge blocks. These people Miss Martin called her "tail" ' boasting that she never went anywhere walking or riding without her 'tail' following her. On leaving the quarry Sir Culling asked her to put a question to the people that he particularly wanted to hear answered. Afterwards he objected that she did not ask it exactly as he stated it. 'No' said she, with colour rising and head thrown back, 'No, because I knew how to put it that our people might understand it. *Je sais mon métier de reine.*' She possessed three riding ponies which on wet days were brought up to the house for her to feed on potatoes. 'One of them is very passionate, and once, the potatoes being withheld a moment too long at the hall door, he fell into a rage, pushed in at the door after her, and she ran for her life and got upstairs. I asked what he would have done if he had come up to her. "Set his two feet on my shoulders, thrown me down and trampled on me." ' After describing further instances of his savage behaviour she suggested that Maria should ride him, even managing to get her up on to his back where Maria looked so miserable that Mr. Martin came to the rescue and lifted her down.

Maria clearly saw that the reign of the Martins in Connemara was nearing its end in spite of their vast territories, their island covered with giant ferns where McHugh was sent to shoot deer for their table, and their private oyster-bed. Though the peasants used to consider Dick Martin not only the lord of all he surveyed but also the lord of their lives, his son was no longer the unrivalled king. Other rich landowners were living in Connemara in fine castles, and rebels who took refuge in the mountains were unsettling the people with their revolutionary ideas. Only a few years back a number of Mr. Martin's tenants were mixed up in a plot to seize Ballinahinch Castle and to drive him and every other Protestant landlord out of the country.

At present things were quiet, Thomas Martin ordering justice week by week in his own fashion and 'when the heat and the crowd in his sessions court are past all bearing, he roars with his stentorian voice to clear the court and if that be not done forthwith, he with his own two Herculean arms seizes the loudest two disputants, knocks their heads together, and bawling as they go thrusts them out of the door'. At home he was the gentlest, most considerate of men, extending his kindness to the valet and lady's maid; to each of them every day he carried 'an excellent glass of port wine'. Like his wife he was very religious, conducting family prayers before breakfast and again before dinner, 'flumping down on his knees' and gabbling his petitions 'without the least stop or reverence' though Maria was convinced there never was a better Christian. During these three weeks while upstairs the patient's sufferings gradually abated and by slow degrees she improved, Maria grew very fond of this honest, simple-hearted gentleman, and in his wife she made a real friend: 'And this is an extraordinary feeling to have made a friend at sixty-six years of age.' Her own fame was known even to the natives of these wilds and one day as she crossed the front hall a stableman, come in for orders, asked Mary if that was 'the great little lady who wrote the books'.

No amount of hospitality and kindness could allay her anxieties or banish her longing to get away, to leave Ballina-hinch behind her and hasten back home to her rents and her agent. There was nothing to soothe the eye or lull the senses in that windswept fastness with the almost inhuman discomfort of its draughty, ill-found rooms looking out upon unkempt wastes and the dreary grandeur of the mountains. It was a relief when at last it became possible to start making plans for the long homeward journey—plans that resulted in Renvyle House, thirty miles on from Ballinahinch, being placed at Maria's disposal by its owners the Blakes and Mrs. Martin arranging with Lord Sligo to put them up for a night at Westport. Finally on 'a wet odious day' and much against their hosts' wishes, they departed accompanied by the Captain of the Waterguard who undertook to see them 'safe out' of Connemara. But the roads to be got over were as bad as the ones they came by and this time there could be no walking. Confined in the narrow, stifling limits of the tightly shut up britzka, Maria and the languishing Isabella had to bear it as best they could.

Four days later as evening drew in and the carriage bowled smoothly along the dear, familiar road from Longford, Maria could hardly control her wildly beating heart. Now every second was bringing her closer to that home that meant all the world to her, bound up in her heart with her father who had created it for the happiness of his large family, animating it with his genius for living and doing and infecting those around him with the same urge. Though he was there no longer his spirit lingered still, to uphold her now that it was upon her that the safety and continuance of his house depended. On her memories of him and the support of those who were left she must always rely—needing, none knew how urgently, the strong, steady guidance of her mother and the affection and approval of her brothers and sisters.

When the carriage turned in at the Edgeworthstown gates, presently through the darkness and the trees she saw with joy and thankfulness lights shining in the windows.

Epilogue

T hough Maria lived to be eighty-two for many years after her adventures in Connemara she went no farther afield than Trim or Dublin, all her energies being devoted to the management of the estate. Though this was often much complicated, and even made positively unpleasant, by the growing animosity of the peasants who, encouraged by the priests, were violently antagonistic to the Protestant landlords, nothing ever persuaded Maria to depart from her father's rule of treating Protestants and Catholics with strict impartiality.

Edgeworthstown continued to attract everyone with literary tastes who came to Ireland and in August 1835 a distinguished American, the Professor of Modern Literature at Harvard, George Ticknor, stayed there. He was amazed at the abandon with which this 'small, short, spare lady of about sixty-seven, with extremely kind, frank manners' and very direct gaze, threw herself into conversation, referring constantly to Mrs. Edgeworth 'and most kindly repeating jokes to her infirm aunt Mrs. Sneyd who cannot hear them'. But much in the same way, she amazed her brother Pakenham's young bride Christina eleven years later, when he brought her to Edgeworthstown in 1846: never, she declared, did she see two such active-bodied, able-minded old ladies as Mrs. Edgeworth and Maria, whose behaviour was still that of a dutiful daughter.

Epilogue

Though *Helen* was very successful and many times reprinted, it was Maria's last book; when she was seventy-five she cut down and entirely rewrote her part of her father's *Memoir*, which was then reissued in one volume. At eighty when the Great Famine was raging and her name at the head of many an appeal, she wrote a short story, *Orlandino*, that was sold for the benefit of the Irish Poor Relief Fund. At all times she worked hard, and, whenever she could, used her influence with her friends in high places, for the good of her poor countrymen, like the loyal Irishwoman she was. That her efforts were appreciated is suggested by the ovation she was given on St. Patrick's Day at Trim in 1843. She was staying there, convalescing after a severe illness, when members of the Temperance Society 'who were honouring the shamrock with temperance rejoicings and music' asked leave to come in to Mr. Butler's lawn 'to play a tune or two for Miss Edgeworth'. And in they came, a glittering brass band preceded by the priest and a great crowd following behind, while Maria, too frail to go downstairs, stood at her bedroom window, 'thanking them as loud as I could, and curtsying as low as my littleness and weakness would allow'.

In 1837 Honora who for many years was her mainstay, married Admiral Francis Beaufort whose wife Alicia had died three years earlier, and went to live in London. Every summer witnessed the return of all the scattered members of the family to Edgeworthstown, and Fanny never failed to come back to Maria then, who much as she longed to return to North Audley Street, did not feel justified in leaving her business for so long. It was not until December 1840 when Francis came to live at Edgeworthstown 'as a resident landlord and magistrate much needed', with his wife and their little brood of half-Spanish Edgeworths, that she felt herself at liberty to go to London. 'I have chosen to go at this quiet time of year', she wrote to Ticknor, 'as I particularly wish not to encounter the bustle and dissipation and lionizing of London. For tho' I am such a minnikin lion now and so old, literally without teeth or claws, still there be, that might rattle at the gate to make me get up and come out and stand up to play tricks for them.'

Old indeed she was, but her appetite for life and powers of enjoyment were as youthful and keen as ever; nor could her many old friends and 'worshippers' make enough of her during her last two visits to the capital: she stayed there from December to April in 1840–1 and again for the same months in 1843–4. In February 1844 she attended the Opening of Parliament and watched young Queen Victoria entering the new House of Lords on the arm of Prince Albert, stumbling against a footstool as she mounted the Throne. Her head, with its diadem of diamonds, was finely shaped, her neck and arms beautifully fair, but though, in Maria's opinion, she read with good sense, 'it was more a girl's well-read lesson than a Queen pronouncing her speech'. Dining at Lambeth Palace a few evenings later she sat on the Archbishop of Canterbury's right hand; Rogers gave a tea-party for her as less exhausting than a breakfast; she was often at Sydney Smith's house in Green Street, putting him right about Irish affairs, each thoroughly appreciating the excellence of the other's talk: 'She does not say witty things,' said he, 'but there is such a perfume of wit runs through all her conversation as makes it very brilliant'; at Lansdowne House she was always welcome, delighting in meeting old friends again and seeing the younger generation. Of the impression she created this winter Joanna Baillie wrote to Fanny: 'So animated, so witty, so good-natured and so gay, she has thrown a grace over old age for which all we ladies of very advanced standing are much obliged to her.'

Epilogue

Her remarkable vitality and recuperative powers brought her safely through a serious illness when she was seventy-six and three years later on she was quite annoyed at finding that she could no longer run upstairs as quickly as she used to. But her pen was still as actively employed as ever it was, writing letters and notes innumerable, and her needle was always busy. Venerated by her family and interested in everything to do with any of them, she went quietly on in no fear of death; enjoying, she said, every moment of life's feast though ready when she was called to quit it. Two who seemed likely to outlive her by a number of years went before her, Francis dying in 1846 and Fanny Wilson, always Maria's best-beloved, following him after a short illness two years later. Yet even from this final blow Maria rallied and tinier and frailer-looking than ever she continued to live to the last as her father had trained her. Her activity and independence often made the others feel anxious, and when she was eighty-two she frightened Harriet Butler out of her wits and earned a good scolding, by climbing up a ladder to wind up a clock.

Three weeks after this little escapade, on the morning of 22nd May 1849, Maria went driving as usual. On her return a sudden sharp pain in her side sent her upstairs to her room to lie down. When an hour or two later her mother looked in, she found her lying very peacefully but strangely still, sunk in a deep sleep from which there was no awakening.

Index

Acland, Lady, 97
Acland, Sir Thomas, 36, 97
Adam, Robert, 137
Adelaide, Queen, 231
Albert of Coburg, Prince, 254
Apreece, Mrs., *see* Lady Davy
Ashburner, Lord, 232
Austen, Jane, 124, 133
Austin, Mrs., 99

Babbage, Charles, 225, 233
Baffin, William, 140
Baillie, Joanna, 83, 105, 114, 145, 182, 201, 224, 254
Baird, Sir David and Lady, 202
Banks, Sir Joseph, 17
Bannatynes, the, 192, 196
Barry, Madame du, 166
Bathurst, 3rd Earl, 119, 141, 181
Bathurst, Georgina Countess, 141, 181
Bathurst, Lady Georgina, 141
Beaufort, Alicia (*née* Wilson), 142–3, 144, 253
Beaufort, Rev. Daniel, 41–2, 50, 90
Beaufort, Frances Anne, *see* Edgeworth
Beaufort, Admiral Sir Francis, 139, 142–4, 154, 189, 191, 216–17, 222–3, 253
Beaufort, Harriet, 50
Beaufort, Louisa, 50
Beaufort, Mrs., 42, 50, 86
Beauharnais family, 168
Beddoes, Anna (Mrs. Thomas), 20, 35, 53, 95, 114, 135–6, 208–9

Beddoes, Henry, 208
Beddoes, Dr. Thomas, 35, 64
Beddoes, Thomas Lovell, 208–9
Bedford, 6th Duke of, 110, 156
Belloc Mme. Hilaire, 177
Bentham, Jeremy, 105, 114, 174
Berry, Mary and Agnes, 105–6, 111, 159
Bessborough, Henrietta Frances, Countess of, 104, 108
Biot, Jean-Baptiste, 166 and footnote
Blackstone, Sir William, 23
Blakes of Renvyle, 250
Boigne, Mme de, 165
Boissy-d'Anglas, François-Antoine, 73
Bonaparte, Napoleon, 70, 75, 82, 94, 167, 248
Bonstetten, Charles de, 176
Boothby, Brooke, 149
Bootle-Wilbraham, Mr., 189
Brandon, Mr., 108
Breton, Joachim le, 69, 82
Brewster, Sir David, 214
Bristow, George, 135
Bristow, Molly (wife of above), 160
Broadhurst, Henrica, *see* Mrs. Sneyd Edgeworth
Broglie, Albertine Duchesse de, 165, 176, 190
Broglie, Duc de, 176
Buchan, 6th Earl of, 83
Bunbury, Sir Henry, 140
Burke, Madgy, 243

R

Index

Burney, Fanny, 31
Burrell, Mr., 182
Bury, Viscount, 119
Butler, Harriet (Mrs. Richard), Maria's kindness to, 116; accompanies Maria to Paris, 162–72; praise of Maria, 167; Maria's good-humour travelling, 174; Maria's popularity at Geneva, 176–7; Beechwood Park, 183; in London, 185–91; Sydney Smith, 190–1; Scottish tour, 192–206; Rev. R. Butler in love with, 210; marriage, 214; Trim Rectory replaces Black Castle for Maria, 237; reads *Helen* to assembled family, 239; scolds Maria for climbing ladder, 255. *Also:* 86, 88, 97, 116, 121, 130, 135, 180–1, 211, 216, 240
Butler, Very Rev. Richard Butler, Dean of Clonmacnoise, 210, 214, 216, 237, 253
Buxton, Fowell, 145
Byron, Lady, 111, 126, 145–6, 190
Byron, Lord, 103, and footnote, 105–6, 112–13, 145

Caledon, 2nd Earl of, 111
Campan, Madame, 71
Campbell, Mr., 204
Candolle, Augustin de, 172–3
Canterbury, Archbishop of, 254
Carr, Isabella, *see* Lady Smith
Carr, Sarah, *see* Mrs. Stephen Lushington
Carr, Mr. and Mrs. Thomas, 156–7, 182
Carrington, 1st Lord, 105, 117 159–, 60, 181
Carrington, Lady, 105, 181
Carysfoot, Lady, 105
Cathcart, Lady, 30, 52
Chapone, Mrs., 182 (footnote)

Charlemont, Anne, Countess of, 106
Charpentier, Jean, 195
Charpentier, Mme, 195
Chenevix, Richard, 55, 93–4, 96, 163, 172, 183
Clarence, Duke of, *see* William IV
Clerk, William, 196 and footnote, 200
Clewberg, Abraham Nikolas, *see* Edelcrantz
Cole, General, 126
Condé, Louis II, Prince de, 67–8
Conolly, Lady Louisa, 126, 141
Constable, Archibald, 204
Constant, Benjamin, 171, 175
Cornwallis, 1st Marquis (Viceroy of Ireland), 48–50
Corry, James, 129
Crampton, Dr. Philip, 98
Crewe, Frances Anne Lady, 105–6
Crillon, Comte de, 73
Crumpe, Miss, 233
Cuvier, Georges, 165–7
Czartowinski, Prince, 166–7

Darnley, 4th Earl of, 105, 156
Darnley, Elizabeth, Countess of, 105, 110, 156
Darwin, Dr. Erasmus, 17
Davy, Sir Humphry, 64, 96, 105, 126, 214, 225, 232
Davy, Lady, 95–6, 103, 105, 112, 126, 132
Day, Thomas, 20, 26, 142, 144
Deffand, Madame du, 71
Degérando, 171
Delaval, Sir Francis, 32
Delessert, Mme Etienne, 69, 71
Derby, Eliza, Countess of, 107 and footnote
Dolgorouki, Princess, 78
Dolomien, Mme, 170
Downshire, 2nd Marquis of, 195

Index

Dumont, Etienne, first meeting with Edgeworths, 69; Maria's description of, 104–5; praises *Tales from Fashionable Life*, 94–5; Mme de Staël's praise of Maria, 118; to criticize *Memoirs*, 134–5; at Bowood, 136–40; friendship with Romilly, 148; at Geneva, 172–77; death, 220. *Also:* 110, 112, 114, 185

Edelcrantz, Chevalier, 72, 74–7, 83–4
Eden, Mrs., 233
Edgeworth, l'Abbé, 70, 79, 166
Edgeworth, Mrs. Anna-Maria, 19, 20
Edgeworth, Anna, *see* Mrs. Thomas Beddoes
Edgeworth, Charlotte, 45, 54, 59, 62–4, 82, 86–8, 90, 219
Edgeworth, Mrs. Elizabeth, 17, 20, 25, 32, 34, 39, 41, 45, 90
Edgeworth, Elizabeth (Bessy), 20, 41, 45
Edgeworth, Emmeline, *see* Mrs. John King
Edgeworth, Mrs. Frances Anne, illustrated Maria's stories, 39; character and appearance, 42; R.L.E.'s courtship of and Maria's disapproval, 42–3; Maria's opinion changes, 43–4; marriage and arrival at Edgeworthstown, 44–5; Maria's devotion to, 45; letter to Charlotte Sneyd, 82; birth of Lucy, 86; 'Maria's *prominent* position', 104; takes William to England, 134. *Also:* 46–8, 59, 62–3, 88, 90, 92, 105, 110, 116, 121, 124–5, 136, 143, 150–1, 180, 209, 211, 213, 241, 252, 255
Edgeworth, Frances Maria (Fanny), *see* Mrs. Lestock Wilson
Edgeworth, Francis Beaufort, Lord Gardner approves of, 117; appear-

ance and character, 237; marriage, 237–8. *Also:* 128, 130, 144, 151, 191, 211, 216, 253, 255
Edgeworth, Rosa Florentina (Mrs. F.B.), 238
Edgeworth, Harriet, *see* Mrs. Richard Butler
Edgeworth, Henry, 25, 37, 45–6, 48, 53, 69, 78–9, 82, 87–8, 92, 103, 136
Edgeworth, Mrs. Honora, 20
Edgeworth, Honora (daughter of above), 20; her character and death, 33
Edgeworth, Honora (youngest daughter of Mrs. Elizabeth Edgeworth), Christmas at Pakenham Hall, 91–2; brings Maria R.L.E.'s last letter, 131; Maria's secretary and reader, 134; accompanies Maria to England, 135–59; marriage, 253. *Also;* 45, 116, 121–2, 130, 182, 213, 242
Edgeworth, Lovell, his delicate constitution, 34; contributes to *Practical Education*, 41; opinion of Maria, 53; Pictet's opinion of him, 59; accompanies Roget to Geneva, 61; taken prisoner, 82; captivity, 119–20; return to Edgeworthstown, 121–3; Maria's criticism of, 122–3; interest in education, 127; inherits Edgeworthstown and starts a school, 132–3; home-life, 209; extravagance and debts, 212 et seq., appoints Maria as agent, 213; gradual deterioration, 238; illness in Dublin and confession to Fanny Wilson, 239; banishment and death, 240–1. *Also:* 20, 37, 45–6, 50, 58, 62, 121, 128, 130–1, 135–6, 151, 160–1, 180, 211, 214, 216, 237
Edgeworth, Lucy, 86, 88, 130, 179, 209–10, 226, 241

R*

259

Index

Edgeworth, Pakenham, 130, 212, 216, 228, 235, 251

Edgeworth, Mrs. Pakenham (Christina), 252

Edgeworth, Richard, 19, 35

Edgeworth, Richard Lovell, character, talents and philosophy, 17–18; his three marriages, 19–20; influence over Maria, 20–1; her all-round training, 24–5; educational theories, 25–6; riding with Maria, 29, 32; as landlord, 27–30; encourages Maria's literary gift, 31–3; grief at Honora's death, 33; hopes that Maria will marry, 33–4, 36; at Clifton, 34–5; on Richard's death, 35; return to Ireland, 37; 'Telegraphic affairs', 38, 68, 83–4; politics, 38–9, 41; *Practical Education*, 40–1, 51–2, 55; death of Elizabeth Edgeworth, 41; determines to marry Miss Beaufort, 42; Maria's disapproval, 42–3; marriage, 44–5; flight to Longford, 46–9; he and Maria become famous, 51; Maria's dependence on him, 52–3; welcomes M. Pictet to Edgeworthstown, 56; a winter in Paris, 61, 68–82; his opinion of Chevalier Edelcrantz, 75, 77; ordered to leave Paris, 79; visits Mme de Genlis, 79–81; at Edinburgh, 83; public activities, 83–4; criticises *Leonora*, 84–5; birthday celebrations, 88–9; admiration of Kitty Pakenham, 89; grief at Charlotte's death, 90–1; at Pakenham Hall, 91–3; sends *The Absentee* to Sheridan, 95; character in old-age, 97; Mr. Parnell Hayes, 97–8; day with William Roscoe, 101–3; Henry's death, 103; Byron's remarks upon, 103 (footnote); at Lady Davy's breakfast, 112–13;

meeting at Freemason's Tavern, 110; experiments for *Harry and Lucy*, 118–19; serious illness, 120–1; joy at Lovell's return, 121–3; *Waverley*, 124–5; health steadily deteriorates, 126; unfaltering courage, 126, 128; Maria disappoints him, 126–8; *Harrington* and *Ormond*, 127–30; last drive to Longford, 130; worries himself about Maria's extravagance, 130–1; death, 131. *Also:* 22, 31, 37, 57–9; 63, 87, 132, 134–5, 142, 151, 177, 218, 251

Edgeworth, Sneyd, 45, 49, 74, 88, 90–1, 92, 95, 115, 130, 135, 213, 224, 237, 239–40

Edgeworth, Mrs. Sneyd (Henrica), 115, 213, 224

Edgeworth, Sophy, *see* Mrs. Barry Fox

Edgeworth, William, 41, 45, 88, 90, 98, 121, 128, 130, 133–6, 144, 177–8, 201, 210–11, 213, 218–19, 243, 248

Elers, Anna-Maria, *see* Edgeworth

Elers, Paul, 19

Elgin, 7th Earl of, 193

Elliot, Lady Anna-Maria, 194

Escars, Duchesse d', 164

Eustace, Major, 49

Evelyn, Mr., 158–9

Fallon, Mr., 30

Fallon, Mrs., 46

Fanshawe, Misses Penelope, Catherine (the poetess) and Elizabeth, 105–6

Farnham, last Earl of, 50 (footnote), 208

Farquhar, Sir Walter, 112

Fay, Léontine, 235

Ferguson, Adam, 200

Fitzgerald, Lady Edward (Pamela), 79, 81

Index

Fry, Elizabeth, 145, 186–8, 190
Forbes, the Ladies, 86
Fortescue, Mrs., 91
Foster, Augustus, 111
Foster, Lady Elizabeth, 78
Foster, John, *see* Lord Oriel
Foster, Judge (Baron of the court of exchequer), 214
Fowler, Dr. Richard, F.R.S., 181
Fox, Lady Anne, 50
Fox, Captain Barry, 208, 216, 222
Fox, Mrs. Barry (Sophy); accompanies Maria to Scotland, 192–206; marriage, 208. *Also:* 86, 88, 130, 216, 222
Fox, Charles James, 106
Fox, Mr. and Mrs. of Fox Hall, 31
Fox, Miss, 105–6
Fox, Richard, 50
Fox-Strangways, Mr., 117

Gardner, 2nd Lord, 117
Gautier, Madame, 69, 94, 165
Gautier, Professor, 199
Genlis, Mme de, 23, 26, 40, 65, 67, 79–81, 170–1
Geoffrin, Madame, 71
George, H.R.H. the Prince Regent, 106, 108
Goodall, Provost of Eton and Mrs., 231
Gower, Lord, *see* Marquis of Stafford
Graham, Mr., 193
Granard, 6th Earl of, 31, 39, 162, 180
Granard, Selina, Countess of, 31, 87, 91, 107, 135, 162–3, 180
Gray, Thomas, 23, 176
Grenville, Lord, 139–40
Grenville, Lady, 139–40
Greville, Mrs., 31
Grivel, Madame, 94
Guilford, Harriet, Countess of, 235
Gustavus III, King of Sweden, 72

Gustavus IV, King of Sweden, 72, 104
Gwatkin, Mr. and Mrs., 230, 232

Hall of Dunglass, 200
Hall, Captain Basil, R.N., 200–1
Hall, Mrs. C. S., 233
Hamilton, Henry, 97–9
Hamilton, Hon. Mrs., 89, 91, 93, 97, 99
Hamilton, Miss, 145
Hardwicke, 3rd Earl and Countess of, 106
Harrowby, Susan, Countess of, 153, 163
Hay, Mr., 232–3
Hayes, Parnell, 97–8
Herschel, Sir John, 190, 214, 225, 230
Herschel, Lady, 230
Hertford, Isabella Marchioness of, 106, 108
Hippolite, Monsieur, 163
Hoare, Mrs. Charles, 22–4, 26, 35–6
Hoare, Samuel, 145
Hodgson, Mr., 222
Holland, Sir Henry, 96, 182, 225
Hope, Thomas, 108, 109 and footnote, 156–9, 229–30
Hope, Hon. Mrs. Thomas, 108–9 and footnote, 156–9, 188, 225, 229–30
Horner, Francis, 113
Hort, Sir William, 140
Houdetot, Elisabeth Comtesse de, 78
Humboldt, Baron Alexandre, 163
Hume, Baron, 199
Huskisson, William, M.P., 222

Inchbald, Mrs., 65

Jeffrey, Francis (afterwards Lord), 199
Jersey, 5th Earl of, 156
Jersey, Sarah, Countess of, 156, 190
Johnson, Joseph, 39, 53, 64, 121
Jordan, Camille, 73, 171

Index

Kater, Captain Henry, 190, 225
Keating, Rev. Mr., 211
Keir, James, 152
Kennedy, Mrs., 206
Kent, Duke of, 110
Keppel, Major, 235
Kerr, Lord Robert, 200
King, Mrs. John (Emmeline), 20, 45, 53, 61–2, 114
King, Dr. John, 62, 114
Kirwan, Richard, P.R.I.A., 247
Knight, Gally, 140, 232–3
Knox, Mr., 77
Knox, Mr. ('a wit'), 128

Laharpe, Jean-François de, 78
Lake, General Gerard, 48
Lally-Tollendal, Trophime G. de, 73
Lancaster, Joseph, 110
Langan, John, 27–8, 52, 57, 88, 168
Langan, Peggy, 111
Laplace, Marquis de, 183 and footnote
Lansdowne, 3rd Marquis of, 69, 95, 105 and footnote, 110, 117–18, 137–42, 148, 178, 224
Lansdowne, Louisa Marchioness of, 105 (footnote), 107, 117–18, 134, 137–42, 148, 188, 224–5
Latuffière, Mrs., 20
Lavoisier, Madame, 71
Leveson-Gower, Lady Elizabeth, 151
Levinge, Lady, 111
Lindsay, Lady Charlotte, 106, 111
Linwood, Miss Mary, 64–5
Lock, Mr., 158
Lockhart, John Gibson, 196, 199, 204 and footnote, 205 (footnote), 211, 239
Lockhart, Mrs., 196, 199, 204, 225
Londonderry, 3rd Marquis of, 189
Londonderry, Frances Anne, Marchioness of, 189
Longford, 2nd Lord, Post-Captain

R.N., 19, 31
Longford, 2nd Earl of, 89, 91–2, 129
Longford, Catherine Lady, 89, 91, 119
Longford, Georgiana, Countess of, 129, 180
Louis XIV, King of France, 94, 169
Louis XV, King of France, 167
Louis XVI, King of France, 68, 70
Lushington, Stephen, 182, 190
Lushington, Mrs., 145–6, 182, 190
Lyndhurst, Lady, 232 and footnote, 233
Lyttelton, Lady Sarah, 107

McGuire, Colonel, 30
McHugh, Mr., 245, 247, 249
Mackintosh, Sir James, 105, 113, 184–5, 198, 228
Mackintosh, Lady, 105
Macpherson, J., 'Ossian', 203 and footnote
Mahon, Lord, 232, 235
Malthus, Rev. Thomas R., 105–6, 112
Marcet, Mrs. Jane, 105–6, 154, 173, 180, 183, 186, 201, 225
Marie-Antoinette, Queen, 68
Marivaux, Pierre de, 23
Marlborough, 1st Duke of, 228
Marmontel, Jean-François, 70
Marshall, Mr., 220
Martin, Mary, 244–5, 247, 250
Martin, Richard ('Humanity'), 242, 244, 249
Martin, Thomas, 244–50
Martin, Mrs. Thomas, 244, 247–8, 250
Mary, Queen of Scots, 197
Mayo, Dr., 136
Meadowbank, Lord, 200
Melbourne, Lady, 104
Milbanke, Lady, 111

Index

Milbanke, Annabella, *see* Lady Byron
Milbanke, Sir Ralph, 145
Moilliet, Mrs. Amelia, 152, 172, 174
Moilliet, Jean-Louis, 152, 172, 174
Moira, Elizabeth, Countess of, 31, 86-7
Molière, 23, 138
Monk, Lady Elizabeth, 108
Montjoye, Madame, 170
Montmorency, Marquis de, 73, 165
Moore, Judge, 211
Moore, Thomas, 148
Moreau, Mme la Maréchale, 165
Morellet, l'Abbé André, 70, 75, 77
Mulso, Mrs. 'Goody', 182

Nangle, Anne, 88
Napier, Emily, 141
Naples, Prince of, 117
Necker, Jacques, 70, 175
Nimmo, Alexander, 201, 214, 243, 248
Nugent, Mr. (of Kilsolla), 30
Nugent, Sir Peter, 52

O'Beirne, Mrs., 122
Opie, Mrs. Amelia, 105-6
Orglande, Madame d', 170
Oriel, Lord, 41, 162, 237
Orléans, Duc d' (Philippe Egalité), 79, 170 and footnote
Orléans, Louis-Philippe, Duc d', 170
Orléans, Duchesse d', 170
Orléans, Duchesse douairière d', 170 and footnote, 171
Orléans, Mademoiselle d', 170
Ortowska, Countess, 163-4
'Ossian', *see* J. Macpherson
Owen, Robert, 193

Pakenham, Hon. Caroline, *see* Mrs. H. Hamilton
Pakenham, Hon. Catherine (Kitty), *see* Duchess of Wellington

Pakenham, General Hon. Sir Edward, 119, 228
Pakenham, Lady Elizabeth, 87, 89, 91, 93
Pakenham, Hon. Henry, 111
Pakenham, General Hon. Sir Hercules, 91-2, 119
Pakenham, Admiral Hon. Sir Thomas, 91, 93
Palmerston, 3rd Viscount, 156
Parr, Dr. Samuel, 112-13
Pastoret, Comtesse de, 69, 71, 94, 164-5
Petty, Lord Henry, *see* 3rd Marquis of Lansdowne
Phillips, Richard, 64-5
Pictet, Marc-Auguste, 55-60, 66, 69-70, 72, 75, 94, 172-3
Pictet-de Rochemont, Charles, 55
Pole, Mrs., 141
Pollard, Mrs., 92
Pompadour, Madame de, 167-8
Portalés, Madame, 94
Powys, Miss Mary, 35
Prévost, Monsieur, 173
Prony, Gaspard de, 69, 71, 166-7, 169

Racine, Jean, 67
Randall, Miss, 175-6
Récamier, Madame, 71-3, 78-9, 165
Reynolds, Sir Joshua, 111, 230-1
Ricardo, David, 178, 190
Ricardos, the, 181
Richmond, 4th Duke of, 141
Richmond, Charlotte, Duchess of, 99
Riou, Comtesse de, 96, 163, 183
Rizzio, David, 197
Robertson, W., 197
Robinson, Fanny, *see* Mrs. Charles Hoare
Robinson, Dr. Romney, 214
Rogers, Samuel, 72, 104, 153, 225, 232-3, 254

Index

Roget, Peter Mark, 53, 61
Roland, Mme, 68
Romilly, Lady, 114, 126, 148
Romilly, Sir Samuel, 112–14, 148, 206
Ros, Lady de, 162
Roscoe, William, 101–3
Roscoe, Mrs., 101–2
Rousseau, Jean-Jacques, 19, 26, 37, 40, 69, 78
Rothwell, Letty, 129 and footnote
Russia, Emperor of, 168
Ruthven, Lord, 197
Rutland, Elizabeth, Duchess of, 109, 112
Ruxton, John, 20, 54, 85, 100, 107, 129, 206, 210
Ruxton, Mrs. (Aunt Ruxton), 22, 33–4, 37, 39, 42, 54, 62, 69, 73, 77, 87, 95, 119, 143, 160, 210, 216, 218, 221, 224
Ruxton, Margaret, 22, 216
Ruxton, Richard, 22
Ruxton, Sophy, 22, 33, 37, 39, 42–3, 54, 62, 75, 77, 85, 89, 105, 109, 110, 123, 127, 129, 217

Sadler, Windham, 97–9
Salis, Henrietta, Comtesse de, 162–4
Salis, Jerome, Comte de, 162–4
Salisbury, Mary Amelia, Marchioness of, 184
Scott, Anne, 196, 198–200, 204, 206, 211
Scott, Charles, 204
Scott, Lady, 195–9, 204–6
Scott, Mrs. (of Kilkenny), 111
Scott, Sir Walter, 87, 114, 125, 192–200, 203–6, 210–12
Scott, Captain Walter, 196, 203, 211
Scott, 'little Walter', 203
Sebright, Sir John, 182–4, 214
Sebright, Lady, 163, 183
Sebright, Misses, 183–4

Ségur, Comte de, 71
Sharp, Charles Kirkpatrick, 196 and footnote
Sharp, Richard ('Conversation'), 157–8, 224
Shepherd, Mr., 102
Siddons, Sarah, 108, 188
Sismondi, Leonard, 176
Sligo, 2nd Marquis of, 250
Smith, Sir Culling, 241–8
Smith, Lady, 241–2, 246–7, 250–1
Smith, Rev. Sydney, 190–1, 254
Smith, Thomas, 178
Sneyd, Miss Charlotte, 39, 42, 45–7, 49, 75–6, 82, 149, 160
Sneyd, Edward (of Byrkley Lodge), 149–50, 152
Sneyd, Mrs. Edward, 111, 149–50, 152
Sneyd, Elizabeth, see Edgeworth
Sneyd, Emma, 149, 150, 152
Sneyd, Honora, see Edgeworth
Sneyd, Miss Mary, 39, 42, 45, 62, 72–3, 149, 152, 160–1, 209, 239, 242, 252
Somerset, Charlotte, Duchess of, 106
Somerville, Lord, 106–7, 110
Somerville, Mrs. Mary, 83, 186
South, Sir James, 235
Spencer, 2nd Earl, 107
Spencer, Lady Georgina, 107
Spencer, Lavinia, Countess, 107, 146–7
Staël, Madame de, 61, 69–70, 81, 84, 94, 104, 113, 118, 165, 171, 175–6
Staël, Baron Auguste de, 104, 175–6, 191
Staffa, Laird of, 195–6, 198
Stafford, Elizabeth, Marchioness of, 150–1
Stafford, 2nd Marquis of, 106, 150–1,
Standish, Mr., 152
Stanton, Sir George, 117

Index

Stewart, Dugald, 82, 113, 142, 148, 193–4
Stewart, Mrs. Dugald, 142, 193–4
Stewart, Sir Henry, 198
Strutt, William, 62, 115
Stuart, Sir Charles, 163
Suard, Madame, 71, 73
Surtees, Mr., 203
Sussex, Duchess of, 104
Swanton, Mlle, *see* Madame H. Belloc
Sweden, Queen of, 165

Talma, François-Joseph, 67, 94
Telford, Thomas, 201–2
Ticknor, George, 252, 254
Tone, Wolfe, 38
Trelawney, Mr., 166–7
Tuam, Archbishop of, 109 and footnote
Tuite, Mrs., 56, 93
Turretin, Monsieur, 173

Ulick, 244

Vallière, Louise de la, 169
Vernon, Lord, 149
Victoria, Queen, 254
Vigée Lebrun, Madame, 171
Vindé, Morel de, 73, 167–9
Vindé, Madame de, 73, 167–9
Villette, Marquise de, 171
Voltaire, François-Marie Arouet de, 23, 79

Wakefield, Mr., 110
Waldegrave, Captain, 189
Wales, Princess of, 104 and footnote
Watt, James, 69
Watts, Mrs. and Miss, 63–4
Webster, Lady Frances, 126
Wedgwood, Josiah, 62, 96
Weddell, Mrs., 105, 111
Wellesley, Sir Arthur, *see* Duke of Wellington

Wellington, Duke of, 89, 90, 119, 126, 141, 222, 226–8, 234
Wellington, Duchess of, 89–90, 97, 108, 111–12, 119, 126, 141, 153, 226–8, 233–5
Whitbread, Lady Elizabeth, 105–6, 146, 153–5, 159, 185, 225
Whitbread, Samuel, M.P., 105
Whitbread, Sam, 159–60, 185, 235
White, Lydia, 96, 188, 190
Whitworth, Earl, 79
William IV, King, 140, 231
Wilson, Captain, 143, 154
Wilson, Lestock Peach, 143–4, 150, 154–6, 217–18, 222–3, 225
Wilson, Mrs. Lestock (Fanny): birth, 64; Maria's adoration of, 116, 206–8; appearance and character, 116; Lestock Wilson in love with, 143–4; Trentham and Byrkley Lodge, 150–2; courtship in London, 153–6; Sam Whitebread's admiration, 159–60; in Paris, 162–72; describes an evening at Neuilly, 170; New Year's Day at Hampstead, 181–2; at Grove House, 185–6; Almack's, 188–9; a year abroad with Sophy and Barry Fox, 208; Captain Beaufort's affection for, 216; disillusioned about life, 216–17; engagement and marriage, 217–18; Maria travels to London with on six months' visit, 222 et seq.; moves to 1 North Audley Street, 223; at the Herschels', 230; Maria at Trim, 237; Lovell confesses his debts to, 239; breaks it to Maria, 239; death, 255. *Also*; 73, 86, 88, 97–8, 116, 121, 130–1, 135, 152, 177, 180–1, 212, 220, 237, 253–5
Wollaston, Dr. William, 183–4, 186, 225
Wordsworth, William, 219–20